Praise for

GOD SLEEPS IN RWANDA

"A thoughtful critique of Kagame's regime. Sebarenzi's tale is a provocative warning to the many outsiders who are ready to canonize Kagame."

—*The Washington Post*

"Sebarenzi's account is valuable to readers seeking to understand the mechanics of ethnic violence, but also the difficulty of securing justice following so enormous a crime. . . . A worthy contribution to the literature of both genocide and conflict resolution."

—*Kirkus Reviews*

"A heartrending account of the genocide."

—CNN.com

"There's a saying in Rwanda: 'God spends the day elsewhere, but he sleeps in Rwanda.' It alludes to Rwanda's physical beauty, but also to the brutality that has sometimes haunted the country. Both of those traits are captured in Joseph Sebarenzi's new memoir."

—NPR.org

"A passionate, heartfelt perspective about the tragedy, and his personal ordeal and survival. Sebarenzi writes with a concise, authoritative voice, and with exceptional clarity of Rwanda's complicated past and present."

—Herb Boyd, author of Baldwin's Harlem

This title is also available as an ebook.

GOD SLEEPS
IN
RWANDA

A Journey of Transformation

JOSEPH SEBARENZI
WITH LAURA ANN MULLANE

ATRIA PAPERBACK

NEW YORK LONDON TORONTO SYDNEY

ATRIA PAPERBACK
A Division of Simon & Schuster, Inc.
1230 Avenue of the Americas
New York, NY 10020

First Atria Paperback edition January 2011

ATRIA PAPERBACK and colophon are trademarks of Simon & Schuster, Inc.

For information about special discounts for bulk purchases, please contact Simon &
Schuster Special Sales at 1-866-506-1949 or business@simonandschuster.com.

The Simon & Schuster Speakers Bureau can bring authors to your live event. For
more information or to book an event, contact the Simon & Schuster Speakers
Bureau at 1-866-248-3049 or visit our website at www.simonspeakers.com.

Designed by Kyoko Watanabe
All insert photographs courtesy of Joseph Sebarenzi.

Manufactured in the United States of America

10   9   8   7   6   5   4   3

The Library of Congress has cataloged the hardcover edition as follows:

Sebarenzi, Joseph.
   God sleeps in Rwanda : a journey of transformation / by Joseph Sebarenzi ;
with Laura Ann Mullane.—1st Atria Books hardcover ed.
      p. cm.
1. Sebarenzi, Joseph. 2. Rwanda—Biography. 3. Rwanda—History—
Civil War, 1994—Atrocities. 4. Genocide—Rwanda—History—20th century.
5. Refugees—Rwanda—Biography. 6. Reconciliation—Rwanda. 7. Rwanda—
Politics and government—1994— I. Mullane, Laura Ann. II. Title.

   DT450.443.S43 A3 2009
   967.57104'31092—dc22
   [B]
                         2008055550

ISBN 978-1-4165-7573-3
ISBN 978-1-4165-7577-1 (pbk)
ISBN 978-1-4165-7581-8 (ebook)

This book is dedicated to all those who work for peace and reconciliation in Rwanda and in other parts of the world. May your commitment and dedication prosper, and may your work yield fruit in nations and in people's hearts.

I also dedicate this book to the brave men and women who took the risk to protect, hide, or rescue fellow Rwandans during the genocide in 1994 and to all the people around the world who endeavor to do good, even in evil times.

Imana yirirwa ahandi igataha I Rwanda.

God spends the day elsewhere, but He sleeps in Rwanda.

Contents

—Ⱥ—

Contents

Author's Note

—⁓—

I N recounting the events during my time as speaker, I withhold the names of several people who helped me for their protection and the protection of their families who are still in Rwanda.

Also, I recount conversations in this book that I had with many different people. Due to the passage of time, these conversations have been recreated to the best of my recollection, but should not be taken as verbatim.

Finally, a note about references to the country of Congo: What is today the Democratic Republic of Congo, which borders Rwanda and is an integral part of its history, has gone through several name changes over the last century. Beginning in 1908, it was colonized by Belgium and referred to as Belgian Congo until its independence in 1960, at which time it first took the name the Democratic Republic of the Congo.[1] In 1965, after a coup led by Mobutu Sese Seko, it was renamed Zaire, which it was called until 1997 when a new government led by Laurent Kabila once again changed the name to the Democratic Republic of Congo.

---

[1] Central Intelligence Agency. The World FactBook. http://www.gov/library/publications/the-world-factbook/geos/cg.html.

Throughout my life in Rwanda, Rwandans continued to commonly refer to this country as Congo and its inhabitants as Congolese, even when its official name was Zaire. Therefore, in these pages I refer to the country as Congo until events after 1997, at which point I refer to it as the Democratic Republic of Congo.

When I use the term Congo in this book, I am referring to today's Democratic Republic of Congo and not the Republic of the Congo, a different country in central Africa.

Prologue

~m~

IMAGES KEEP coming to me.

I'm a young boy and hiding under our neighbor's bed with my mother, my three-year-old brother John, and my niece. We're trembling. It's dark so I can't see my mother's face, but I can feel her tight embrace, her shaking body, her quick, shallow breaths, her whispered prayers, "O mighty God, please protect us from harm . . ."

Men are at the door with machetes and spears. "We know Kabogora's family is hiding here," they yell. "Send them out! We're going to kill them!"

In the distance, we can hear our house being destroyed. We hear machetes ripping through our corrugated metal roof. We hear the crackling of flames that engulf our cooking house. We hear the voices of the mob as they steal our food and loot our home. We hold each other and pray—for ourselves, for our neighbors, for my father and other brothers and sisters who were scattered with the violence. "O mighty God, please protect us from harm . . ."

Another image is of my father hiding deep in our banana plantation. A Hutu neighbor takes me to find him, to tell him the violence has passed. We run together down the hillside to my father's hiding place. We don't call out. All my father hears is the sound of footsteps running—and thinks men are coming to kill him. When we reach him, his entire body is trembling; his eyes are wide with fear. I have never before seen my brave, strong father afraid, and it cuts me to the core.

These are the images that come back to me in haunting detail two decades later, in the spring of 1994, as I watch television reports from Rwanda of Hutu extremists chopping people with machetes, of rivers swollen with bloated bodies, of the dead piled on top of one another inside churches, of terrified people trying to flee. I can feel the terror that grips the back of their throats. I can hear their hearts pounding. I can taste the sweat running down their foreheads and into the corners of their mouths. From the safety of my apartment seven thousand miles away, I watch as my homeland falls apart and know—with crushing certainty—that my family is dead.

My parents don't have a phone. No one in our village does. I can't call them to find out what's happening, to tell them I love them. When the violence first began, some family members were able to reach my brother-in-law at his office just twenty miles from my parents. But he knew nothing. Then one day, he stopped answering his phone.

I sit and watch. Hour after hour, day after day, the same news. I think of my brother John, now twenty-four years old. He lived with me in Rwanda when he was still in school. He is like a son to me. I remember pleading with him to leave Rwanda, but he refused. "I'm staying with my parents," he had said. "If they're killed, I'll be killed with them." Now as I watch the violence, I worry that his promise is being fulfilled.

Then, I see the impossible: I'm watching footage of the French military rescuing a Tutsi family and see that it is my step-sister. Next to her is John—I'm sure of it. I videotape it and watch it over and over again to make sure. Yes, it's John—he has survived! It's as if I was dead and brought back to life. For the first time since the violence erupted, I feel hope that maybe my family survived.

In July, after the violence has ended, the death count begins to emerge. At least eight hundred thousand Tutsi and moderate Hutu dead in just ninety days. Some estimate the killings at closer to one million. Hutu militia managed to kill at least one-tenth of the Rwandan population and three-quarters of the Tutsi population in only three months using nothing but machetes and small arms. Entire generations of families are destroyed in the blink of an eye.

My brother in Africa returns to our village in Rwanda to find our family. He calls to tell me what he's found. But I already knew. In some ways, I always did.

Chapter 1

The Drum Beat and We Were Saved

—⟋⟍⟍—

The most horrible and systematic massacre we have had
occasion to witness since the extermination of the Jews
by the Nazis.

—BERTRAND RUSSELL

I'M NOT a storyteller. In Rwanda, it's too dangerous to tell stories.
There are thousands of stories to tell—about birth and life, and
far too many stories about death. Stories that wrap around the
hills and skip like stones across the abundant lakes and rivers. Stories
that whisper through the banana and coffee plantations and eucalyptus groves. Stories that are carried on the heads of women walking
barefoot to market, or swaddled on their backs with their children.
Stories that run through the sweat of men as they cultivate the land,
rhythmically turning the rich soil with their hoes. Stories that sing
with voices raised at church.

But you don't tell stories. You listen. You listen to your parents.
You listen to your teachers. You listen to the drumbeat that echoes
from hilltop to hilltop before an official announcement is made. But

above all else, you listen to your leaders. In the United States, a presidential address gets less attention than a football game. Unless there is a crisis, most people don't really care what the president has to say. In Rwanda, when the president speaks, everyone listens. In rural areas where radios are scarce, people gather at neighbors' houses to hear what he says. And you listen closely, for what he says could mean the difference between life and death. When you hear him, you don't form opinions. You nod your head in agreement.

So you listen. You don't tell stories. You don't need to. Everyone knows you. Everyone knows your family. Everyone knows if you are sick. Everyone knows if you need help. And they will help. They will take turns carrying you on a stretcher for the two-hour walk to the hospital. They will give you milk from their cow if yours is dry. They will share their cassava if you are hungry. They will share their beer, brewed from bananas, to celebrate a wedding. They will work side by side with you in your fields. They will give you shelter. But the very thread that knits Rwandans so closely together is the same one that can so quickly unravel the country.

I first learned what Hutu and Tutsi meant when I was not yet a teenager, sitting on the floor of our cooking house with six of my brothers and sisters while my mother prepared our evening meal of beans and cassava. The glow of the fire and the oil lamp cast long shadows on the walls. My father sang his evening hymns next door at the main house, his voice traveling the short distance between the two mud-and-brick buildings. We could hear our cows breathing quietly in the paddock in front of our house, where they were enclosed for the night. Outside, a blanket of stars spread from horizon to horizon.

It was March 1973 and this night was like any other, except it wasn't. Something was wrong. My mother and older siblings were unusually quiet. As my mother worked, she focused entirely on her chores, rarely looking up. The light in the cooking house was dim, so I couldn't see her face very well, but I could tell she was worried.

As my sister Beatrice and I joked with each other, my mother pointed a stern finger at us. "Keep quiet!" she snapped.

We stopped talking and looked at one another, wondering what we had done wrong. My mother was rarely strict with us. It was my father who was the disciplinarian of the family. For her to snap at us when we had done nothing wrong was unlike her. Our older brother and sisters kept their eyes down.

Then my mother looked at me, her eyes wide with warning. "Did you know that I spent nights hiding in the bush with you when you were a baby?"

This seemed ridiculous to me. We had a nice home—I couldn't imagine why we would sleep in the bush, where poisonous snakes hid in the tall grasses. "In the bush?" I asked. "Why?"

My mother looked down at her cooking and said simply, "Because if we stayed at home, we would have been killed."

I had never heard anything like this before. I was shocked. "Killed?" I asked. "Why would we be killed, Mama?"

My mother's voice became small. Her eyes did not meet mine. "Because we are Tutsi," she almost whispered, as if she wanted no one around to hear, not even herself.

"Because we are Tutsi?" I had heard the word before but didn't know what it meant, and could see no reason someone would want to kill us because of it. "Why?"

My mother said nothing.

"Who?" I asked. "Who would kill us?"

Again, my mother's voice was low. "Hutu."

"Who are Hutu?" This was another word I had heard, but I had no idea of its meaning.

My mother paused. "Abraham and his family are Hutu," she said.

This did nothing to clear my confusion. The Abrahams were close family friends. Before I was born, my father gave Abraham a cow—a strong symbol of friendship in Rwanda. Cows in Rwanda were not used to work the land. They were not bred for meat or even milk (although we do drink it), but for beauty. And giving someone a cow as a gift was cause for great celebration. Abraham called my father

Rutabeshya, meaning "truthful," in admiration of their friendship. My younger brother played with Abraham's grandchildren. I couldn't begin to understand why they would want to kill us.

"The Eliackims, the Nyakanas, and the Ngarambes are also Hutu," she said.

These were also good family friends. It didn't make any sense. "So the Abrahams and the Ngarambes want to kill us?" I asked.

Beatrice jumped in, "Oh, Mama, the Abrahams are very good, I don't think they would kill us."

"No, I don't mean that they will kill you," my mother said. "Not all Hutu are bad. When I hid with you in the bush, the Abrahams hid our things for us so they wouldn't be stolen. They're good people. But some Hutu may try to kill us because we are Tutsi."

I couldn't understand what she was saying. We had always lived peacefully with our Hutu neighbors. We shared drinks with them. We worked our fields together. We celebrated weddings and births together. Hutu would come to our aid and we would come to theirs. We felt welcome in each other's homes. What she was saying didn't make any sense. Again I asked, "Mama, why? Why would they want to kill us? Because we are Tutsi? What did we do?"

My mother took a slow, deep breath and waved her hand as if she was shooing a fly. "Oh, this child, asking so many questions. Eat your dinner and then go to bed."

With that, my mother stopped talking. She didn't tell me more about how she hid in the bush with me as a baby in the early 1960s, while tens of thousands of Tutsi were killed and hundreds of thousands were driven into exile. She didn't tell me how she watched as homes were burned and Tutsi neighbors were beaten. She didn't tell me how loved ones—including my father's brother—fled with their families to neighboring Congo. She didn't tell me about Tutsi men, women, and children being killed with machetes. She didn't tell me that it was about to happen again; that word of violence was spreading through the country; that it was only a matter of time. She didn't tell me how afraid she was there in the cooking house, preparing the evening meal with her small children around her. She told me none of this. Perhaps she didn't need to. I would soon learn it all myself.

One of my fondest memories of my childhood in Rwanda is of swimming in Lake Kivu as a boy. It's the largest of Rwanda's twenty-one lakes and serves as the boundary between Rwanda and Congo. My family's land bordered the lake and on weekends, I would bring our cows there to graze on its banks and drink from its waters. While the cows rested, I would dive into the lake and feel its cool wash over me. I would turn over and float on my back, stare up at the vast expanse of blue sky spread above me and listen to the waves lap against the shore.

From the lake I could climb a steep hill to our house, which was surrounded by avocado trees. Eucalyptus trees dotted the farm, their sweet scent carried on the breeze that slipped between its branches and blew across our banana and coffee plantations. We were considered a wealthy family in our village of Butimbo in the Kibuye province. We had no electricity or running water. Every day we would descend the steep incline to the lake, fill our jars with water, and carry them on our heads back up the hillside to the house. We had no cars, no tractors, no bicycles. In fact, my first car ride would not be until I was sixteen years old. We traveled everywhere on foot, padding along the narrow paths that linked homes and villages. A walk to the market took two hours, so we went no more than twice a month to buy small things like sugar and sell our crops. All other food we grew ourselves on our land. But we were rich in ways most Westerners don't understand. My father owned what was considered a large amount of land in a country where land was scarce. Rwanda is one of the smallest countries in Africa—roughly the size of Maryland or Belgium, its former colonizer—but the most densely populated on the continent, with 9 million residents, or 547 people per square mile. Land was like gold. And just as blood has been spilled all over the world to acquire that precious commodity, so has it been spilled in Rwanda for land. My father also owned about thirty cows, another symbol of wealth and status in Rwanda. Our roof was corrugated metal—a luxury in a village where most homes were covered in grass or wide, sturdy banana leaves.

My father was a self-made man. He had inherited a small piece of land from his father, but through hard work he was able to purchase more. He was a respected man in the community, someone other villagers would turn to for advice and help. Like other wealthy men in Rwanda, he had three wives, who had given him a total of sixteen children. Although polygamy had been frowned upon since Christian missionaries first began arriving in 1910, it was still practiced. But few men could afford it. In Rwandan culture, no more than one wife could live in a house, so for a man to have more than one wife, he had to have enough land and money to build homes for each one. An additional tax on multiple wives was further disincentive, ensuring that only wealthy men could afford it. My father, who was a devout Christian, did not intend to have three wives. But when his first wife was unable to bear children—suffering repeated miscarriages—he felt that he had no other choice. So he met and married my mother, a decision that cost him his teaching job at a Seventh-Day Adventist school. Soon after he married my mother, his first wife got pregnant; then my mother discovered she was also pregnant. Within a few weeks of each other, both his first wife and my mother delivered beautiful baby girls. He married his third wife in the 1960s, after his brother fled to Congo. My father asked the local government official to grant his brother's land to him so it would stay in the family. The official agreed, on the condition that he marry a third woman who could live on it. So my mother helped him find his third wife: one of her cousins. My stepmothers, as I called them, and their children lived in other homes adjoining our property, just a few minutes' walk away. Although we lived apart, we would interact daily, borrowing food or doing chores together. My relationship with them was similar to most Americans' relationships with their aunts and cousins.

To reach their homes, I would descend another hill. As I walked, I could see Lake Kivu stretch all the way to where its shores became Congo. Beyond it I could see the imposing volcano range that divides east and central Africa. Even as a boy, before I had traveled more than a few miles from my home, I knew that I lived in one of the most beautiful places on earth.

Our ancestors knew it, too. Before European colonizers arrived in Rwanda at the turn of the twentieth century, Rwandans thought their country was the center of the world. They thought their kingdom was the most civilized and their monarchy the most powerful. When Europeans arrived, they were impressed by the efficiency and organization of its government, its politics, and its military. It was that organized and obedient military that so fiercely protected the nation. Slave traders were pushed back from the borders. Few immigrants settled there. It was one of the few African nations to live virtually in isolation from other cultures. Rwandans spoke one language—Kinyarwanda—worshipped one God, and answered to one king.

That king was a Tutsi. It is unclear when Tutsi, Hutu, and Twa—the native hunting and gathering pygmy populace—first arrived in Rwanda. Most historians estimate the cattle-raising Tutsi arrived sometime between the tenth and fourteenth centuries. Somehow Tutsi established a monarchy led by an all-powerful *mwami,* or king, who was not mortal, but a divine creation. The *mwami* not only ruled Rwanda, he *was* Rwanda. If he was sick, it was believed that Rwanda would suffer. If he was threatened, the entire country was thought to be at risk.

The king appointed both Hutu and Tutsi to positions of authority in his administration and in local communities, but Tutsi enjoyed more power, social status, and influence than Hutu. Despite this, the two groups lived peacefully together—working together, marrying one another, having children together. The only large-scale violence in the country was within the ruling Tutsi clan, specifically during a coup d'état at Rucunshu in 1896. But relations between Hutu and Tutsi were peaceful. Unlike other tribal nations that have endured centuries of sectarian violence, the people of Rwanda—whether Tutsi, Hutu, or Twa—saw themselves first and foremost as Rwandans. There is an ancient Rwandan saying, *Turi bene mugabo umwe,* meaning "we are the sons and daughters of the same father." For centuries, Rwandans believed this and lived accordingly.

Then in 1885, in a distant land no Rwandan even knew existed, white men sat down with a map of Africa and pencils and started drawing borders and writing names. It was the Berlin Conference, and although no European had ever set foot on Rwandan soil, the country was given to Germany. It wasn't until 1894 that the first white man officially visited the country, a German official who politely informed the surprised *mwami* that his kingdom had been under German rule for the last nine years.

Germany established a few government offices in Rwanda, but largely ignored it, having little interest in this small landlocked farming country. Because Germany governed through the existing monarchy, few changes were imposed on the day-to-day lives of Rwandans. More changes were brought by the incoming Catholic and Protestant missionaries who established schools and hospitals and, of course, churches.

Then came World War I, after which Rwanda was taken from the defeated Germans and given to Belgium. Belgium took a keener interest in this country of rich soil and mild weather that sits just below the equator. The Belgians marveled at Rwanda's cohesive government and strong national identity. In the 1950s, the missionary Monsignor Louis de Lacger wrote in his history of Rwanda, "One of the most surprising phenomena of Rwanda's human geography is surely the contrast between the plurality of races and the sentiment of national unity. The natives of this country genuinely have the feeling of forming but one people."[1]

Belgian colonizers put an end to that. They were fascinated by the physical differences between Tutsi and Hutu and decided to make a "scientific" study of them: their height, their weight, their eye color, the width of their noses, and even the texture of their hair. Using rulers and calipers, scientists set about classifying these differences, determining that not only were Tutsi physical features more European but they were nobler and more intelligent than Hutu, and

---

[1] Quoted in Gourevitch, Philip. *We Wish to Inform You That Tomorrow We Will Be Killed with Our Families.* New York: Picador, 1998.

therefore the natural rulers of the country. While stereotypically Tutsi are taller, thinner, and lighter-skinned than Hutu, in reality not many Rwandans fit these portraits. But the Belgian colonizers didn't see it this way.

As a result of the data they collected, Belgians stripped Hutu of any authority they had been granted by the Tutsi king, and all leadership positions in the colonial government were given to Tutsi. Admission to schools to prepare for government jobs was reserved predominantly for Tutsi; only a handful of Hutu could go. The only truly accessible education for Hutu was the seminary. As if this weren't enough, in 1935, Belgium institutionalized ethnic identity cards in one of history's first incidences of large-scale, state-sponsored racial categorization. Ethnicity descended from the father, so a person with a Tutsi father was a Tutsi, even if his mother was Hutu. Despite this imposed ethnic division, Hutu and Tutsi continued to live an integrated existence, sharing the same neighborhoods, the same schools, the same churches. But the seeds of discrimination and resentment were sown, and Rwanda's strong national identity began to erode.

It eroded further when decolonization spread throughout Africa in the 1950s. In the latter part of the decade, the Tutsi elite claimed Rwanda's independence from Belgium. Out of anger at their Tutsi subjects—and out of a desire to extend their stay in the country—the Belgian colonists shifted their support to Hutu. Under the guise of social justice, the Belgian government systematically took away power from Tutsi and gave it to Hutu. The colonists helped Hutu leaders take political and military power—often by force—in the years leading up to Rwanda's independence in 1962.

While Hutu leaders had every right to seek equality and compete for power, their methods—and the complicity of the colonists—were unjust. Between 1959 and 1967, twenty thousand Tutsi were killed and three hundred thousand fled to neighboring countries to escape death.[2] The worst massacres occurred in the space of just two

---

[2]International Panel of Eminent Personalities. *Rwanda: The Preventable Genocide.* OAU. 2000.

months, between December 1963 and January 1964, leading British philosopher Bertrand Russell to describe it as "the most horrible and systematic massacre we have had occasion to witness since the extermination of the Jews by the Nazis."

Violence would erupt periodically, usually in retribution for the attacks of Tutsi rebel forces living in exile in neighboring countries. The state would paint the victims as the aggressors, telling Hutu that the Tutsi planned to exterminate them, and if they didn't kill them first, then they would be killed themselves. "Clear the bush" was the call to Hutu to incite them to kill—and without fail, some did.

These rounds of massacres used to be called *muyaga*, meaning "wind." It was a fitting description of the nature of the violence. It would come suddenly and forcefully and then, just as suddenly as it came, it would stop. Those who were killed were gone, and those who survived would continue to live with their persecutors as if nothing had happened. Part of this was because those who survived had no other choice. But it also demonstrated Rwandans' strong obedience to authority. Rwandans kill when they are asked, and stop as soon as they are told.

In addition to periodic ethnic massacres, a state-sponsored system of discrimination was put in place. Hutu leaders had taken the injustice they suffered during colonization and replaced it with another injustice. Tutsi could make up no more than 10 percent of a business's workforce. Their access to military service and the government was also severely limited. Members of the military were unofficially forbidden to marry Tutsi. Intermarrying among nonmilitary citizens still existed, but the Belgian practice of establishing ethnic identity based on paternity continued, and discrimination persisted. In schools, teachers were tasked with taking a census of all the Hutu and Tutsi students in the classroom. They would ask all Tutsi children to stand or raise their hands, and then ask all Hutu to do the same. Hutu children who were old enough to understand ethnicity would stand to be counted with a beaming sense of pride, backs and shoulders straight, heads held high.

When the Tutsi children stood or raised their hands, they looked ashamed.

History lessons were biased and politically motivated. Instead of honestly recounting events in a way that would foster reconciliation, the lessons fueled the *us against them* mentality. I believe that children can be taught in a way that prepares them to live in peace with each other and to become good leaders. Sadly, in most schools, teachers would tout the heroism of Hutu revolutionaries who helped Rwanda gain its independence from Belgium and topple the Tutsi monarchy. They would dehumanize the Tutsi and deify the Hutu, making all Tutsi into aggressors and all Hutu into victims. This message was reinforced through radio and newspapers, particularly on national political holidays. Tutsi were referred to as *Inyenzi*, meaning "cockroaches."

The discrimination in the classroom extended to the accessibility of education. Rwanda didn't have enough schools to educate its population. While all Rwandan children, regardless of their ethnicity, could receive an elementary school education, only about 10 percent of the population could go on to high school. Of that 10 percent, the government made certain that virtually all were Hutu. Rare was the Tutsi child who received the great honor of attending high school. One of my earliest memories is of overhearing my father ask a Hutu friend who held a position of influence in the local government if he could secure fake Hutu identity cards for his children. My father knew that the best chance his children had to receive an education beyond elementary school was if we could "pass" as Hutu. His friend looked at my father and then at me and shook his head. "Your children are too Tutsi," he said. "They would be caught." He was right. We all had undeniable Tutsi features. I didn't understand it at the time, but I knew enough to know that being Tutsi was somehow a bad thing, and I felt ashamed.

Despite all this, my parents never said a harsh word to us about Hutu. Our Hutu neighbors were our friends. They never told us we had reason to fear them, or that we should hate them. They never told us we were ethnically inferior or superior. I was raised believing we were all equal human beings. We were Rwandans.

I feel as if my childhood ended the night my mother told me that people wanted to kill us for being Tutsi. For the first time I had a sense of "other." When the day began I innocently believed that I lived in a peaceful, secure world. There was no "us" and no "them," only "we." Now that had forever changed.

That evening, after we finished our dinner, we went to the main house to get ready for bed. Each night before we went to sleep, we sang and prayed together. It was an important ritual, one that kept us united as a family through our shared faith in God. Rwanda is predominantly Christian—with a slight majority Catholic, about a quarter Protestant, and just over a tenth Seventh-Day Adventist. Muslims account for only about 5 percent of the population. We were Adventists, and each evening we would sing the hymns we learned in church. Then each child would offer a prayer, followed by my parents. Usually my mother's prayers were simple. She would thank God for His many blessings and then ask Him to give us a peaceful night's sleep and keep us healthy. If we were planning a big event like a wedding, she would ask for His help. But this night my mother's prayers were very powerful. She asked for God's protection during the violence that was brewing. She prayed that we would all survive whatever came. I still didn't understand what she was talking about. My world was safe and when I went to sleep, I slept soundly.

In the morning, my mother went room by room to wake us all for school. Every morning, as we did at night, we would sing and pray together as a family. Again, my mother prayed fervently for our protection. As she led us out of the house for our five-mile walk to school, she told us, "Violence may be starting soon. Be very careful. Be prepared. I'll keep praying for you to be safe."

My brother, sisters, and I left for school. Beatrice and I still did not fully understand what my mother was talking about. Despite what she had told me the night before, life seemed normal. I couldn't grasp the idea that our Hutu neighbors might kill us. I couldn't imagine that human beings would kill other human beings.

We ran to school that morning. We were late and if we didn't make it to school on time, we would have to endure a painful beating by switch at the hands of the school principal. I had suffered a few beatings before and had no interest in another one.

We arrived at school on time and the day proceeded as usual. At our morning and midday breaks, I played with my Hutu and Tutsi friends. I ate lunch with them. We played soccer. My brother and I were good players and usually picked the teams. We would pick the best players—we didn't care about their ethnicity. Our teacher showed no sign of anxiety or concern.

Then, at our afternoon break, as I was walking outside to the playground, I heard the shouts of my other classmates who were already out the door. "Look! Over there! Look what's happening!" I ran outside and followed their pointing fingers to a hillside far in the distance and saw it: burning houses dotting the hillside. Huge billows of smoke filled the air. I had never seen anything like it. I remembered my mother's story from the night before, her prayers, her warning as we left for school. I still didn't grasp everything that was happening, but I knew it was Tutsi homes that were burning. Everyone began talking, trying to figure out whether they were Hutu or Tutsi. I approached one of my best friends, a Hutu, and said to him, "These houses are being burned because they belong to Tutsi."

"I don't think my family is Tutsi, so our house won't be burned," he said. Then he asked me, "Is your family Tutsi?"

"Yes," I said, remembering my mother's quiet voice the night before.

He looked at me sadly. "Your house will be burned then."

Then the principal's whistle blew and we all retreated to our respective classrooms, where we were dismissed early, without any word about why. It was clear from the flames on the hillside that the situation had gotten worse and we all needed to return to our families. But still, we were children, so as we made our way home, we played on the road, kicking the soccer ball among us as we ran.

When we reached home, my mother was anxiously waiting for us. "Things have gotten bad," she said. "The burnings have started." We listened much more attentively than we had the night before. "We have to be ready," she said. "We won't stay in the house tonight. It's too dangerous."

That night, my mother and siblings snuck into the bush, down the hill not far from the lake. I spent the night with my father a few miles away, where he had bought a beautiful piece of land surrounded by Lake Kivu on three sides and built a farmhouse. Its soil was rich and so were its grasses, perfect grazing for our cows. He wanted to make sure the house and cows were safe, so we stayed there, singing and praying together.

"You have a very good voice," my father told me.

I beamed with pride. I always remember this night alone with my father with great tenderness. It felt special to be with him by myself, keeping watch over our house and cows together. I was not his oldest son, so I felt even more important being asked to go with him. My father was a very strong man and I admired him immensely. A birth defect outturned his left leg and he walked with a limp, but I never thought of him as disabled. It seemed as if there was nothing he couldn't do, and I always felt safe with him. But I was careful around him, too. He was a strict disciplinarian. If any of us children did something wrong, he would tell us to go pick out a stick. We would lie on the ground and he would hit our backsides with it eight times. In Rwanda this wasn't abuse, it was discipline. I remember the time he caught me staging a fight between two cows. I wanted to show my friend how much stronger my cow was than his, so I brought his cow into our field. When two cows that don't know each other are introduced, they circle each other and butt heads to establish dominance in the herd, and that's exactly what these two cows did. I didn't realize that my father was watching from some distance away, and I paid a painful price for it.

In my eyes, my father was all-powerful. Whatever terror was taking place outside our farmhouse that night, I was with my father, sleeping in the same bed—protected. I had no worry that something bad could happen to me.

In the middle of night, my father tapped my shoulder. "Sebarenzi, Sebarenzi, wake up. I want to show you something," he said.

We walked outside and he pointed to the village across the lake. The hillside glowed with the flames of burning houses. "We need to stay awake because anything can happen," my father calmly said. "We need to stay faithful. We need to keep praying so nothing will happen to us." We stayed awake the rest of the night, waiting for the shouts of the approaching mob. But they didn't come.

Early the next morning we returned to our house, where my mother and siblings were waiting for us. Our village was spared. Our home was still standing. Our belongings were still there. Our family was safe. My mother told us about their terrifying night in the bush, how quiet they all stayed, how even my three-year-old brother John, the youngest, didn't cry.

But the violence wasn't over.

Later that morning, a very close Hutu friend, Eliezer Ngarambe, came to our house. He told my father that the Hutu mob was coming to our village. "No one will kill children or women," he said. "But with men, you never know. You should hide."

He helped my father find a safe place to hide in our banana plantation. "Stay here until I come for you," he said. "I'll come get you when it's safe." Then, Eliezer left us and joined the Hutu mob as it began roaming our village and destroying Tutsi homes. It didn't seem strange to me that Eliezer would join the mob. It was his duty, like an act of patriotism. Here was our good friend destroying the homes of our neighbors. The houses with corrugated roofs were cut with machetes. The houses made of grass were set on fire. I remember watching an excited crowd of Hutu running and shouting, burning house after house. It was strange to watch. They were not angry, as I thought they would be, but happy. It was like a party. Burning the houses was like some sort of amusement for them. Because of this, I still wasn't afraid. I was standing on top of the hill overlooking our home with my mother and other Tutsi families as they helplessly watched their homes being destroyed. We just stood there. The Hutu mob could see us, but no one threatened us. They seemed to be having some sort of celebration, and we were the spectators. A Hutu neighbor, Kayugushu, saw us and approached my mother before the Hutu crowd reached our house. "Don't worry, don't worry, nothing will happen to you," he said. "We will protect you, you are very good people." Then he said, "I need matches to burn houses."

My mother looked down. "I don't have matches," she said.

Kayugushu said again, "Give me matches."

"I don't have any," my mother replied.

"I know you have matches," he said, his voice becoming more threatening. "You are a rich family—of course you have matches. Give them to me!"

My mother knew that defying him would put us all at risk, so without saying another word she hurriedly went down the hill to our house and returned with a box of matches. Her eyes didn't meet his as she gave them to him, waving a dismissive hand in his direction with a look of disgust on her face and saying, "Take them." He did, and then ran to join the mob.

A short while later, they reached our house. Kayugushu was with them, and so was our friend Eliezer Ngarambe. They began shouting, "This is Kabogora's house!" referring to my father, Daniel Kabogora. "He's is a good man! Don't touch that house!" And they didn't. They walked right by it. Eliezer and Kayugushu had kept their promise: Our house was spared, as was that of a widowed neighbor. Because she had no husband, they decided to leave her house alone. It was a rare display of compassion on a day filled with hatred.

After the violence of the day finally ended, Eliezer came back to us. "Come with me to get your father," he told me. "It's safe now. Let's go tell him."

We ran together down the hill to where my father was hiding. I can only imagine what his day must have been like—huddled silently among the dense banana trees, hearing shouts in the distance and wondering if his family was safe. Every insect's call, every animal's scurry, every branch cracking in the breeze must have stood his hair on end. I imagine the loneliness he must have felt. The discomfort of his gathering thirst and hunger. The doubts running through his mind about whether he should leave his hiding place in the trees and find his family.

And then, a sound. What was it? Another branch snapping? No, footsteps. This time he knew they were footsteps. And they were not the footsteps of a single man. There was more than one. And they were running at him fast. *This is it,* he must have thought. *This is where I will die.* His eyes darted right and left, but there was no escape. Anywhere he ran would be out of the cover of the trees. He stood, trembling. He couldn't stop the trembling. It started in his legs and rolled like a wave up his body. His eyes dilated. Every sense, every muscle told him to flee. But he couldn't. He could only stand and tremble.

And then two figures appeared. "Don't worry, don't be afraid," said one. An arm reached out and grabbed his. "It's over. Nothing will happen to you. You're safe."

My father saw his friend and his son standing before him. And he wanted to break down crying out of relief and fear and anxiety. But he couldn't. He just trembled.

This is how I imagine it, but I don't know for sure, because he never told me. All I know is that for the first time in my life I saw my brave, strong father shaking with fear. It was an image that would stay with me for the rest of my life. As a boy, seeing my all-powerful father tremble made me tremble, too. I realized then how serious this was. I realized that we could be killed.

That night, my father and I returned to the farmhouse to protect it, as we had the night before. In the morning, I went back home, leaving my father behind. As I was walking home, I saw a group of people on the neighboring hill running. I wondered why they were running—wasn't the violence over? I couldn't believe it was already starting again.

A few yards from my house, I saw my mother and siblings running in different directions. I followed my mother, who was running with my brother John in her arms and my niece Esperance beside her. "What's happening?" I asked.

"They want to kill us," my mother said. "They're coming for us! We have to run fast." So we did. We ran toward the house of the Abrahams, our longtime Hutu friends. When we reached the door we were scared and out of breath. Without hesitation, they hurried us inside. "You must hide," they said, corralling us into the next room. The four of us scrambled under their bed, a traditional Rwandan bed with enough space under it to sit. It was dark. I could see nothing. Our breathing was rapid and shallow. My throat was dry. I tried to swallow, but couldn't. Our house was close enough to Abraham's that we could hear the mob destroying it. We could hear machetes rip through the corrugated metal roof; the crackling flames engulfing our cooking house; the cheering of the crowd.

Suddenly, we heard three Hutu men at the door of the Abraham's, machetes and spears in hand. "We know that Kabogora's family is hiding here," they said. "Send them out! We're going to kill them!"

Under the bed, my mother whispered prayers over and over again. "O mighty God, please protect us from harm." Because it was dark, I couldn't see her face, I could only feel her tight grip around my shoulder and her trembling body. I imagined she looked just as my father had when I found him hiding in the banana plantation—vulnerable, weak, scared.

"Send them out!" the Hutu men called again.

Fortunately, Abraham had two young, strong sons named Bunyenzi and Segashi, who stood at the door with their machetes, ready to protect us. "They won't come out of this house!" they shouted back. "If you try to come in here we'll kill you!"

My mother kept whispering her prayers, asking God to protect us and our Hutu friends, who were risking their own lives trying to save ours. The argument with the mob continued, voices rising with each exchange.

"Send them out! We're going to kill them!"

"No!" Bunyenzi and Segashi yelled again. "If you come into this house, we'll kill you!"

I thought for sure we would be killed. Abraham's sons were

strong, but there were only two of them. The three men at the door could easily overpower them, and there were many more in the mob who would gladly come to their aid. I didn't see how we could survive.

Then the drum beat. A methodical thud reverberated through the hills.

In rural areas of Rwanda, where telephones were nonexistent and even radios were rare, the drum was a major means of communication. The sound of the drum told people to listen for a message that was then shouted from hilltop to hilltop. At that moment, the drum beat and the message came: *"Ihumere . . . ihumere . . . ihumere . . ."* "It is time for peace." With that, the violence stopped. Immediately. The *muyaga* was over. The men at the door turned around and walked away.

Later we would learn of the reason behind this *muyaga*. The massacre of Tutsi had been going on for several weeks in other parts of the country, precipitated by fighting within the Hutu leadership and growing dissatisfaction with the president's regime. In an effort to rally support for himself, the president mobilized Hutu against a common enemy: the Tutsi. The plan was enthusiastically embraced by the president's supporters as well as his opposition, who thought the violence would serve as justification for a coup. This cheap grab for power cost thousands of Tutsi their lives in 1973—and thousands more fled the country.

But the drum beat and we were saved.

We hid under the bed for a few more hours until Abraham's sons finally came to us and said, "It's safe to come out. The mob has left. You can go home."

But home, as we knew it, no longer existed. We arrived at what had been our house to find our food, furniture, and clothes gone. Our cows and calves had been taken. Our main house had been severely damaged. The metal roof was hacked apart. Our cooking house was in ashes. Our house had been targeted, we learned later, because of a Hutu man named Marere. When I was younger, Marere stole cassava from our property. My father had him arrested and Marere spent a few days in jail. When he heard our house had been spared in the previous day's violence, he was livid. He saw destroying our home as a chance to get his revenge—and he did.

We had no food and no money. The rainy season was at its height and we had no roof over our heads. There was no humanitarian assistance, because according to the government, nothing had happened. We couldn't report the crime to the authorities, because the authorities had sanctioned it. We could do nothing but suffer.

But still, we knew that it could have been far worse. My father, siblings, stepsiblings, and the rest of my extended family emerged safely from their hiding places. Some people were beaten, but unlike other parts of the country, not a single death was recorded in my village. Had the violence continued, Tutsi in my area—including ourselves—would surely have been killed. The *muyaga* always followed the same path: first looting, then burning houses, and then mass killings. The logic of the killers went like this: They could loot under the cover of state-sanctioned terror. After they looted, they began to worry what would happen when the violence ended. Would the people they took from come to get their things back? Would they come seeking revenge? So they concluded that the only way to keep their newly acquired possessions safe was to kill the rightful owner. But it was not enough to kill just that person, they also had to kill anyone who would have a legitimate claim to his property, so his family was also murdered. And so the cycle of violence was the same, over and over again: loot, burn, kill. It had happened periodically between 1959 and 1967. It was happening this time in other parts of the country. It would have happened in my area, too.

Eventually the authorities ordered the looters to return the stolen things. We managed to get our cows and some of our furniture back. We were fortunate that our cows were returned, so we had milk to drink. But our beans, the staple of our diet, were gone. We had bananas from our plantation, but they were grown to make beer, not to eat. My mother did her best to make these bananas edible by putting them in the hot atticlike space to ripen, or cutting pieces and drying them. We also had cassava, but the freshly picked roots are bitter. Cassava root contains a naturally occurring cyanide that can be deadly if it's eaten before it is completely dried. The drying process took several days, however, and it was hard as children to wait. We were so hungry. So we would eat it before it was ready. Luckily, no one got sick.

Day in, day out, we ate cassava and bananas. Yet even this was not enough. We did not have near enough food and my mother constantly worried about how she was going to feed all of her children. But at least we had something to eat. Other families had nothing and were seriously starving. We were lucky.

When the rain came, it poured into our house. It was impossible to repair the corrugated metal roof, but my father tried to cover the damaged parts with banana leaves. We would sleep under the parts of the roof that were patched, but still, rain would soak our clothes and mats. Everything was wet. We had to sit, eat, drink, and sleep in the wetness. We used a straw broom to push the water out, but still, our house was wet. It was awful, but we had nowhere else to go. It was several months before my father was able to buy more metal to replace the roof.

Soon after the *muyaga* passed, life slowly returned to normal. Schools reopened and interactions with neighbors began again. When the bananas were harvested and beer was brewed, we would go to one another's homes to drink. Tutsi and Hutu would eat together and help cultivate one another's fields. At school, we would once again pick our soccer teams on the playground without paying any attention to ethnicity. But even though our actions were normal, our feelings had changed. I began to pay attention to the ethnicity of people in my neighborhood. Whenever I was unsure if a particular person was Hutu or Tutsi I would ask my parents or surreptitiously ask another Tutsi. I was not alone. I later learned that all children—Tutsi and Hutu alike—did this. We were wary of one another. We didn't know whom to trust. At school, students would spontaneously gravitate into small groups based on their ethnicity, and then come back together as if nothing had happened. Yet still, we all worried about what would happen next.

• • • •

Through all of it—the terror, the hunger, the wet, the suspicion—my parents never taught us to hate Hutu. Even after all they had been through, I never heard them vilify Hutu as a group. Instead, my parents taught us never to hurt others. They taught us specifically never to shed blood, because *"amaraso arasema"*—which means "shedding blood curses the perpetrator." They taught us the passage in King Solomon's proverbs: "The Lord blesses everyone who is afraid to do evil, but if you are cruel, you will end up in trouble." I believed it then, and still do. I wanted to live in peace.

Chapter 2

If We Are Killed,
You Will Survive

—ᴍ—

Peace is not the absence of conflict but the presence of cre-
ative alternatives for responding to conflict—alternatives
to passive or aggressive responses, alternatives to violence.
— DOROTHY THOMPSON

I T WAS early afternoon on a Saturday in August. I loved Saturday. It
was our Sabbath. Our day of rest. No school. No chores. We would
spend our morning in church and then come home for lunch.
After lunch, I would go swimming with my brothers and sisters in
the lake. But on this day, as I sat in the cooking house finishing my
lunch, my father's voice called to me from the main house. "Sebarenzi!
Come here." In Rwanda, you are given one name at birth. Sebarenzi
was the name my father chose for me. It was his grandfather's name
and means *chief shepherd*. I never asked my father why he named me
Sebarenzi, but I know he admired his grandfather, and I also think it
reflected his aspirations for me: that I would be a chief shepherd—a
good leader. "Sebarenzi!" he called again.

I walked into the house to find him and my mother seated at the dining room table. "How are you?" he asked. He was smiling, but there was an air of seriousness about him. He didn't usually call me in to talk like this, especially on a Saturday, when he would not have chores for me.

"I'm fine," I said, searching his and my mother's faces for a sign of what this was about.

"Here, sit," my father said, gesturing to the chair next to him.

I sat. My parents had just finished their lunch. The sun was high and warm in the sky, but the thick mud walls kept the house dark and cool. A breeze blew through the small window. It was the summer of 1974, more than a year after the violence had passed, and life in Rwanda was good. President Kayibanda, who had ignited the violence in an attempt to rally support for himself, was ousted in a coup d'état and arrested. Juvénal Habyarimana, a Hutu from the northern part of the country, took over. With his regime came hope for Tutsi. We would listen to his speeches on the radio as he called for peace and unity, for Rwandans to live together as one. The term *Inyenzi* was no longer acceptable. Rwandans called Habyarimana *Umubyeyi*—our father, provider, and protector. At long last, it seemed that Tutsi would be able to live without fear. Although state-sanctioned discrimination against Tutsi in the workplace and schools still existed, we were left alone. There were no more burnings or lootings or killings. You could almost hear the collective sigh of relief spread among Tutsi across Rwanda. *Finally,* we thought, *we can live in peace.*

So I was surprised at what my father had to say. "I want you to go to Congo to go to school," he said evenly. "There are no opportunities for you here. I can't get you into secondary school in Rwanda." I knew this to be true. Rwandan middle and high schools were few and far between. Only about 10 percent of children could expect to go. Of that 10 percent, all but about 1 percent were Tutsi. My father had already tried to get a false Hutu identity card for me so I could have a chance to go to school, only to be told I was "too Tutsi" and would never be believed.

My mother quickly added, "Going to school in Congo will mean more opportunities for you. You'll have a better future."

"Yes, it will be better for you there," my father said. But what he said next surprised me: "And it's not safe here. Violence could erupt again at any time. If you get an education, you can escape. If we are killed, you will survive."

Why does he think we will be killed? I wondered. Things were peaceful. We socialized with our Hutu neighbors again. We had a president who called for peace and uttered no negative words against Tutsi. The idea that violence could erupt again seemed ridiculous. But I didn't say this. I trusted my father and nodded as he talked.

"My brother's wife lives on the island of Idjwi," he said, looking at the table. "You can live with her while you study." Then he looked me in the eye. "Will you go?"

I didn't hesitate. "Yes," I said. It was an honor to be asked to go to school. I would be the first one in the family to get an education beyond elementary school. I would make my father and my family proud. "Yes," I said again, "of course I will go."

A broad smile spread across my father's and mother's faces. My father stood and put his arm on my shoulder. "*Uri umugabo sha,*" he said. "You are brave, my child." I wasn't sure what he meant by that, but I knew he was proud of me, and I quietly reflected that pride in myself and basked in the glow. "We'll make arrangements for you to leave in a couple of weeks."

As I left the kitchen house, my heart raced. *I am going to go to school,* I thought. *I will get to see another country.* In my lifetime, I had traveled only a few miles from my home and had never spent a night away from my family. The idea of going to another country and actually *living* there was very grown-up. I felt like a man. It seemed almost too good to be true.

I left the house trying to contain my excitement. When I met my brothers and sisters who were beginning to descend the hill to the lake, they bombarded me with questions. "Why did Papa want to talk to you?" "Are you in trouble?" I smiled and proudly told them, "He asked me to go to school in Idjwi."

My older brother Samuel spun his head and looked at me. "And you agreed?" he asked.

"Yes, of course," I answered.

Samuel broke into a deep laugh. "Are you crazy?" he asked me. "Do you know what Idjwi is like?"

In truth, I didn't. I knew that the island of Idjwi sat in the middle of Lake Kivu, equidistant from Rwanda and Congo, to which it belonged. But that was it.

"Have you not seen the fishermen from Idjwi?" Samuel continued. "They don't wear clothes."

I had seen them come to Rwanda's shores to sell their fish and they *did* wear clothes, but not much. They wore only loincloths, a primitive way of dressing that was almost never seen in Rwanda.

"And do you know how you have to get there?" Samuel asked again.

"In a boat," I replied tersely. I wasn't stupid, and I didn't like Samuel treating me as if I was.

"Yes, in a boat. If you're lucky, you survive."

I knew what he was talking about. Lake Kivu is like the Great Lakes of the United States. It is more than a lake; it is like an ocean. When you stand on its shore you can't see the other side. A trip to Idjwi took about four hours of rowing in a dugout canoe—and that's assuming nothing went wrong. The canoes were small and the huge waves of Lake Kivu could easily topple them. I had heard many stories of people drowning on trips across the lake. This was the journey I would have to make to go to Idjwi. My boundless excitement at the prospect of going to school ran smack into a wall.

Samuel continued, "You know, Papa asked me and David to go, but we refused," he said. "I would never live in Idjwi." David was my other older brother. Now it made sense why Papa asked me: if they refused, I was the next boy in line. He did not want to send his daughters so far away, so I was the next logical choice.

I was silent the rest of the walk to the lake. *Where was my father sending me?* I wondered. *Is this why he called me brave?* When we reached the banks of the lake, I looked across and saw the same view I had seen since I could remember: nothing but water. The idea that I would soon cross that vast expanse in a canoe to live somewhere I'd never been, with people I hardly knew, made my stomach sink back against my spine. *But I will go to school,* I told myself again. *That is what matters.* Few of Idjwi's children went to school, so there was space in the classrooms for foreigners. Whatever else was wrong with the place, I would get an education. I held on to that fact like a prayer.

I waded into the water with my brothers and sisters. We began splashing and taunting each other as we always did. Our shouts and laughter reverberated across the water and rose up to fill the sky above us. For a moment, I forgot about Idjwi.

After swimming, we began to climb the hill back home. My sister Beatrice fell in step next to me. "So you're going to Idjwi?" she asked.

"Yes." I wondered if she could sense my trepidation.

"I'll miss you," she said simply. Beatrice and I were only a year apart, but we had lived like twins. We did everything together. "Who will I swim with?"

I gave her a feeble smile. "I will miss you, too."

We walked the rest of the way home in silence.

The night before my boat was to leave for Idjwi, my mother helped me pack my sack with clothes and notebooks. "You'll make it," she said, sensing my uneasiness. "Your uncle's family will take good care of you." My uncle had died, so I would be living with my aunt. I tried to act brave, but inside I was scared. I had never been away from my parents and brothers and sisters. It all seemed like too much to leave behind.

Then my mother said, "I have something for you." She left the room and returned with a pair of shoes. "Here," she said, handing them to me, "these are for you."

I broke into a smile—my first smile in many days. Shoes! I had never worn shoes before. In fact, no children I knew wore shoes. Only adults had them and even they saved them for special occasions like church. "Thank you," I told my mother as I slipped them onto my feet. The leather felt tight on my foot. When I walked, the thin soles were slippery. I walked around the dirt floor of the house and my excitement about going away to school once again surged to the surface. *I am becoming a man,* I thought.

The day came for me to leave. In the late afternoon, I descended the hill from our house to the shore of the lake with my parents, brothers, and sisters, where a canoe waited. The sun was getting low in the sky. It would soon be dark. My mom held tightly to my arm as we walked. "Be a good boy," she told me. "Be strong and brave. And you must always remember to keep your good character. No matter what others do or say, you must do the right thing." By the end of the sentence she was choking back tears. Despite my mother's words over the last two weeks encouraging me to go and telling me I would be fine, I could tell she was uncertain. My mother had no formal education. She was illiterate. I don't think she was convinced that an education was worth the risk I was taking by leaving. She knew what Idjwi was like. She knew how dangerous the boat ride to the island was. She composed herself and said again, "Keep your strong character."

My father interrupted her. "There's no need for that," he said, putting his arm on my shoulder. "I trust my boy." His confidence buoyed me.

When I saw the boat, my stomach did an excited flip in my gut. *I really am going,* I thought. I would make the trip with three other boys who were also going to school in Idjwi and two adults who would row us the four hours across the lake to the island. We greeted each other, and then I turned to my family to say good-bye. My mother looked desperately sad. Her eyebrows were furrowed and the corners of her mouth were tight. I reached out to shake her hand, as is the custom in Rwanda when you say good-bye. She took my hand and held it a bit longer than normal. I did the same with my brothers and sisters. All of them looked sad, but none more so than Beatrice, who averted her gaze as she shook my hand. Then I turned to my father, who betrayed no emotion other than pride as he shook my hand and then gestured to the boat, telling me it was time to go. I climbed aboard and took my place on a bench toward the front. My father and my brother Samuel pushed the boat into the water. I could feel the firmness of the earth release the canoe and the uncertainty of the water embrace it. I watched my family grow smaller as the oars pulled us away from shore.

Our boat rowed along the shore of the island of Idjwi. It was morning. We had spent the night on another island that was still part of Rwanda—only an hour's journey from my home—and then set out for Idjwi with daylight. Three hours later, we were making our way up the shoreline. I looked at the island and couldn't believe I would be living there. In fact, I couldn't believe *anyone* lived there. Mountainous contours rose up in jagged formations. Dense jungle covered nearly every square inch. Chimpanzees swung from tree to tree, calling to one another in screeching voices. I couldn't imagine a place like this had homes, much less schools.

When we finally reached the inlet that was our destination, the men rowed the canoe close to shore. The other boys and I jumped into the water to push the boat onto firm land. The water lapped against my knees and I could feel the earth of Idjwi beneath my feet. After we unloaded the canoe, we began walking along a footpath toward my uncle's house about four miles away. Other than the dense jungle, it felt the same as Rwanda. The air and smells were the same. We saw people who were dressed similar to Rwandans. Others wore only loincloths, but at first glance it didn't look as bad as I had imagined. But then, suddenly, a snake the size of my arm slithered across my path. I jumped and let out an involuntary screech. The man with me laughed. "Get used to it," he said. "You'll see much bigger snakes than that here. This is not Rwanda."

He must have seen the look of horror on my face. Snakes in Africa are deadly. I knew that one bite could kill me. "Don't worry," he said comfortingly. "When you're bit, they have healers here. You'll be fine."

When I'm bit? Healers? This did little to ease my worry. *I'm living in a jungle and I'm going to be killed by a snake,* I thought. I never knew how much I could miss home, and I'd only just arrived. I tried to push the negative thoughts out of my head. *We'll be to my uncle's house soon,* I told myself. *It will be better there.*

But it wasn't. When we finally reached the house, I couldn't believe what I saw—a small round house made entirely of grass. In Rwanda, we used these grass huts to house our calves at night. Virtually everyone in Rwanda lived in homes made of mud, except for the poorest families, particularly Twa. The thought of living in this hut deepened my despair.

My aunt emerged from the house with a welcoming smile. I had met her before and it was nice to see a familiar face. She looked Rwandan and dressed like a Rwandan, except for the numerous bracelets that adorned her arms, something I had never seen before. I had remembered her as a kind but stern matriarch who ruled with supreme authority. I knew I had to be careful not to offend her. I returned her smile and hugged her warmly. Whatever my reservations, this was my family and they were very kind to offer me their home. I could be nothing but appreciative. Her daughter and four children also lived with her. Seven of us would be living in a house that was only about seven hundred square feet.

"You must be hungry," my aunt said, as she retreated to the kitchen area of the house.

I *was* hungry—the long boat ride had ensured that—and the prospect of eating made my stomach growl in anticipation. When she returned with a plate of food, the growl turned to a lurch. A row of shiny *indugu* eyes stared up at me. Similar to sardines, *indugu* are a bony fish that are eaten whole—heads, bones, and all. In Rwanda, only poor people ate *indugu*. Inwardly I cringed. But I knew that I must be polite, so I thanked my aunt and reached down to take a bite. I was in for another surprise. When I put the food to my lips, an intense burning overtook my mouth. The fish were saturated in hot pepper, something I had never eaten before. It burned my mouth like hot ash and seemed to set fire to my throat as I swallowed. But that was not the end of the suffering. As anyone who has eaten unusually spicy foods knows, the revenge it exacts is fierce and unforgiving. For days after my stomach tried to recover, but every meal dealt it yet another blow. I began ignoring my hunger pangs and eating less. As if that weren't enough, my aunt had no cattle so we had no milk, which had been a staple of my diet since I was a small child. *This is not Rwanda,* the man from the canoe had told me. I had a feeling I would be uttering those same words to myself over and over again.

That night I lay down to sleep on the floor of the house next to the children. They were younger than me and spoke only the island's native language, Mahavu, which was unfamiliar to me. We would try to talk to one another but understood very little. As I lay on the floor, my stomach burned from the meal. Everything felt different. The language was different. The food was different. The house was different. For one of the rare times in my life, I was going to sleep without drinking milk. I missed it almost as much as I missed my family, and I missed them with an intensity I hadn't known existed. I thought of them back in Rwanda. They, too, would be going to sleep. They would be gathered together in the main house, saying their evening prayers and singing hymns. I closed my eyes and imagined their faces glowing in the light of the oil lamp. I imagined my mother gently touching my temples and telling me good night. I imagined my sisters and brothers laughing as they lay down for the night. I imagined the soothing low of our cattle. I imagined it all, and fell asleep.

I only spent a week at my uncle's house before I was told I would be moving to my cousin's home. He was married and had only two small children, so there would be more room for me. When I arrived at his house, my spirits lifted a little. It was a mud house with banana leaves for a roof, much like traditional Rwandan homes. It was one of the nicest houses in the area, and much more comfortable. But it came at a price. Life there was desperately lonely. I had spent my entire life up to that point surrounded by sisters and brothers close to my age. Now I was living with two adults and two young kids. I had no one to talk to. I had no one to play soccer with. I had no one to share my long list of chores with. Every day I had to carry water from the spring, help care for the children, and take care of the goats, with their beady eyes and greedy bleating. I thought of our cows back home—how I would lean on them and feel their warmth. I knew each of our cows like I knew my brothers and sisters. I knew what they liked and didn't like. I knew their habits. They would come to me when I called them. These goats, on the other hand, would run from me, their short legs ferrying them away on a choppy stride. In Rwanda, taking care of the cattle was an honor. Caring for goats was a chore. In addition to fetching water and caring for the children and goats, I had to collect firewood almost every day. Soon I would add schoolwork on top of that—and about a five-mile walk to school.

Each night I would go to sleep with an aching sadness deep in my chest. I worked long hours every day. I felt as if my cousin and his wife didn't show me enough affection. We did not pray together or laugh together. I did not feel like a member of their family; I felt like a servant. It was not that my cousins were bad people, it was just the reality of the situation: I was a guest, not a close family member. I always had to be polite and watch what I said. In Rwanda, if I finished my meal and was still hungry, I would ask for more. Here, that would be rude. So I would go to sleep with a low growl in my belly. On school days in Rwanda, my mother would come to me in the morning to make sure I was ready. She would make sure I had combed my hair and put lotion on my face. Here, it was as if I were living alone. No one checked on me. No one hugged or comforted me. I realized for the first time that the closeness of family cannot be replicated with others. As I fell asleep each night, I would think of home and count the days until I could return for Christmas break. I had been in Idjwi only a couple of weeks, and already I was dreaming of home. A prison sentence would have seemed more tolerable.

A week before I was to start classes, my cousin and I walked to the school with a goat, a cask of beer, and a branch of bananas. It was the custom in Idjwi to bring these gifts to the principal in exchange for admission to the school. In essence, it was a bribe, but everyone did it and it was the only way to ensure a spot in school. So one late August day, we made the five-mile trek to see the principal and give him his gifts.

When we reached the school, my cousin and I sat with the principal. As the two men exchanged pleasantries, I looked around me in amazement. The school was by far the nicest I had ever seen. It was constructed of brick and had cement floors. In Rwanda, the schools were made of mud, with dirt floors and dilapidated furniture. This schoolhouse had nice chairs and desks. It looked like an official government building, not like a school for children. For the first time the excitement of getting an education returned and I thought for a moment that I had made the right decision by coming to Idjwi.

My cousin presented the gifts and the three of us shared a beer. Then the principal looked at me and smiled. "Be ready to come to school next week," he said. And with that, it was official. I would be going to school. I would begin in the fifth-grade class. I had just completed sixth grade in Rwanda and done well, but my French—the dominant language in Congo—was not good enough to move to the seventh grade. So not only would I have to learn the local language, I would have to learn French as well.

The night before my first day of school my stomach performed somersaults and other acrobatic feats as I lay down to sleep. I would be going to a school where I didn't speak the language well and knew almost no one, except for the two Rwandan boys who I was told would be in my class. I prayed for God to guide me and be with me. I asked Him to help me understand the lessons and do well. And I asked Him to protect me.

The next morning I began the journey to school, walking first along a footpath and then to a main road, just like my cousin had showed me when we had gone the week before. I thought back to Rwanda and how I would walk to school with my brothers and sisters, kicking a soccer ball among us. This walk seemed desperately lonely by comparison.

When I got to my classroom I went through the lessons in a bewildered fog. I tried hard to understand the teacher, recalling my French lessons from back home, but it wasn't easy. At recess, I retreated with the two other Rwandan boys from my class to a corner of the playground, but several bigger children found us. "One Congolese equals five hundred Rwandans, plus the president and his wife!" they chanted. It was their way of asserting Congo's superiority over Rwanda, which is a speck on the map compared to Congo. Many Congolese determined that Rwanda's small size (nearly one hundred times smaller than Congo) meant that that Rwandans were backward and inferior. Of course, in Rwanda, we thought people from Idjwi were backward and inferior, but my friends and I didn't say this. We kept our eyes down and endured the taunts.

This would not be the end of it. Every day children would seek us out and tease us. Their bullying didn't stop with words. They would also try to pick fights. We would scare them off by telling them we would fight them with *inkoni*—cow-herding staffs that were used for fighting in Rwanda. Men would hold two *inkoni* like swords: one to defend themselves and the other to strike. In Congo, people fought with fists, not *inkoni*, so the idea of an angry Rwandan coming at them with a long stick was enough to keep them away. In truth, I was not much of a fighter and I'm glad no one took me up on my threat. My other defense was to stay as quiet and as invisible as possible, but it wasn't easy. My Tutsi features and the fact that I didn't speak the local language made me stand out. I might as well have had "foreigner" stamped on my forehead. But I did my best to keep out of trouble, focusing all of my energy on improving my French and doing well in school.

After school I would walk home, do my chores, eat dinner, and go to sleep. Day after day, it was the same. And day after day, my longing for home grew more intense. Whenever I heard that a boat was going back to Rwanda, I would hurry to write a letter to my parents. I knew my father would be the one to read it because of my mother's illiteracy, so I chose my words carefully. I told my father how much I didn't like it there and the hardships I endured, but I never said the one thing I so desperately wanted to say: I want to come home.

Summer near the equator doesn't arrive like it does in other parts of the world. The seasons don't really change. There are no budding trees or longer days to herald its arrival. If it weren't for calendars, summer would have little to distinguish it from the rest of the year. But for me, summer was everything. Summer meant going home. I had been home at Christmas and Easter, but summer was different. I would be home for two full months. I spent the waning days of June imagining life in Rwanda. I could see the footpath leading up from the lake to my home. I could see the faces of my brothers and sisters and parents. I pleaded in my prayers that the remaining days on Idjwi go fast and that my days home creep by.

The night before the boat left, I could barely contain my happiness. I practically ran to the shore where the dugout canoe waited to ferry me to home. I spent the night on the lake's banks with the two men who would row me to Rwanda. At about five o'clock in the morning, when the water was calm and darkness still blanketed the sky, one of the men woke me up and told me it was time to go. I leaped to my feet with the excitement of a child on Christmas morning.

The trip was becoming commonplace now. This would be the sixth time I was rowed across Lake Kivu. I still knew it was dangerous, but our previous trips had been uneventful, so I began to relax and approach the journey like a seasoned traveler.

Our trip this day started the same as the others. The gentle rocking waves. The rhythmic sound of the oars slapping the water. The warm breeze. But about three hours into the trip, after the sun had warmed the sky into daylight, things changed. With the sun came wind, huge gusts of it. Waves began crashing into the side of the boat.

"Row! Row!" the men shouted to me.

I picked up an oar and began frantically rowing, trying to keep the canoe from tipping. I had never seen waves like this. They pounded relentlessly. The hull of the boat would rise almost straight up in the air before it crashed down again. The force of it knocked me from the bench and onto the floor of the canoe. As soon as I righted myself, I would be knocked down again. It seemed certain that the boat would capsize. Then it became clear that if capsizing didn't kill us, sinking surely would. I looked down and water covered my ankles. One of the men barked at me to stop rowing and start bailing. I dropped my oar and began scooping the water out with a wooden bucket. But it was futile. With every bucketful dumped over the side, another wave would crash over us and replace all the water I had just thrown out.

When the waves finally stopped more than an hour later, I sat in an exhausted heap. I put my head in my hands and wiped the water from my eyes. My hands shook and my heart raced. I lifted my eyes and looked around me. For as far as the eye could see there was nothing but water. No land. No other boats. If our canoe had capsized, we would have undoubtedly drowned. The prospect sent a chill up my spine and I quietly closed my eyes and thanked God for protecting us.

The strong winds had thrown us off course. We had been in the water for about four hours and were still far from land. The men and

I finished bailing the water from the canoe, and they began rowing again. One hour later, land came into view. As we rowed to shore, I looked up the hill to my house. In a few moments, I would be with my family again. My heart filled and I had to force back tears of joy. I stepped from the boat, still shaken from our journey. My feet sank into the soil—Rwandan soil. I had never been so happy to set foot on earth in my life.

I rushed up the hill. As I reached the house I began shouting, "Mama! Papa!" My mother came running out of the house and embraced me.

"Oh, Sebarenzi! You're home." She stood back and examined me, her arms on my shoulders. Quickly her look of happiness changed to worry. I knew why. I had lost a lot of weight since she last saw me. My homesickness had suppressed my appetite, and any appetite I did have was hard to satisfy. Plus, I had to walk about ten miles each day to and from school, as well as do my daily chores, which were physically taxing. I was burning more calories than I was eating, and it showed. She had noticed that I had lost weight when I visited at Christmas and Easter, but it had only gotten worse.

"Sebarenzi," she said shaking her head. "You are too thin."

I cringed at the words. In Rwanda, as in many developing countries, thinness is equated with poverty. My family's status meant their children should be well fed. My meager frame belied my father's wealth. I quickly changed the subject. "Where's Papa?" I asked.

"At your stepmother's," she answered. "Come in, sit." She led me into the house.

Soon my brothers and sisters began pouring into the house with questions about my trip and life in Idjwi. I told them about the boat nearly capsizing. "See," my brother Samuel said. "That's why I'll never go to Idjwi!"

I laughed at his teasing. I didn't care what anyone said. I was home.

My mother brought me a cup of *ikivuguto*, a kind of milk that would be set aside for three days, until a thick layer of fat had settled on top. Then she would stir it until it was thick and creamy. I swallowed it in satisfied gulps.

I spent the day with my brothers and sisters, and then visited my

stepmothers' homes to see them and their children. When I saw my
father, he embraced me proudly. "Sebarenzi, it's good to see you," he
said. He made no comment about my weight loss. I knew he noticed
it, but he did not want to say anything that would discourage me.

That night, I ate dinner with my family. We prayed together and
sang together, as we always did. I felt the warmth of home wrap
around me and held on to it, never wanting to let it go. After dinner,
my father left to spend the night at my stepmother's house. As I got
ready to go to sleep, my mother came to me. "Sebarenzi," she said,
holding my hands and looking at me with worried eyes, "you don't
look well. You need to eat more."

"Mama, the food in Idjwi is not good. And there's not enough—"

"Well, while you're home, you need to catch up. Get fat while
you're here so you can go back with some meat on your bones."

With the mention of going back to Idjwi, tears came to my eyes.
I hadn't expected them to come so easily, but they did. "I don't like it
there, Mama," I told her, wiping the tears from my cheeks. "It's hard.
There's not enough food. The work is very hard. The boat ride today
nearly killed me." I looked down and said the words I had wanted to
say for the last year, "I want to come home."

She put her arm around me. "Then you should come home," she
said.

I looked up at her, surprised.

"You are not happy there. You are too thin. You're going to get sick
if you keep losing weight like this. It's not good for you to be there."

Relief washed over me.

"Besides," she continued, "if you don't go to school it doesn't mean
you won't have a good life. Look at your father, he doesn't have an
education. He's successful and happy. I want you to go to school, but
not if it will cost you your health."

"But Papa says it's not safe here."

"If we are killed, we'll die together," she said quietly.

I nodded solemnly, thinking of the terrifying night we had spent
hiding under our neighbors' bed.

"We'll talk to your father tomorrow."

That night I went to sleep with a contentment in my heart that

I hadn't felt since last summer. *I don't have to go back*, I kept saying to myself over and over again. *Thank you, God. I will be home again. Thank you.* I fell into a deep and dreamless sleep.

The next morning, my father came home. My siblings and I were all in the house with Mama, getting ready for the day. When my father walked in, my mother immediately turned to him, "Do you see how thin Sebarenzi has become?"

My father shrugged. "Oh, he's not that thin."

"Yes, he is," she said. "He has lost too much weight."

Again, my father brushed her off. "You're exaggerating."

I jumped in. "No, she's not exaggerating," I said.

My father cut me a look, and then my mother. He sensed an ambush.

My mother spoke first. "I don't think Sebarenzi should go back to Idjwi," she said. "He's not well. If he stays there, he's going to get sick."

My father looked at me. "Please, Papa," I pleaded, feeling emboldened by my mother's support. "I don't like it there. I don't want to go back."

He shook his head. "No," he said quietly. Then more forcefully, "No. You will go back." It was as if he hadn't heard a word we said. He didn't even stop to consider.

"But, Papa—" I began to protest.

He raised his hand to quiet me and looked at my mother. "What are you telling him?" he asked her. "What ideas are you giving him? He must go back. You know that. He has no future here."

"What future does he have there if he is weak and sick?" my mother shot back. "Look at him! He's too thin."

My father shook his head again. "No, he must go back."

I knew his word was final and with it, my heart ripped open again. He must have noticed because he softened his voice and looked at me. "Sebarenzi, your education is the most important thing. There's no future for you here. You must go back to Idjwi and graduate from high school. It is your only chance for a better life."

My brother Samuel, who had been listening in rapt attention with my other siblings, said quickly, "It's not worth it, Papa. No education is worth being so miserable."

My father didn't waver. "Education is always worth it." He turned and looked at me again. "Sebarenzi, when summer is over, you must go back."

I nodded, but inside I was screaming. *I don't want an education if it means going back to stupid Idjwi!* Besides, Rwanda was a peaceful nation now. I thought my father was being irrational. I could live and work on the farm for the rest of my life. What was wrong with that? Why couldn't that be my life?

Two months later I climbed into the canoe and traveled back to Idjwi. I would spend three more years there. After that I would go to boarding school in Goma, a city on the mainland of Congo, and then to college. Rwanda was at peace the entire time. But I didn't know then what my father knew. He knew that, despite the new president's speeches espousing peace and unity in Rwanda, neither existed. The peace of President Habyarimana's regime was a negative peace. Although Tutsi were physically safe, they were still discriminated against and treated as second-class citizens. Tutsi children, like myself, were still largely barred from attending secondary school. Discrimination in hiring still persisted.

For the Tutsi who had lived through the violence of the 1960s and 1973, these terms were bearable. "At least we are left alone," they would say. "No one burns our homes or tries to kill us." But my father knew that in any country where one part of the citizenry is oppressed, violence is sure to come. He also saw other disturbing signs. Papa would point out that during the 1973 massacres, Habyarimana was minister of defense. Papa rightly wondered how he could serve as minister of defense and not play a role in government-sanctioned killing. This suspicion was validated when Habyarimana took power and held no one accountable for the massacres. Also, Habyarimana put the former president under house arrest and imprisoned dozens of his aides. At the time, rumors swarmed that they had been killed. My father figured if Habyarimana could kill his own people, then he could certainly kill Tutsi.

Papa also pointed out that Habyarimana did not abolish the use of ethnic identity cards that had been established under Belgian rule. If he really wanted to unify Rwanda, would that not be the first step? And celebrations of national holidays were still fueled with venomous rhetoric. During Rwanda's Independence Day celebrations, Tutsi felt that it was not so much a celebration of victory over the colonial government as a celebration of victory over Tutsi. But the holiday that Tutsi anticipated with dread each year was the Kamarampaka holiday on September 25, which celebrated the abolition of the monarchy. The Kamarampaka celebrations that followed Habyarimana's rise to power were saturated with the same offensive words and tone as in previous years. On Independence Day the following year, the tone of the celebrations had changed little. I don't think it was a coincidence that my father suggested I go to Congo shortly after those celebrations. He saw that a year into Habyarimana's rule, it was still acceptable to chip away at Tutsi's dignity. This was not a good sign for a regime that claimed to cherish unity and reconciliation.

I learned all of this in bits and pieces over the years, when I returned home from school and he would talk to me about government and politics and caution me to be wary of nice words from dictators. The more I listened to him, the more I understood why he had sent me to Idjwi. But I think there's another reason my father pushed me to go to Congo, one he never talked about. I think it was that day in 1973 when he hid in the banana plantation and thought men were coming to kill him. I think it was the story of my mother, brother, niece, and I hiding under our neighbors' bed, waiting to be killed. I think it was our burned cooking house and the destroyed homes of so many others. I think it was the hunger we faced after our food had been looted. That was the first time violence had come so close to our family. What's more, the massacres of 1973 had come after a period of peace. Everyone thought civilians would be safe. No one believed Tutsi would be targeted again. When my father realized how wrong they were, I don't think he ever trusted periods of peace in Rwanda to last. I think he knew that a cosmetic peace hiding the blemishes of discrimination *could not* last. He was right. Violence did come again, and this time it was far worse than anyone could ever have imagined.

Chapter 3

No One Knows How War Will End

~~~

Mankind must put an end to war, or war will put an end
to mankind.

—JOHN F. KENNEDY

WHEN THE soldiers came to my house in Kigali to arrest
me, I did not feel fear. It seems odd to think of it now,
but I had anticipated my arrest for so many days that
when it finally happened, I was not afraid. Fear is in the anticipation
of danger, not in danger itself. So when they loaded me into their
jeep, telling me I was accused of treason, fear disappeared. I simply
thought, *It is in God's hands now,* and I had faith that He would protect me. I reminded myself that even if I was powerless, God was not.
He could make the impossible possible. I prayed that He would.

It was October 1990, and until that point, life had been very good.
I was married to a wonderful woman named Liberata, whom I had
met while attending college in Congo. She was studying economics
and I was studying sociology. When I met her, I thought she would
one day be my wife. There was a kindness about her, a down-to-earth

quality that few other women I knew possessed. When I asked her to marry me and told her I wanted to move back to Rwanda, she told me, "I love you, but I cannot live there." She was from a Tutsi family who had fled the violence in Rwanda in the early 1960s, when she was just a baby. They had lived as refugees in Burundi ever since. I assured her Rwanda was now a peaceful nation. "Go for a visit," I told her. "If you don't like it, we won't live there."

"No," she said. "I won't set foot in that country. My family barely survived living there. I won't go back."

I begged her to give it a chance, and she reluctantly agreed. So I took her to Kigali, Rwanda's capital. At the end of our visit, I asked her hopefully, "So? What do you think? Can we live here?"

"It's better than I thought it would be," she admitted. "But I still don't think it's a good idea." She regarded me soberly, sighed, and shook her head. "I will move here because I love you. But I'm still not convinced it's completely safe."

I smiled and hugged her. "We will have a good life in Rwanda," I told her. "I'll make you very happy."

So in April 1989 we married and began our life together in Kigali. I worked first as a high-school teacher and then as a researcher and trainer for a nonprofit organization. We also owned a small store that was quite successful. And in February 1990, our first child, a son we named Respect, was born. My youngest brother, John, was living with us while he attended school, and he, too, was like a son to me. Our life was good and I felt confident I had made the right decision in coming back to Rwanda.

Then one evening I was walking home from my teaching job with a man from the neighborhood. Our walks home were similar and we would often fall in step together and talk. He was also Tutsi and we had become friendly over the last few months. As we descended the hill to our homes, we were passing time talking politics, as we often did, when he told me casually, "Bene wacu"—our brothers—"are going to attack this country. They're going to end Habyarimana's regime."

My eyes widened in disbelief. "No," I said, shaking my head. "That is a very bad idea."

He looked at me quizzically. I suppose he thought that because I was also Tutsi I would support the idea of launching a war.

"If the Tutsi refugees attack," I said, "it will only mean reprisal killings of Tutsi living in Rwanda."

"But we must fight," he said. "Habyarimana will never allow Tutsi to have equal rights—"

"Yes, I know," I said, cutting him off. "But a rebellion is not the answer. You know as well as I do that if there is an attack, massacres of Tutsi will begin."

My friend shook his head. "Not if we win."

"We cannot win! Habyarimana has the support of France, of Belgium, of Congo," I said. "If Tutsi attack, all of these countries will step in to protect the government. There is no way we can win!" I reminded him of the French saying, *On sait comment la guerre commence, mais on ne sait pas comment elle se termine*—one knows how war begins, but no one knows how it will end. I was more worried by the reality of a war we could not win and by the massacres it would trigger than by the intrinsic weakness of the war. There is no such thing as winning a war in a divided society. Intercommunity violence results in death and destruction and, for the defeated, in humiliation and resentment. The resentment eventually boils over and turns violent. It was a vicious cycle, and I saw no winners.

"So what should we do? Continue to live oppressed like this?"

"Of course not," I said. "But we should try to change it peacefully, democratically. A war will only result in bloodshed." He knew what I meant. In the past, Tutsi rebel groups had launched assaults in the provinces, and innocent Tutsi paid the price. In 1962, shortly before Rwanda gained independence, a group of Tutsi attacked the province of Byumba in the northeast. In retribution, the government massacred an estimated two thousand Tutsi men, women, and children. Their huts were burned and looted, and their property divided among the Hutu population. The same thing happened again, in the space of a couple of months at the end of 1963 and the beginning of 1964. Only this time, an estimated ten thousand Tutsi were slaughtered.

I told my neighbor that peaceful efforts to restore democracy to

Rwanda were beginning to emerge—efforts that stemmed more from dissent among Hutu than Tutsi. Tutsi were resigned to their fates, at least outwardly, but Hutu from the south were clamoring for an end to Habyarimana's dictatorial rule. Rumblings of democracy were rippling through the country. This dissent, I believed, would ultimately result in change—change that would benefit Tutsi.

We argued the rest of the way home—he insisting that fighting was the answer, me countering that it would only result in more suffering for Tutsi. As we reached the bottom of the hill and parted ways to go to our homes, he shook my hand and said, "We will talk about this again."

When I returned home, I didn't tell Liberata of the conversation. I didn't want to worry her unnecessarily. Rumors of rebellion were common, and I hoped maybe this was just another one that would quietly fade away. I put the conversation out of my mind and didn't think of it again until several months later, in October. I had begun working for a nonprofit organization located in central Rwanda. Every day I would take a small commuter bus to my office, about an hour's drive from the capital. On this day, as the bus made its way along the road, I saw roadblocks guarded by soldiers on the outskirts of town. "What's going on?" people on the bus began to ask one another.

Then a man toward the back of the bus said, "Didn't you hear? The *Inyenzi* have attacked."

Immediately I recalled my conversation with the man from my neighborhood. So it had happened. The Tutsi refugees had launched their assault. *Oh, my God,* I thought. *This is going to be terrible.* I thought of Liberata and Respect at home. I knew how terrified Liberata would be when she heard the news. I needed to get back home to her.

I was late arriving to work. The roadblocks had slowed us considerably. When I arrived, I went to my boss, Umutesi, a Hutu woman who was always very kind to me, and asked her if I could go back home. "Of course," she said without hesitation, "go home to see your wife and son."

So I boarded the commuter bus again, expecting to be home in an hour or two. But as we got closer to Kigali, traffic slowed to a crawl. Soldiers stopped cars at checkpoints, searching vehicles for weapons—or rebels who might be sneaking into the city. The tension on the streets was palpable. From the conversations on the bus, it was clear that this rebel attack was more successful than those in the past. In the 1960s, rebel forces were ill-equipped bands of inexperienced fighters. This time, the rebels were organized, equipped, and trained. I thought of my conversation with my neighbor and his assertion that this time the rebels would win. I didn't see how it was possible; now I wondered if he was right. But I knew that before they won, Tutsi would suffer immeasurably. On the long ride home I thought of what to do. I knew that I had to get Liberata and Respect out of the country. Her family members were refugees in Burundi; she could go stay with them until this ended. But how would it end? *On sait comment la guerre commence, mais on ne sait pas comment elle se termine.* The truth of this statement rang in my ears.

Seven hours later, I got off the bus and rushed home. When I walked through the door, Liberata was standing in the living room, holding our son. She gave me a cold kiss. "I knew this would happen," she said. Her words were harsh, but her voice was soft. I could tell she was more frightened than angry. "I knew we should not have come to Rwanda."

I had no reply. She was right, after all.

"What are we going to do? Things are only going to get worse," she said.

"You and Respect must leave," I told her. "I think you should take Respect to your parents'. You'll be safer there."

She looked at me warily. "And what about you? It's not safe here. You should go, too."

"No," I replied, "it's better if I stay behind and leave later. It will give me time to sell the store. And I can keep my job if I stay here. Besides, this might blow over."

"And what if it doesn't?"

"It will be easier for me to run and hide if I am alone. You and Respect should leave now. I'll join you later."

What she said next surprised me. "No, I won't go," she said.

"Mama Respect," I said, calling her the customary Rwandan name for a spouse after the first son is born, "you must go."

"Not if you won't go, too."

"I don't think you know how serious this is," I said, my voice rising. "You could be killed. You can't stay!"

"Either we leave together or we die together," she said plainly. "I'm not leaving without you."

"Yes, you will!" I said forcefully. For the first time in our marriage, I demanded that she do something. "You will take Respect and go to Burundi. This is not a choice. You must leave."

She said nothing. She just stared at me.

I softened my voice. "I know this is hard," I told her. "But it won't be for long. After things quiet down, I'll meet you in Burundi. I promise." I understood her fear of being separated. Crossing into Burundi without me could be dangerous for her and Respect. Also, although she didn't say it, I knew she wondered what her life would be like if I were killed. In Africa, a widow's life is hard. Few can make a sufficient living to support themselves and their children, and even fewer have hope of remarrying. She was risking a lot by leaving without me.

The next day we went to consult with some good friends, asking them if they thought Liberata should leave. This is customary in Africa, where few decisions are made individually—family and friends always have a say. We told them the situation: I explained why I thought Liberata should go; Liberata explained why she thought she should stay. Our friends agreed with me. "Liberata," they said, "take your son and go. It will be safer for you. Joseph will join you later, but you should leave now before things get worse."

Liberata, who had so reluctantly agreed to come to Rwanda, now reluctantly agreed to leave it.

The next day, on the third of October, Liberata, Respect, and I walked to the bus station. Respect was swaddled on Liberata's back. I carried her luggage. Our walk was silent. We both retreated into ourselves, knowing that this good-bye could be our last. As I watched her step onto the bus and take her seat by the window, it felt like my heart would burst through my chest. Everything I loved was on that bus, and now it was being taken away. I swallowed my tears as I waved to them. As I looked at my eight-month-old son sitting on my wife's lap, words flashed through my mind: *If I am killed, you will survive.* The same words my father had spoken to me so many years ago were now the words I silently said to my son as I watched the bus roll away.

The night after they left, my brother John and I were awakened by explosions in the distance and the cracking of gunfire.

"Quick—under the bed," I said to John, thinking the blasts could get closer to the house.

"What's going on?" he asked.

"I don't know. I think the rebels are attacking the capital." I thought of Liberata and Respect, who by now would be in Burundi. *Thank God they are gone,* I thought. *Thank God they are safe.*

We stayed under the bed part of the night, listening to the alternating booms and pops grow closer. Then in the morning, it was silent again. John and I decided to venture outside to see what had happened. Maybe, we thought, the rebels had won. Maybe Habyarimana's government was defeated. "If they won," John said optimistically, "that would be very good."

I offered a wan smile. *Yes,* I thought, *but if they lost, things will get very bad.* I didn't say this to John. He seemed so young and vulnerable. I didn't want to scare him.

We walked the streets and saw the same Hutu soldiers who had been patrolling them for the last four days. I looked at John and shook my head. "The rebels have lost," I said. "This is not good."

Later, as we walked around Kigali, we noticed something strange: No buildings were destroyed. Nothing was burned. No bullet holes pocked walls. We returned home and listened to the radio, which claimed that rebels had attacked the capital and been defeated by government troops. But if they had attacked, why was there no evidence of it? It didn't make sense. Over the next several days, we talked with other friends and neighbors who had noticed the same thing. Then it became clear: The rebels had not attacked Kigali. The government staged the fighting to galvanize Hutu against Tutsi. Voices on government-run radio stations would implore, *Put aside our differences and unite against the common enemy—Inyenzi. We must remain vigilant. The* Inyenzi *are cunning. They hide everywhere. You might think you've found them, but there are always more hiding.* So Tutsi were once again *Inyenzi*. What's more, there was no distinction between Tutsi rebels and Tutsi citizens. We were all lumped together as one.

I imagine that Habyarimana was secretly happy that the rebels attacked when they did. A democracy movement spearheaded by Hutu from the south was emerging. It seemed to be only a matter of time before his regime would end. But now, all attention was on Tutsi. He could shore up support for himself by whipping the country into a frenzy over the Tutsi enemy. Habyarimana saw this war as a chance to get rid of the opposition once for all.

Just as I expected, en masse arrests of Tutsi and Hutu who opposed the regime immediately began. But that was not all. Rumors spread that in some regions of the country near where the attacks took place, Tutsi civilians were rounded up and murdered. Security in Kigali took on the feel of a vise grip. Travel to other districts was heavily restricted. Checkpoints spread like fungus. Soldiers manned the street corners.

I thought of the last time I had seen my father, about nine months earlier. During our conversation, he again expressed doubts of the fragile peace that knitted Rwanda together. Although Rwanda had been peaceful for seventeen years, he still did not trust Habyarimana. By this point, I needed little convincing. Despite early hopes that Habyarimana would be the "father" of our country and unify Hutu and Tutsi, it was clear he had no intention of making Tutsi equal citizens. Under Habyarimana's regime up to this point, not a single Tutsi served as a provincial governor or mayor. Virtually no Tutsi served as officers in the military, and Hutu officers were discouraged from marrying Tutsi women. Only one Tutsi would serve in Habyarimana's cabinet and only one Tutsi would serve in parliament at any given time. No Tutsi filled an ambassadorship except in the late 1980s, when one was appointed to the Vatican. Although Tutsi were safe and able to go about our daily lives undisturbed, we were not free. Our aspirations were suppressed and our questions—*Why can't we hold high offices in the army or government? Why can't our children have the same access to schools?*—unanswered.

If that weren't enough, Habyarimana showed little respect for power sharing and rule of law. Elections were held every five years, but they were a fraud. Each time, Habyarimana would win with more than 99 percent of the vote. It was a single-party, single-man rule. He also showed little regard for human life. The government officials he had imprisoned after the coup—President Kayibanda and fifty-six of his former aides—all died mysteriously while under the government's control. President Kayibanda starved to death while under house arrest. Despite my anger at Kayibanda for his evil policies, and my firm belief that he should be held accountable for his actions, he did not deserve to die like that—no one does. All human beings, regardless of the evil they commit, deserve dignity and respect, and it is a disservice to humanity when either is denied.

Habyarimana took other steps to solidify his dictatorship. He changed Rwanda's Independence Day celebration from July 1 to July 5—the day he took power. It was ridiculous. Independence Day cannot be subordinated to an individual, especially one who makes an undemocratic ascension to power. Habyarimana was not elected by the people; he overthrew the government in a coup. But Habyarimana's biggest mistake was his negligence in addressing the issue of Tutsi refugees. When Rwandans who had fled the country during the violence of the 1960s and 1973 asked permission to return, Habyarimana rejected them, saying that the country was too small to accommodate the hundreds of thousands of Rwandans living outside the country's borders. This enraged exiled Tutsi, who rightly felt entitled to return to their homeland.

Among those in exile were my relatives on the island of Idjwi whom I had lived with while I was in school. My uncle and his family had fled to the island following the first wave of Tutsi massacres in the early 1960s. They were forbidden to return, even for a visit. Despite this, my uncle would sneak back into the country occasionally to visit his aging mother—my grandmother. He would row across Lake Kivu under cover of darkness and arrive on the shores of Rwanda deep in the night. He would then fill his boat with water to sink it, so it would not raise suspicion, and sneak to my grandmother's house, where he would hide the entire length of his visit. Leaving the house would be too dangerous. If he were seen, he would be severely punished, as would my family, for harboring a refugee. So each of his trips to Rwanda was the same—a midnight crossing, a sunken boat, a stealthy visit. As a child, I watched this and learned firsthand that refusing people the right to return to their homes only breeds anger and resentment. My grandmother died without ever seeing her grandchildren or great-grandchildren on Idjwi—all because Habyarimana asserted that the country was not large enough for everyone. My family was only one of hundreds of thousands who had the same experience. Liberata's family was another. Time and again, the government drew a border between families that could never be crossed.

Eventually, many of these refugees organized and formed a rebel force, threatening attacks on Rwanda if a peaceful solution to the refugee crisis was not found. Habyarimana disregarded them, the attacks began, and Rwandans were once again suffering. It is not that I didn't understand the Tutsi refugees' reasons for starting the war. I did. But I didn't—couldn't—agree with them. The price war exacts on a population is too high.

Life in Kigali was tense. The rebels were making progress, and the rhetoric on the airwaves became more venomous. More rumors circulated about Tutsi being slaughtered in the provinces. About eight thousand Tutsi from Kigali were rounded up in the national stadium and then dispatched to prisons. *This is only the beginning,* I thought. *More will follow.*

I continued going to work and trying to live my life as normally as possible, but it was hard. I still had hope that a negotiated settlement could be reached and Tutsi would be able to live undisturbed again. Then one day a Hutu neighbor told me my name had come up in a local meeting. "They say you were involved in plotting the attack," he said. "They say that you knew it was going to happen. Be careful."

I felt as if I had been punched in the gut. "But I had nothing to do with this!"

"I know," he said, "but others say you did."

This was how it always happened in Rwanda. Any time a crisis erupted, finger-pointing—or *gutunga agotoki*—began. It started as little more than gossip, then became rumors, and then everyone believed it to be true. "Who is saying this?" I asked him.

He told me it was another neighbor, a Hutu man who frequented my store and owed me money. "He says that you sent your wife and son away before the attack, so you knew it was going to happen."

"But it's a lie! Liberata and my son left two days *after* the rebels attacked," I told him. But I knew that the man who was accusing me didn't have any need for the truth. He was trying to get out of his debts. If I were imprisoned or killed, he wouldn't have to pay me the money he owed me. This is also common in Rwanda during times of crisis. People use the government-induced frenzy to get back at people against whom they held personal grudges.

"Well, he's saying they left before the attack. And he says you told him that your brothers were going to rise up and overthrow the government."

I shook my head in disbelief.

"Just be careful," he said again. "Watch your back."

I thanked him and immediately began wondering what I could do to get out of Kigali. If this man were spreading these rumors and others believed him, it was only a matter of time before I was arrested. It was a certainty. Each day I would walk through the streets feeling the weight of every soldier's eyes on me.

So when the soldiers finally knocked on my door to arrest me, it was almost a relief—*so this is how it will happen,* I thought. There was no more suspense. No more looking over my shoulder. I climbed into the jeep as I was told and sat on the bench seat next to two other men who were friends of mine from the neighborhood. Makombe was a teacher; Kaberuka was a statistician. Neither struck me as a conspirator. But I had the feeling that facts mattered little to the government at this point.

The jeep arrived at a district government office building that housed the offices of the mayor, who was also a lieutenant colonel in the military. We were taken out of the vehicle and led into a small room that looked as though it had once been a storage area. Now it was a makeshift cell. About seven other men were sitting on the floor when we walked in. A small window gave the room its only light. We were released into the room and the door closed behind us. I heard the crisp clack of the bolt locking us in. I walked to the window and looked out. The building was surrounded by a fence. Armed soldiers patrolled the perimeter. It was clear there was no escaping—not that there would have been much point. Roadblocks were everywhere. Even if I had escaped, I would most certainly have been caught.

I thought of John. He would come home from school and find me gone. Surely one of the neighbors would tell him what had happened. And then it struck me just what *had* happened: I had been arrested. It was absurd! What was I doing in jail? I had done nothing wrong. I thought of Liberata and Respect and said a silent prayer thanking God that they were safe in Burundi. I imagined what Liberata would say if she knew I was in jail. *I told you so* would have been completely justified. She was the one who did not want to live in Rwanda. She was the one who told me I should go to Burundi with her. I had promised her I would be fine. I was wrong.

Each day in jail passed the same as the next. I would sit with my friends. We would whisper back and forth to each other, careful not to reveal too much to our fellow inmates. "They could be spies," my friend whispered to me shortly after we arrived. "We can't trust anyone." So we continued our whispering, theorizing about what was going on in the outside world, wondering aloud about our fates. We had nothing to read—not a single newspaper, magazine, or book. There was no television, no radio. We had nothing to do except look out the window to see who was coming and going. We would curl up on the floor at night and try to sleep, but sleep rarely came. The soldiers, however, did. Every few days, they would come to the cell and take one of the other men away. Often, whoever they took would never be returned. We would whisper among ourselves about what might have happened and come to the same grim conclusion: They were killed. We each silently wondered when they would come for us.

We were given no food by our captors. If it weren't for my brother John, who brought me food each day, I would have gone hungry. He was the only one of my family and friends in Kigali who came to see me. Not that I could blame the others for staying away. Visiting me—a suspected conspirator—put them at risk of being found guilty by association. If that weren't enough, to visit me meant walking a gauntlet of soldiers. Despite this, John never once failed to come. Every day he would bring me food and discuss ways to get me out of there. My best hope was through Hutu friends. "Contact my boss, Umutesi," I told him. "Also talk to Pierre Legrand." Pierre was a Belgian citizen who married a woman from my area. He had become a friend and I knew he would do what he could to get me released. "And find Major Mugemana." Mugemana was a major in the army and worked in President Habyarimana's office. I knew if anyone could get me out of jail, it would be him. Liberata and I rented property from him, and each month I would collect rents from his other properties and deliver them to him. He appreciated my honesty and we had become friendly. Although his rank in the military ensured a certain distance between us—he was very much an authority figure who treated me like a boy of sorts—he respected me and I hoped that respect would be enough to convince him to do something to secure my release.

As the days wore on, other men were brought into our cell and we would ask for news from the outside. Fighting with the rebels continued, making our situation more precarious with each passing day. After we had been in the cell for more than a week, my friends and I engaged in one of our hushed conversations. I was tired and frustrated and fearful. "What wrong have Tutsi done to deserve this?" I asked. "We've endured thirty years of persecution—and why?"

"Don't worry," replied Makombe, the teacher. "The war will end soon and we'll get out of here. Don't lose hope."

Kaberuka shook his head. "Don't be so sure. They will kill us this time. This time we won't survive. Prepare for the worst."

Makombe quieted him. "We shouldn't talk anymore. We don't know who's listening," he said as he furtively glanced at the other men in the room.

He was right. We all were silent once again.

One day, after spending nearly two weeks in jail, I was called from my cell. "Someone is here to see you," the soldier said, leading me outside into the yard that surrounded the building. Waiting there was a car and inside it, Major Mugemana. My heart leaped when I saw his face. I leaned into the car window to speak with him.

"*Bite, mwa?*" he asked, *How's it going, guy?*

I'm guessing he could tell the answer by looking at me. I had lost weight and my eyes were bloodshot from lack of sleep. "Not well," I said. "I need to get out of here."

"Yes, I've been looking into the charges against you," the major said. He was friendly, but more reserved than before. I could tell he wasn't sure whether I was guilty. "This man who accuses you, he said you told him the day before the attack it would happen. He said you told him, 'Our brothers will rise up and defeat the government.' "

"I know," I replied, shaking my head at hearing the absurdity of the story again. "But it's not true. I didn't know the attacks were planned. I had nothing to do with this."

"Well, he's adamant that you told him the day before the attack. He said he looked at the calendar on the wall of your store the moment you told him and saw that it was September 31."

"What?" I asked.

"He said the day you told him the attacks were going to happen, it was September 31. He's certain of it. Then the rebels attacked on October 1."

A smile spread across my face. "But there is no September 31," I replied, barely able to contain my joy at having discovered my accuser's slip.

"What?"

"There are only thirty days in September. How could he look at a calendar and see September 31? He's lying! There's proof!"

The major let out a booming laugh. "Yes, you're right!" He leaned forward and said to his driver, "I knew this man was not a traitor! I told you he was an honest man." And then he turned back to me, "I'll talk to the mayor and see what I can do."

As I turned from his car to walk back to my cell, I felt like I was floating. *Surely now I will be released,* I thought. For the first time since my arrest, I felt real hope.

The next morning dawned like every other. I rose from the floor after another uneasy night of sleep. My good mood from the day before was still with me, but doubt had once again crept into the corners of my mind. My friends and I had heard murmurs the day before that the rebels had been defeated. We weren't sure what this meant for us. We hoped that it would mean they had no reason to keep us—but what if they decided to make examples of us?

Later that morning, we saw through our window the mayor standing in the yard of the complex dressed in his military uniform. Soon after soldiers came to our cell and escorted all of us into the yard. The mayor stood inspecting us and then went down the line, asking each of the men, "You, what's your name? What are you accused of?"

Each prisoner would stammer a response before the mayor moved on to the next person. "You, what's your name? What are you accused of?"

When he came to me, I began my response: "Joseph Sebarenzi. I—"

Before I could finish, he said simply, "Go home."

So the major has made good on his promise, I thought. I could hardly contain my joy.

The mayor then told my two friends that they were also free to go.

We walked out of the gates of the compound with smiles stretched tight across our faces. We were free men again.

. . .

As soon as I returned home, I began to make plans to get out of Rwanda. It wouldn't be easy. Security was growing tighter. Although the government had indeed crushed the rebellion, the rebels who had survived had fled to Uganda and reorganized. They had to if they were to have any hope of winning. Before their defeat, the rebels were trying to fight a conventional war. They thought they would win in a matter of weeks. After all, these Tutsi refugees—who were calling themselves the Rwandan Patriotic Front, or RPF—had been fighting in the Ugandan bush for years. The Rwandan army, on the other hand, had not fought any major battles in more than twenty years. The rebels figured their opponents' skills would not be as sharp and that the Rwandan government would quickly fall. Habyarimana, on the other hand, assumed the rebels would be easily defeated because they didn't have the support of stronger nations. They were both wrong. While it was true the rebels could not win a conventional war—after all, Habyarimana had the support of Belgium, France, and Congo—they could potentially win a guerilla war. The RPF knew that for Habyarimana's government to engage in a guerilla war meant more casualties, both military and civilian. A guerilla war was messier and harder to manage. Neither side was guaranteed victory.

Most Tutsi in Rwanda, including myself, were still unhappy that the RPF had started a seemingly useless war. But as Habyarimana's government grew more desperate, the rhetoric more vitriolic, and as more innocent Tutsi were slaughtered in retribution, sentiments began to shift. More young Tutsi fled the country to fight in the rebellion, or parents who were too old to fight sent their sons. The divide between Hutu and Tutsi in Rwanda grew steadily wider. I worried my country had started down a path from which we could never return.

I needed to get out. But no one could know. I returned to my job and tried to go about life as normally as possible. As part of a condition of my release, I had to report to an intelligence officer once a week. Each week, I would show up at his office. Some days I would wait and wait, only to be sent away without ever talking to him. Other days I would be grilled with the same accusatory questions: "Where did you go this week? What type of work do you do? Who did you talk to?" Each time I would answer the same: "I went to work at a non-profit organization, where I do research and conduct training. I talked to the people that I work with and my brother." It was a tedious drill, but frightening all the same. Every time I went to his office I worried that he would be in a foul mood and, on a whim, send me back to jail.

At least once a week, I would talk to Liberata on the phone and could hear the desperation in her voice. Each time I called her, I would tell her that I would join her in Burundi soon. But she did not believe me. "It's too risky to cross now," she would say. "You'll be killed." Her fears were justified. As fighting with the RPF intensified, any Tutsi trying to cross the border was assumed to be leaving to join the rebellion. I reassured her that I would not get caught and I would not be killed. Only silence would answer me on the line. I couldn't blame her for doubting me. After all, had she not been the one to tell me we should not live in Rwanda? Had she not told me to leave when she took the bus to Burundi? I had spent almost two weeks in jail because I didn't listen to her. Of course she doubted that I could cross into Burundi—now, when things were much worse than they had been. But what choice did I have?

I spent the next several months arranging a way to leave the country. Travel was heavily restricted throughout Rwanda, with official permission required to cross between districts. To make my commute to work easier, I moved out of my house in Kigali and found an apartment closer to work, which I shared with a colleague. John needed to stay in the capital to attend school, so I enrolled him in boarding school there. One day in May I went to visit him.

"I'm going to try to go to Burundi," I told him when we were alone together.

He looked at me with worried eyes.

"I'm worried that this intelligence officer is going to send me back to jail. And the situation here is getting very bad."

Still, he said nothing.

"If I make it across, I'll find a way to get you there, too. We can't cross together; it's too dangerous. But I'll find a way to get you out once I'm there."

"Yes, okay," he said.

When I left him, I shook his hand, gave him some money, and told him I would be in touch. He looked so young, standing before me. He was a man now, but as my younger brother, he would always be like a son to me. I wanted to protect him from whatever harm might come to him—and I worried it inevitably would.

The river was about a hundred feet wide. My feet were on Rwandan soil, but I was looking across to Congo. Soon, God willing, I would be on the other side. And once I was in Congo, I could easily get to Burundi. Crossing into Burundi directly would have been impossible. Relations between Burundi and Rwanda had been strained for many years. Although there was no open conflict between the two nations, they didn't trust each other. Congo, on the other hand, was an ally of Rwanda's. Its border was not as tightly controlled. So I would cross first to Congo. But not tonight. Too many guards dotted the riverbank. I would most certainly have been caught. And if I was caught, I would be killed.

I was standing with my friend François, a teacher who was a Tutsi refugee who had gained citizenship in Congo. He had kindly offered to help me cross. He knew the river and the roads and the best places to cross undetected. He agreed that on this night, it would be too risky. "Find a place to stay tonight," he said, "and we'll try tomorrow." With that, he crossed a bridge into Congo (as a citizen, he could do so easily) to stay the night with his family, promising to return the next morning to shepherd me across.

As I walked to a nearby hotel, I thought of the web of lies I had created to get to this border town in southwestern Rwanda. I had told my boss that I was going to visit my parents in Kibuye for the weekend.

"I'll be back on Monday," I told her, feeling shame at lying to someone who had been so good to me, yet knowing I had no choice.

"Okay, have a good trip," she said without a trace of suspicion. "Please tell your parents hello for me."

"I will," I said with a smile. I wondered if I would ever see her again.

In order to travel, I needed a government pass for each district I would travel through. I told the official that I would travel to Kibuye by way of southwestern Rwanda, so I received a pass for both areas. That morning I packed a small bag with some clothes and a few important papers (a large suitcase would have led to questions), closed the door of my apartment, and left, never expecting to return.

Now I stood in the lobby of a border town hotel, booking a room. As I waited, I heard someone call out behind me, "Joseph!" My back muscles tightened. "Joseph!" I heard again. I turned slowly to see a man I knew from Kigali walking toward me with a smile.

I shook his hand and smiled as warmly as I could.

"What are you doing here?" he asked amiably, just as surprised as I was to see a familiar face so far from Kigali.

"I have a work meeting here tomorrow," I said casually, hoping he could not hear the thudding of my heart. This man knew my wife and son were in Burundi. I worried he would begin to suspect that my visit to a border town had nothing to do with work.

"Oh, okay, good," he said. We exchanged a few more words and then he left.

As I walked to my room I reassured myself that I had acted casually and that he wouldn't suspect anything. Besides, he was a good man. Even if he did suspect something, he wouldn't tell anyone. Would he?

I lay down to sleep, but did little more than roll from one side to the other. My thoughts jumped from the river to the soldiers to the man in the lobby. I tried to force them out of my mind by envisioning Liberata and Respect, who was now fifteen months old. This river that I would cross was the same one they had crossed eight months earlier. But fortunately they had fled before things had grown so tense. They were able to walk across a bridge into Congo. I would have to be smuggled in a canoe. I prayed, asking that God protect me, asking that He reunite me with my wife and son. My son. I thought of the day he was born. How small and fragile he was. How could something so small bring with him so much hope—hope for a better future, for a life freely lived, for peace? I named him Respect as part of that hope. Tutsi had been treated without respect for so many years. In giving him the name of that which Tutsi had been denied, I hoped he would embody it—respect for others, respect for himself. I closed my eyes and finally drifted off to sleep.

The next morning I met François at the hotel. We both forced a smile to put each other at ease, but neither of us was very convincing. He led me to a small path that followed the river. "This is where smugglers cross to Congo," he said. "We can find a canoe here that will take us across." My heart beat quickly, but I was not afraid. *I am in God's hands,* I thought.

Soon we stumbled upon a man loading contraband into his canoe. We said nothing. We just handed him some money and climbed into the boat. As the boat pushed away from shore, I thought how this would be either the beginning of my life, or the end of it. A soldier could see me in the canoe, arrest me, or aim his gun at me and fire, and that would be it. All the months of preparation came down to these few moments. But no soldier saw me. No shots were fired. We crossed the river in just a few short minutes. When we reached the other side, I scrambled out of the canoe and felt the solid ground beneath me. I had made it! I couldn't believe it. I had finally made it! My joy practically leaped out of me. François and I found a path leading away from the river and quickly followed it. The farther away from Rwanda I got, the safer I would be. As we hurried away, I turned my head and looked over my shoulder to Rwanda one last time, wondering if I would ever return. Then I turned my back and rushed forward to find my wife and son.

François took me to a bus station and shook my hand as I boarded. I thanked him and tried to convey in a glance how grateful I was for his help. I could not have crossed without him, and he had put himself at risk for my sake. It was the hallmark of a true friend, and I wished I had the words to let him know how much I appreciated it.

As I made my way to find a place to sit on the bus, I wondered if it would be able to move. Every square inch was occupied. Those who could not find a place to sit stood sandwiched between the others. Years later when I was in the United States I would hear the phrase "packed like a can of sardines" and would remember this bus ride. The bus lurched forward. Traveling like this on flat, paved roads would have been dangerous enough, but we were traveling on winding, narrow, dirt roads that twisted through mountains and skirted steep cliffs. With each bend in the road, the bus would list precariously to the side. I would peer out the window and see a hundred-foot drop rising up to meet us before the bus would right itself again. I once again implored God for His protection. I had thought crossing the river would be the most dangerous part of my journey; now I was beginning to wonder if I had survived that only to be killed in a bus crash.

About two hours later, the bus arrived in a border town of Congo. There I boarded another bus bound for Bujumbura, the capital of Burundi and the town where Liberata lived and worked. It was approximately a fifteen-minute drive, yet my anticipation of again seeing Liberata and my son seemed to extend it interminably. My excitement rose through me and spread in a wide smile across my face. The bus stopped and I jumped from it. As soon as my feet touched the ground, I asked for directions to the gas station where my wife worked as a bookkeeper.

I made my way to the gas station in long, ground-covering strides. When I walked in, I approached the counter and said to the person standing behind it, "I'm looking for Liberata."

As soon as I said it, I saw her out of the corner of my eye, sitting at a desk with her eyes down, doing her work. When she heard my voice, her head snapped up in disbelief. Our eyes met. She jumped from her chair and rushed into my arms. As I held her, I felt her body shake. It took me a moment to make sense of it, and then I realized that she was crying. In Rwanda, tears are shed in private. Liberata had never before cried in public. But now sobs wracked her body as she wrapped her arms around me and buried her head in my chest. "I can't believe it!" she said through her tears. "I can't believe it!"

I couldn't believe it either. I was holding my wife. At last, we were together again. But she was not the same woman who had boarded the bus in Rwanda eight months earlier. She had lost weight and lines of worry etched the skin around her eyes. She seemed like a shell of the woman I once knew.

"I can't believe you're here! I can't believe you're alive! I thought you would be killed." Sobs overwhelmed her again.

"I'm here," I said, fighting back my own tears. "I'm here. We're safe."

As I stood there with her in my arms, I did not know what the future held. I did not know the hell that awaited my country, that the war in Rwanda would drag on for another three years, culminating in genocide. I did not fully understand the havoc that war wreaks on communities. Yes, war kills—I knew that—but that is only part of its destructive path. War makes widows and orphans. War cuts off arms and legs and rips emotional wounds that never fully heal. War drives people from their homes—in this case, hundreds of thousands—and dooms them to lives of poverty and displacement. John F. Kennedy once said, "Mankind must put an end to war, or war will put an end to mankind." As I held Liberata in the gas station, I did not yet know what this meant. The war launched by the rebels in 1990 would forever alter Rwanda's history. If that war had not been started, the genocide would never have happened—at least not on the scale it did. *One knows how war begins, but no one knows how it will end.* Countries rush to war thinking it is the quickest, easiest solution to conflict, only to find themselves still entrenched years later, suffering more losses than they expected and asking themselves, bewildered, "How did we get here?" There is no "winning" a war.

But I knew none of this yet. All I knew then was that I was alive and I was holding my wife—and soon I would hold my son. Nothing else mattered.

Chapter 4

A Tragedy Beyond Belief

———〰———

> Many ethnic and internal conflicts are triggered by self-
> obsessed leaders who will do anything to get and keep
> power. They often incite ethnic violence of the most hor-
> rific kind for their own political ends.
>
> —MICHAEL BROWN

THE BODIES were piled on top of one another in the church at Ntarama, a village outside of Kigali. The grim details of the massacre were well known by this point: The Hutu militia threw grenades through windows and doors. After they exploded, the mob went into the church to finish their work, hacking survivors to death with machetes or beating them with *masus*, clubs studded with nails, until there were no more left alive. In the end, it's reported that about five thousand people were killed here. The bodies, mostly women and children, were skeletons by this time. Bones and belongings littered the floor a foot deep. I looked at the skulls, some with teeth still sitting inside them. I looked at the arms and legs that had been separated from their bodies by machetes. I looked at all of it—and walked out. I didn't need to see any more. It was a year after the killings and I had returned to Rwanda to start a new life, not to dwell on the dead. But not dwelling on the dead was difficult in a country ravaged by genocide. Every familiar face on the street was met with an embrace and praise to God for each other's survival, followed by inquiring about common friends and relatives and hearing the same response: "No, she is dead." "He was killed." "My whole family is gone."

The church at Ntarama was the first mass grave I had seen since returning a few months before. It was beyond belief. Seeing the bodies in that church and knowing what had happened—knowing that people had fled here seeking refuge in the one place they thought certain was safe, only to be brutally murdered—was devastating. And knowing that this horror had played out over and over again throughout the country was almost unbearable. During previous violence against Tutsi, churches had been a haven, somewhere people could hide and know that they were protected. No one, no matter how deep the hatred, would kill someone in a church. But not this time. Story after story emerged of families' fleeing to churches to find protection, only to discover they were herded there like sheep to slaughter. The killers were not shy about invading holy places in pursuit of their targets; shedding blood at the altar; butchering helpless men, women, children, priests, and pastors in the shadow of the cross.

I walked out of the church feeling a mixture of deep grief for the dead, and their families, and anger—anger at the killers and anger that the world stood by and watched it happen. I thought of the refrain after the Holocaust—"never again"—and yet here was proof: It had happened again, in front of our own eyes, on our televisions, and yet nothing was done. How was it possible?

I was in Detroit, Michigan, on April 6, 1994, waiting to go to Canada when I heard news that the plane carrying Rwandan president Juvénal Habyarimana had been shot down. Immediately I knew that massacres would follow. The situation in Rwanda was so tenuous, the government's anti-Tutsi campaign at such a fevered pitch, that the death of the president would surely make everything explode.

Tutsi were blamed for the death of the president. A curfew was established. Checkpoints blocked every road. Radio Mille Collines, the radio station of Hutu extremists, began calling for the death of all Tutsi and their Hutu accomplices. Killings began immediately, first in the capital of Kigali by Hutu militia and the presidential guard, and then spreading to the rural areas. Tutsi weren't the only targets: Hutu known to oppose genocide were also murdered, starting with Hutu who were active in the opposition and preached a united and democratic Rwanda. And the militia weren't the only killers: As the violence spread, ordinary Hutu participated, murdering Tutsi neighbors and, in some cases, family members.

Every morning I would wake up and turn on the television. And every day I saw the same images: piles of bodies, burned-out cars, rivers choked with corpses. I would read reports about atrocities that were so brutal they were beyond comprehension: Babies were torn from their mothers' arms and killed. Women and girls were raped in front of the pleading eyes of their husbands and fathers before they were killed. It all seemed too barbaric to be possible. I thought of the country's future. How could Hutu and Tutsi ever live together again? Previously, with the passing of the *muyaga* everyone would return to life as if nothing had ever happened. We would go back to socializing with our Hutu neighbors and playing soccer with our Hutu friends. I could not imagine a future in Rwanda like that again. After this, how could we act as if nothing had happened?

At night, I would fall into a fitful sleep, dreaming of men with machetes chasing me, or of hiding under the bed with my mother as a boy. I would dream of my family being hacked to death and trying desperately to help them, but failing time and again. I would hear their pleas for mercy and their screams. I would wake in the morning drenched in sweat, my heart vibrating in my chest. Then I would turn on the television to watch the nightmare all over again.

The media tried to explain why the violence had erupted. Many erroneously attributed it to centuries of tribal violence between Hutu and Tutsi—which was pure fabrication. Anyone with a knowledge of Rwanda's history knew that the animosity between the two groups began with colonization and never erupted into violence until 1959, just thirty years before the genocide. Others explained the genocide as a sudden reaction to the assassination of a Hutu president. But in reality it was not a surprise. Almost two years before, Radio Mille Collines had begun broadcasting hateful messages, labeling Tutsi as enemies. The government was training and equipping a special militia—the *Interahamwe*—to kill Tutsi. Progovernment newspapers openly incited violence against Tutsi, one even going so far as to publish "Ten Commandments of the Hutu" dictating that Hutu should have no relations with Tutsi. The assassination of President Habyarimana was a trigger, not a cause. Although I don't think the killing would have reached the gruesome level it did had he been alive, it is clear that the seeds of genocide were being planted long before his death.

When the violence finally stopped in July, after Tutsi rebel forces took control of the capital, the body count began to emerge: at least eight hundred thousand dead—some estimate up to one million—in just ninety days. Three-fourths of Rwanda's Tutsi population and one-tenth of the country's entire population was destroyed. The massacres took place in every part of the country. Neighbors killed neighbors. Armed militia and soldiers would intervene where local mobs were unable to finish the job. The weapons were traditional arms such as machetes, spears, and clubs, and then guns and grenades. Despite the crudeness of their tools, the efficiency of the killers was unprecedented—the speed outpaced the Nazis' slaughter of the Jews three times over.

The international community chose to not help because Rwanda didn't matter to them. We had no natural resources to mine; no port to protect; no strategic importance. All we had were people. Apparently that was not enough. I remembered watching footage of U.N. jeeps and buses driving away as Rwandans chased after them, pleading to be taken; others pleading to be shot so they wouldn't have to face the machete. I remembered the desperation in their faces, like prisoners being led to their execution. My stomach turned in disgust. How could the world turn its back so easily?

I thought of how lucky I had been to have escaped. Two months before the president's plane was shot down, I was living in Burundi, working for a nonprofit organization. Although I was living outside Rwanda, I knew it was only a matter of time before widespread violence erupted. The anti-Tutsi campaign was so aggressive that simply being on the other side of a border did not ensure safety. Violence would spill over—it already had. Hutu-Tutsi violence was escalating in Burundi. I had seen enough *muyagas* to know what was coming.

Liberata and I made a plan. I would apply for a visitor's visa to the United States. If the whole family applied for visas, it would raise suspicion that we were trying to flee the country, and our visas would likely be denied. There was a better chance that they would grant a visa only to me. After all, I had a good job in Burundi, a wife, and two children (Liberata had given birth to our second son, Pacifique, the previous year). Why would I want to leave permanently? Assuming I got the visa, I would go first to the United States and then to Canada, where we had some friends. Once there, I would have a better chance of getting the paperwork for Liberata and my sons to join me. We agreed it was a good plan, and the quickest way to get us to a country where we would finally be safe, where we would have opportunities for a better life, where we could live in peace.

I went to the American embassy in Burundi and applied for the visa. So many visas were being denied at the time, I was surprised when mine was actually approved. *It is going to work!* I thought. *Our plan is going to work!* But the reality that I would be leaving my wife and two young sons behind set in. Respect was only four years old; Pacifique, our second son, was not yet two. We knew enough about the immigration process to know it would be a long time before we were reunited. It would be at least a year, probably two. My sons wouldn't recognize me when they saw me again. How could I leave them, especially in such an unstable country? When I told Liberata that I had been granted the visa, I could tell she was thinking the same thing.

"How will we join you?" she asked. "When will I see you again?"

I didn't know the answer, but I knew that our only chance to have a better life was to get out of Africa. "It will work out," I told her. "This is the best chance we have to get to Canada." I embraced her. "I think I have to go."

"Yes," she said with her usual stoicism, but I could detect a tremble in her voice. "I know."

So on a warm March day in 1994, my wife, my two sons, my mother- and father-in-law, my brother Emmanuel, and two of my sisters and brothers-in-law took me to the airport to bid me farewell. As I boarded the plane, I turned to wave, soaking in their faces one last time. I wondered when I would see them again. A month later, the genocide began. I knew that Liberata and my sons had to get out of Burundi, whose president was also assassinated and where violence was escalating. I called her and we feverishly discussed a plan. "Go to Uganda," I told her. "You can stay with our friends. It will be safer there." She agreed, said good-bye to her family in Burundi, and flew to Uganda with our boys.

Once she was safe in Uganda, we would talk on the phone about everything that was happening in Rwanda. As our culture dictated, we didn't cry. We didn't have to. Our grief enveloped our words. I would ask her if she had heard from any of our family in Rwanda. "Nothing," she would say quietly. "There are no communications from Rwanda. Everything has been cut off."

"How are the children?"

"They keep asking for you. 'Where's Daddy? Where's Daddy?' I hear it all the time."

My heart sank back in my chest. "We'll be together again soon."

"I know," she would say.

I would hang up the phone and wonder when that would be. By May I had left the United States and was living in Canada among other Rwandan refugees. We would spend our days talking about unfolding events and sharing bits of news we heard from relatives still in Africa. We were mostly Tutsi, but there were some Hutu in the community as well. I could tell they felt ashamed about what was happening in Rwanda. They bore no responsibility for the killings. They were good people and, like us, they were suffering.

They, too, were far from their homeland and their families. Many had Tutsi relatives and friends who were most likely dead. The reach of the genocide was far and wide. No one could escape its grasp.

Meanwhile, the RPF began advancing through Rwanda. The RPF had been formed by Rwandan exiles in Uganda, Burundi, Congo, and many other countries around the world. I, and many other Rwandans, thought they were the country's only hope. If they were successful in defeating the extremist government, the killing would stop and finally a government would be established that would allow Tutsi to live free of discrimination. Those who survived would no longer live in fear. Those who had lived in exile for so many years could return. Rwanda would be whole again. I held on to this belief. *At least it is something*, I thought.

But still, the television was there with its needling reminders of death. One day in June, as I watched the most recent reports, I saw something that made my heart skip a beat. The reporter was recounting the only notable intervention by the international community: the French-led Operation Turquoise. It came late in the violence, after most of the killing had taken place, and its humanitarian value was marginal at best. The stated goal of the operation was to create a "safe zone" in the southwest part of the country. But the motives of the French government were suspect. France had been a strong supporter of President Habyarimana's government. In fact, the president's plane had been a gift from French president François Mitterrand. Although the French government said it was on a humanitarian mission to save lives, it was also apparently on a mission to bolster the position of the Hutu government and push back the RPF, which had already gained significant ground. When France announced plans to launch this operation, it was met with fierce opposition from both the RPF and Tutsi living abroad—including myself. I would have wholeheartedly supported intervention by a neutral force, but France was not neutral. I had even taken part in a protest outside the French embassy—certain that their intervention would mean victory for the Hutu extremists. Despite the opposition, on June 23, the first of 2,550 French troops entered Rwanda.

On the news they showed footage of a Tutsi family being rescued by the French military. I couldn't believe what I saw: my stepsister Brigitte and her family! Next to her was my brother John. They had survived! Tears came to my eyes and I folded my hands in a prayer of thanks. *They are alive!* I had been videotaping the news, as I had done since the genocide began, and when the report ended, I rewound the tape and watched it again. I looked at their faces, making sure I was not mistaken. I wasn't. It was them!

I felt deep gratitude then for the French, although the impact of their mission is still strongly debated. President Mitterrand claimed that French forces saved "tens of thousands of lives," while critics noted that not only did they arrive too late to be of much use, but the slaughter of Tutsi continued inside the supposed "safe zone." In addition, the French never seized a transmitter of Radio Mille Collines that was moved into the area during the occupation. Yet they inarguably saved some lives, including my sister's. My feelings toward the French government were terribly conflicted. I was angry that it had supported the regime that had oppressed Tutsi for so many years, yet grateful beyond description that they had rescued John, my sister, six members of her family, and a number of other Tutsi.

Thank you, God, I whispered over and over again. *Thank you, God, for protecting them.* I felt as if I had been raised from the dead. For the first time since the violence had started more than two months before, I felt hope. *Maybe more have survived,* I thought. *Maybe others escaped.*

When my brother Emmanuel Niyomugabo, who had been living in Burundi during the violence, called me in July and told me he had returned to our village in Rwanda to find our family, I knew as soon as I heard his voice that my hope had been false.

"It was a catastrophe," he said plainly. "They're dead. All of them. Mother, Father, Samuel, David, Edith—"

"What about John?" I interrupted. Ever since I had seen the footage of him being rescued, I had been eager to find him. "Did you find John?"

"No, Joseph." He paused. "He's dead."

I couldn't believe him. "No, he's not. I saw him on television. He escaped."

Emmanuel said again, "No, Joseph, he's dead."

"But that's impossible! I saw him! He's alive. I saw him being evacuated." Then I pressed further, "Is Brigitte alive? Because if she is, John is with her."

"Joseph, I saw his body. He was killed. He's dead, Joseph." Emmanuel told me how he found John's body on a hillside a few miles from our home—running away, he suspected, toward the home of one of our stepsister's Hutu in-laws in search of safety. Emmanuel was told that as he was running he met the grandson of that same family, who murdered him with a machete. The man I saw in the video was a friend of my sister's family, he told me. It wasn't John. My heart broke open anew. I couldn't swallow. I thought of how a short time before the genocide broke out, after John had left Kigali and returned to Kibuye to continue his education near my parents, I had sent a message to him through a friend, asking him to leave Rwanda and join me in Burundi. The friend relayed to me his response, "I'm staying with my parents. If they're killed, I'll be killed with them." And he was.

Emmanuel continued. He found the bodies of my mother and two of my sisters, Martha Ilibagiza and Budensiyana Mukankundiye, in the bush, where they had been hiding with my two stepmothers, my sister-in-law, and their young children for two weeks before they were hunted down and butchered. Emmanuel was told that they spent those two weeks singing and praying together. They knew they would be killed, but they had nowhere to go, so they turned to God and prayed for a miracle. It never came.

My father's body was found near our house. His head was found some distance away. They had all been killed in April, early in the violence, so the decomposition of their bodies had already begun.

Still, my brother Emmanuel said, he recognized them. "I looked at Papa and it was still his face. I was looking at him."

My sister Beatrice Mukamunana was dead. She had been living in Gikongoro in southern Rwanda working as an elementary school teacher. Her husband was killed first, shot to death in front of her, their five-year-old son, and three-year-old daughter. Later, they came for Beatrice. By some miracle, her children escaped and were evacuated to Congo. I thought of the last time I saw Beatrice, just nine months before. I was living in Burundi and working for a nongovernmental organization. In October I accompanied my boss to eastern Congo and southwestern Rwanda for work. While we were there, Burundi's president—a Hutu—was killed by Tutsi soldiers in a coup attempt. When we heard the news, we knew things would get bad very quickly. Immediately, all roads to Burundi were blocked. The only way to get there was by plane from Kigali, and we were a half day's drive from the capital. But we knew if we had any hope of getting out of the country, we had to get to the airport. It was a terrifying drive. Tensions were high. Men with guns patrolled the roads. *Muyaga* seemed imminent. One of the more frightening parts of the drive was through Gikongoro, an area where Tutsi had been slaughtered by the thousands in the 1960s. As our car cautiously made its way along the narrow road, I happened to see Beatrice walking alongside it. I told the driver to stop the car and jumped out. "Beatrice!" I called and ran to hug her. She was only a year older than me and we had always been close. Seeing her that day felt like a small gift from God amid all the fear. But she was not the same Beatrice I had known. She hugged me quickly and immediately chastised me for being there. "What are you doing here?" she asked angrily. "You shouldn't be here. It's too dangerous." Her eyes darted from side to side, looking to see if anyone was watching her talk to this tall Tutsi man riding in a car with foreign plates. I tried to tell her what was happening, that I was trying to get to the capital to fly back to Burundi, but she wouldn't listen. "You shouldn't be here," she kept saying. "Leave. It's not safe. Please go. Find a way to leave as soon as you can." We hugged again and that was the end of our conversation. I got back in the car, the terror in her eyes and the desperation in her voice imprinted on my mind like a photo negative. I waved to her through the rear window as we drove off, but she was already walking away.

Emmanuel also told me stories of our other brothers and sisters—stories that had been pieced together from the accounts of survivors and Hutu neighbors. He told me of our stepbrother David, who was sick in the local hospital when the violence started. He decided to leave the hospital and go home to our village to be with his family. Because we had always been protected by our neighbors in the past, he thought he'd once again find protection there. Instead he found his mother, wife, and four school-age children dead. He went to Abraham's house, the same Hutu family who had saved our lives in 1973, asking for protection. Abraham's grandsons killed him. At this news, my stomach turned in newfound disgust.

Emmanuel told me of our other stepbrother, Gérard, who lived in a suburb of Kigali. Gérard was strong and tall—over six-foot-three. He played volleyball and rode motorcycles. When we were children, girls were always falling in love with him. In high school, one girl—whose father was Hutu—finally captured his heart. They married before they had even graduated from high school. Before the violence started, he sent his wife and two children to stay with his wife's family, knowing that because they were Hutu, they would be safer there. He could have gone, too, but he had a pistol and decided to stay and fight. Before the violence, I told him to leave Rwanda, that it wasn't safe. He refused. "If I die, then I die," he told me. "But I'll kill them first. They won't take me without a fight." And they didn't. Gérard defended himself against the Hutu attackers, firing his pistol until it was empty. Then he was killed.

Emmanuel told me of our older brother Samuel Bitahurugamba, whose two daughters and son were killed in the early days of the violence. After his children were killed, his wife Tabitha fled to a church, where she was murdered. Samuel went to Bisesero, a rugged, mountainous area of Kibuye, where my mother was raised and where a strong Tutsi population had successfully defended itself against past attacks by Hutu. It had always been a region of Tutsi warriors, and this time was no different. It was the one of the few areas of the country where Tutsi were organized and fighting Hutu with spears, stones, bows, and arrows. Samuel joined the fight. He was a strong man who bravely fought the advancing Hutu. But during a battle he was shot in the foot. As he was in the mountains with no medical care, the wound became severely infected and ultimately killed him.

My brother-in-law Amos Karera also fled to Bisesero. The husband of my sister Edith, Amos had asthma and had always been sickly. In Bisesero, running was the strategy for survival. The cold of the mountains and the constant running to elude Hutu took its toll on Amos. After several days he told his friends that he couldn't run anymore. But he didn't want to wait to be killed—he wanted to die quickly. So as his fellow warriors ran away from the gunfire of the approaching militia, Amos ran toward it and was shot dead.

His wife Edith Yehofayire—my sister—and her three daughters sought refuge at their Adventist church complex in Mugonero, where other Tutsi had gathered and where she thought she would be safe. She wasn't. On April 16, the Hutu militia arrived at the complex and, in just eleven hours, slaughtered roughly eight thousand men, women, and children there.

As Emmanuel continued the litany of stories of who had died and how, I interrupted him. "Don't tell me who's dead. Tell me who is alive." Sadly, the list was much shorter. There was my stepsister Brigitte and her family, three of my stepsisters who were married to Hutu men, and my sister Agnès, who survived by fleeing to Congo with her Hutu husband and children. But that was it. My parents were dead. My stepmothers were dead. Of my mother's ten children, seven were dead. Of my father's six children from his other wives, two were dead. Most of these children had children of their own, ranging in age from five to twenty-five years. Few of them survived. My family was, by and large, gone.

Emmanuel gathered the bodies of those killed in the area and dug a mass grave on our land. Because of the carnage he couldn't always tell which parts belonged to which body. Still, he gathered them all and prepared to bury them. My wife, Liberata, and sons had returned to Rwanda and were living in Kigali with her family, who had returned after living thirty years in exile. She made the trip to Kibuye to take part in the ceremony. I was still in Canada, grieving for my family, grieving for myself, grieving for the hundreds of thousands of dead. I watched the video of John—of the person who I thought was John—being rescued with my sister and was still convinced it was him. *How could I not recognize my own brother?* I thought. *It is John, I'm sure of it.* I thought Emmanuel must have been mistaken. He didn't find John's body. It was someone else's. He was seeing their bodies three months after the killings. How could he be sure the face he was seeing was John's? Here I was, watching him on television, very much alive. I held out hope that by some miracle, he had survived. I kept waiting for a phone call or a letter with news of his survival. But none came. Only news of more dead.

I watched footage on television of hundreds of thousands of Hutu fleeing Rwanda. The RPF had taken control of Rwanda and the Hutu were now afraid for their own lives. I watched as an estimated 1.7 million Hutu fled to Congo, where they died of cholera by the thousands in refugee camps. I wondered what curse had befallen Rwandans? I knew that not all these refugees were guilty. The innocent were suffering, too. Children were dying. The old and crippled were dying. My niece Patricia, whose father was Hutu, was among the refugees who died of cholera. People who had done nothing wrong were paying for the sins of the rest.

I spent the first few months after the killings treading in a deep sea of grief and anger. For the first time in my life, my belief in God was shaken. I thought of the ancient Rwandan saying, *Imana yirirwa ahandi igataha I Rwanda,* meaning God spends the day elsewhere, but he sleeps in Rwanda. Where was God when men, women, and children, the old and the weak were being mercilessly slaughtered? He *was* asleep, it seemed to me. My mother and sisters and all of the other people who were killed had prayed for protection—was God listening to their prayers? Or was He in a deep slumber, oblivious to the suffering of nearly a million people?

My life felt meaningless. I didn't know what to do. I thought

about returning to Rwanda but everyone told me I was crazy. They
said it would never be safe, that my return would be a mistake. Why
leave Canada, a beautiful, peaceful country, to return to war-ravaged
Rwanda? I dropped the idea for a while, but then in February 1995, I
decided that I had to go back. The country was all but ruined. Most
of the Tutsi had been killed and many Hutu had fled the country. I
thought of my father's words more than two decades earlier when he
sent me to Congo to get an education: "If we are killed, you will survive." He was right. I was now the oldest surviving man in my family.
I was educated—an education that had come at great sacrifice to my
parents. Maybe I could make a difference. I loved my country—I always had—and I wanted to help rebuild it. Besides, the immigration
process to bring Liberata and my sons to Canada was progressing
at a snail's pace. After all the death and destruction, being apart no
longer seemed acceptable. I called my wife and told her that I wanted
to return to Rwanda.

For a moment, she was quiet. "Why?" she asked. "After all the
terrible things that happened here, why do you want to come back?"

"I want to help my country," I replied.

"Who are you going to help? No one is left."

"I know," I said. "I can't explain it. But I have to go back. I don't
have a choice."

"No," she said. "No, you can't come here. We've been through too
much for you to come back."

I knew what she meant. Through all the violence and turmoil and
fleeing across borders to escape the threat of death, she held on to
the belief that soon she and our sons would be safe in Canada with
me. She had no interest in starting a life in a place that had been a
killing ground.

But I told her that it was my responsibility—my duty—to go back.
I told her that I had survived for a reason—to help my country rebuild and start again.

When I told the other Rwandans living in my community in
Canada, they, too, were shocked. "What are you going to fix?" they
would ask. "Everyone is dead or has fled." The only Rwandans return-

ing to the country were those who had been given leadership positions in the new government. I had no high-level connections and no promise of a job. But still, I wanted to return. I wanted to start a life there. When they realized my mind was set, they came together to bid me farewell—Hutu and Tutsi alike—and took up a collection to pay for my airfare. It reminded me of the Rwandan saying, *Turi bene mugabo umwe:* "We are the sons and daughters of the same father." It was time to go home.

My plane touched down in the neighboring country of Uganda in early March 1995. I couldn't find any direct flights to Rwanda; Uganda was the best I could do. As my plane rolled to a stop, there was Liberata, who had traveled from Rwanda to meet me, standing with her niece and a family friend. We embraced and I felt the dampness of her tears on my cheeks as we kissed. For the first time since I learned of my family's death, I felt love and warmth and life. But death was our constant companion. She told me of her return to my family's village for the burial ceremony and the devastation she witnessed—dead bodies, destroyed homes, and a vast emptiness where people once lived and worked. "Your entire family is gone," she said. "How can it be possible?" She told me of her own sister who was killed along with her four children, and of her niece's husband, who was also killed.

The following day we took a bus into Rwanda. The bus was small—smaller than a school bus—and packed with many more people than it should carry. We sat shoulder to shoulder for the five-hour ride into Rwanda, stopping along the way at roadside vendors to buy food and enjoy a respite from the bad smell of too many bodies in too tight a space. Despite the cramped quarters, everyone was kind and patient with one another. Tragedy has a strange way of bringing out the humanity in people. It's as if we all suddenly realized the preciousness of life and the gift we'd been given in survival.

As we crossed the border into Rwanda I was immediately struck by an image I had never seen before: Tutsi soldiers. When I was growing up, the military and police were always Hutu. And now, everywhere I looked, I saw Tutsi men standing with guns. For the first time since I was a boy, since I had first learned what Hutu and Tutsi meant in the cooking house that night so long ago, I felt safe. When we arrived in Kigali, I marveled at the fact that I could approach soldiers without fear. For the first time I felt no rigidness in my neck and no uncomfortable self-awareness when an armed man walked by. For the first time I had relatives who were serving in the military. I realized then the importance of feeling protected by one's government. I also realized the feeling for Hutu was just the opposite. Now it was *they* who felt fear. A Tutsi friend recounted a Hutu asking him, disbelieving, "Is this what it was like for Tutsi? Did you live in fear for the last thirty years?" My friend bluntly answered, "Yes!" Now the tables were turned and Hutu felt the same lack of security we Tutsi had felt for so many years.

But while I recognized this change, I didn't yet recognize the Hutu's suffering. When I heard about the persecution of Hutu, I attributed it to the postwar crisis and said that it would pass. I had faith in the new government, and I admired Paul Kagame, the military leader of the RPF. I thought that finally, Rwanda would see peace under a democratic government that represented all people, Tutsi and Hutu alike. Little did I know then the role that I would play in that government, and the bitter disappointment I would feel in realizing its hypocrisy.

But now, I knew none of that. I had only a soaring optimism for the future. I imagined a long, happy life in Rwanda with my family. Maybe we would own a store, as I once had. We would have more children. I would someday take them to my village to swim in the lake as I had as a child. And although I had lost my own parents, I had my wife's family, with whom I had always been close. My mother-in-law once told me that I should think of her not as my in-law, but as my mother. Those words took on special meaning now that my own mother was gone. Seeing them again helped to fill the hole in me that had been gaping since news of my family's death. They embraced me like a son—not only out of love for me, but out of relief that their daughter would once again have her husband. We were all together. Home.

I began to look for a job and was hired in a few consulting positions, including one as a research assistant and interpreter for Laurel Rose, an American woman working for the United States Agency for International Development (USAID) to assess Rwanda's fragmented legal system. Together we would tour the country and visit prisons where Hutu accused of murder were being held. It was a daunting task. Nearly one hundred thousand people were confined to makeshift prisons throughout Rwanda. We would walk into these jails overflowing with men and women who had room to do little more than sit. The conditions were filthy. The smell of sweat and sickness hung in the air. In the smaller jails in the countryside, it was even worse. Sometimes when the door of the jail opened, the smell was so sickening, I couldn't bring myself to go inside.

In one of the larger prisons in Kigali, as I walked with Laurel among the sea of people, I heard someone say my name. "Sebarenzi," a thin voice said.

I turned and, to my surprise, came face to face with the mayor of my family's village. He looked equally surprised to see me. He had once been a good friend of my family, and now he sat accused of giving the order to slaughter the Tutsi who lived there, including my family. I was told that he had encouraged the Hutu of our village to kill, telling them that the land of their dead neighbors would be theirs for the taking. He used this incentive to mobilize the mob to kill every last Tutsi, reminding them that any surviving family member would have a legitimate claim to the land.

Now here he stood in front of me. He was a shell of a man: gaunt and sick, his two desperate eyes sunk back in his head. If I had imagined this scene before, I would have felt nothing but rage. I would have imagined screaming at him or cursing him. But to my surprise, now that I was face to face with him, I didn't want to do any of those things.

"How are you?" I asked.

"Not well," he replied. That was clear. We exchanged some more small talk and then I asked him directly, "Were you involved?" I didn't have to say what. He knew.

"No, no," he said adamantly. "I was not involved. I'm innocent."
I knew he was lying, but I said nothing. As we talked, all of the anger and bitterness I had felt for the last year sat idle as another emotion slowly rose to the surface: compassion. Not anger, not hate—but compassion. I couldn't explain it, but there it was all the same. Despite what he had done, I felt sorry for him. As we said good-bye and I turned to leave, I reached into my pocket, pulled out some money, and gave it to him. "For food," I said.

"Thank you," he choked in reply.

"Of course." And with that, I left. I never saw him again. I heard that he died in prison a few years later.

Laurel, the American from USAID, later wrote about this encounter, "I wondered whether Joseph believed him to be innocent, did not care about the accusations, or just decided to treat him as a fellow villager in need." It wasn't a heroic gesture. I wasn't trying to prove a point or demonstrate a holier-than-thou piety. In truth, I didn't really think about it at all. I saw another human being in need and offered help—nothing more, nothing less. I knew that regardless of what he had done, I had to help him. I knew that my behavior could not be dictated by his.

I didn't realize it then, but that encounter changed my life. Seeing the mayor and realizing the depth of his suffering—and realizing that I could look beyond my own suffering to help him—changed something in me. I began to realize that life in Rwanda would not be as I had envisioned: a blissful place where the guilty would be brought to justice and the innocent would rebuild. There were too many guilty. The extremist Hutu government had made certain of this by involving as many people as possible in the killings. If everyone had blood on their hands, who could be blamed for the deaths? It didn't help that no one was confessing. Everyone we met would tell us they were innocent. Of course, that's not possible. You can't have a country of nearly one million slaughtered and no killers. I believed they had to be punished, but the detention conditions were unacceptable; unconditional release was also unacceptable. I began to realize that we needed a flexible justice: one that was tough on those who planned the genocide but more lenient on the masses. But most important, I realized that we had to find a way to forgive and move on. No, we had to find a way to forgive so we *could* move on.

When I first started working with USAID's consultant, my wife was upset that I would be meeting and talking with murderers. She worried that they would attack and kill me inside the prison, where security was virtually nonexistent. I told her that I wanted to hear what the genocide suspects had to say. I thought that seeing and talking with them would help me make sense of the senselessness of genocide. That didn't happen. There were no facts, no conversations that could make sense of the terror so many people had endured. During the genocide, the Hutu government and *Interahamwe* had rallied normally kind, caring people into a bloodthirsty frenzy. Good people were driven to do savage things. I thought of our neighbors' children killing my stepbrother David. I thought of the grandson of my stepsister's in-laws killing John. I thought of the mayor's role in the genocide. I thought of all of the other thousands of stories of how friends and neighbors became murderers and asked myself, *How can it be possible?* There was no satisfactory answer.

But in that space where I sought an answer, something else emerged that was, in some ways, much more important: I began to look outside my own suffering and see the suffering of others. I began to once again see Hutu as my neighbors and friends—as fellow human beings in need.

After the job with USAID ended, I began working for a nonprofit organization, traveling to rural, mostly Hutu areas of the country where I would hear their stories of grave human rights violations at the hands of Tutsi rebels. Previously, I would hear these stories and dismiss them. "Tutsi would never do something like that," was my thought. "Hutu are lying to get sympathy." Now I began to realize that they were not fiction; that Tutsi were also capable of cruelty; that the RPF I had put so much faith in had done terrible things.

I saw Hutu struggling to support their families. I saw Tutsi survivors and returnees struggling to overcome poverty and create a life for themselves. I saw Hutu helping their Tutsi neighbors rebuild. I saw Tutsi survivors caring for their Hutu nephews or nieces whose parents had fled or died. I saw Tutsi wives working to free their Hutu husbands from prison. I saw all of it and realized that our existences were intricately intertwined. I realized that we would sink together or survive together. We were all in this together. Now I just needed to find a way to make a difference.

Chapter 5

It Was God's Plan

—⟶⟶⟶—

> He raises the poor from the dust and lifts the needy from
> the ash heap; He seats them with princes and has them
> inherit a throne of honor.
>
> —1 SAMUEL 2:8

I WATCHED THE woman sway, the weight of her body shifting
from one foot to the other. Her eyes were open and her face was
lifted toward the ceiling. She sang. I don't remember the song,
but I do remember her. One of her arms was missing, but she looked
more whole than any person I had ever seen. I could tell she was at
peace with God, and I envied her.

I had come to this small, dimly lit church in Kigali to find that
wholeness. I looked around and watched the others sing and sway,
arms and faces lifted. The song came from more than their voices.
Their whole bodies seemed to sing; it was as if their souls reached
through their throats and stretched toward heaven. I had never seen
people worshipping so passionately. In Rwanda, where Catholi-
cism and Seventh-Day Adventism are the dominant religions, I
was used to services that were more orderly, with parishioners
quietly following the liturgy. I had never seen people so moved by

87

song and prayer. *This is what I want,* I thought. *This is who I want to be.*

God had always been part of my life, but I had never really felt His presence. Like many children raised attending weekly church services and praying with their families, I felt that God was something abstract and far away. I was religious, but not a person of faith.

After the genocide, whatever faith I had was gone. I felt abandoned by God. I could never understand why He had allowed so many innocent people to suffer such horrific fates. I asked God *why* many times, and heard only a hollow silence in reply. Nor could I understand how so many members of the clergy could be complicit in the genocide. I would hear stories of Catholic priests and Adventist pastors who stood by and watched as their congregations were slaughtered—or worse yet, participated in the massacres. Were these not men of God? How could I put my faith in church leaders whose hands were stained with blood? The all-loving God I had been told about as a child was lost to me.

Then I went on a business trip to Kinshasa, the capital of Congo, to attend a training seminar with other representatives of nonprofit organizations. I shared a hotel room with a man from Congo, Muller Ruhimbika, who was attending the same seminar. Every night before he went to bed, he would pray. In the morning, he would wake up and pray again. It reminded me of my childhood—how my own family would gather each evening and morning to sing hymns and pray together. I watched Muller and could tell from the kindness he showed others and the peace he seemed to carry with him that he was a man of faith. I thought of how much I missed that faith in my own life. Although I was able to abstain from seeking revenge on my family's killers and to support reconciliation, every day it was a struggle. One night I asked Muller, "How can I have the faith that you have?"

He smiled gently and replied, "You must live a life of prayer. You need to surround yourself with people who pray and love God."

"But where do I find them?" I did not know any people of faith in Rwanda. My stepsister Brigitte was very faithful, but I could not learn it from her. I would see her and think, *We come from the same family;*

we have the same background—how can she have true faith? As it says
in the Book of Luke: "No prophet is accepted in his hometown." This
was how I felt about my stepsister. Although she was a very good and
kind woman, it was hard for me to believe that she had something
special. I could not believe that this person I had played with as a
child could know God more than myself.

"I know some people in Rwanda that you can talk to," Muller said
to me. "I have a friend who is a pastor of a church in Kigali. I'll put
you in touch with him."

When I returned to Kigali I contacted the pastor, who invited me
to his church.

So here I was. The spirit of the people moved me beyond words. I
knew I had found something—something I had searched for longer
than I realized.

As the months passed and I became more involved in the church,
my faith grew. It watered the roots of my soul. The answers I had
sought for so long began to slowly and quietly emerge. I realized
that, like a child who asks a parent "why" but doesn't understand the
answer, I could not understand God's answer to my repeated, desperate entreaties asking why my family and so many others had been
killed. I realized that "mystery is not the absence of meaning, but the
presence of more meaning than we can comprehend."[1] After all, isn't
God sovereign? Isn't faith believing in the unseen? I was beginning
to understand that.

One day my pastor, Manasse Ngendahayo, told me that while he was
praying for me, he had a vision of me leading people as a high-level
government official. "I think it is your destiny," he told me.

My destiny? For so many years the thought of a Tutsi serving as a
government leader seemed impossible—but now, things were changing. Maybe he was right. Not now, but many years from now. "We'll
see," was my reply. "One never knows God's plan."

---

[1] Covington, Dennis. *Salvation on Sand Mountain.* New York: Penguin, 1995.

Soon after, I was eating dinner with a close friend I had known since my childhood in Kibuye. "You should join the Liberal Party," he told me.

"The Liberal Party? Why?" I asked.

"There aren't many members left. They were all killed in the genocide. You're one of the few Tutsi with an education who survived. You can help the country. You could even be appointed to a cabinet position."

I responded with a noncommittal smile.

"You should join," he said again. "At the very least, you can start to get involved so people will get to know you."

I thought maybe he was right. Since my return to Rwanda, I had become increasingly disillusioned with the country's new leaders. The RPF was the ruling political party of the transitional government that had been established after the genocide. They chose a president: Pasteur Bizimungu. Although Bizimungu was named Rwanda's president, he was not the most powerful man in the country. That distinction belonged to the vice president, Paul Kagame, the brilliant but ruthless military commander of the RPF. After the RPF took control of the country, everyone expected Kagame, a Tutsi, to become president. But as a military man who had a modest education and no prior experience in Rwandan politics, Kagame chose not to be president of a country in desperate need of reconstruction and reconciliation.[2] So Bizimungu was selected instead. It made sense. As a Hutu, Bizimungu would present a unified face of Rwanda—critical to the rebuilding of the country. The fact that he was Hutu meant he had a better chance

---

[2] Kagame is also believed by some to have ordered the shooting down of former president Habyarimana's plane, igniting the genocide, while others maintain it was the work of Hutu extremists. In 2006, a French judge issued international arrest warrants for Kagame and nine other Rwandan officials, implicating them in the crime: Major General James Kabarebe, joint chief of staff; Brigadier General Faustin Nyamwasa Kayumba, ambassador of Rwanda to India; major General Charles Kayonga, infantry chief of staff; Brigadier General Jackson Nziza, former head of the department of military intelligence; Samuel Kanyemera Kaka, former chief of staff; Major Rose Kabuye, Kagame's chief of protocol; Lieutenant Colonel Jacob Tumwine; Captain Frank Nziza; and Eric Hakizimana. In 2008, Major Rose Kabuye was arrested and, at the writing of this book, is standing trial in France.

of convincing the more than two million Hutu who had fled Rwanda out of fear for their lives to return. Plus, he was married to a Tutsi woman. He would help bridge the Hutu-Tutsi divide. He was also well educated and spoke fluent French and English. So Bizimungu was named president, but Kagame wielded all the power. Nothing significant was done without Kagame's tacit approval.

Once the RPF had control of the country, it became clear that its governance was tantamount to a dictatorship: Human rights were violated and ordinary citizens' voices were not heard. Of course it was too early to judge, but nevertheless these telltale signs made a number of Rwandans whisper: *Ababyinnyi barahindutse ariko imbyino iracyari ya yindi*—the dancers had changed, but the dance is the same.

And then there were the stories. When I traveled to rural, mostly Hutu areas of the country for work, I would hear from impoverished farmers and villagers terrible stories about the suffering of their families at the hands of the RPF. At first, I didn't believe them. I had my own prejudices; I couldn't believe Tutsi would behave in this way. But again and again, stories would surface—many reported by Amnesty International, Human Rights Watch, and the United Nations. They became harder to ignore. I would see the faces of men and women who pretended to be fine but were fearful that they would be killed or imprisoned. One told me, "Any one of us can be singled out, and that would be it." Looking at them, I saw myself being led away to jail on false accusations. I remembered the constant fear that followed me throughout my life, and knew now that this is what the Hutu were feeling. I knew that the RPF and Kagame were taken as saviors by Tutsi, but that they were the opposite for Hutu. This is the paradox of "victory" in divided societies. The human rights of Hutu were violated, just as the rights of Tutsi had been violated for decades.

With this knowledge came the sad realization that everyone was capable of evil, no matter their ethnicity, religion, wealth, or poverty. There is evil in all of us. A Cherokee Indian story describes it this way: An old man was explaining to his grandson the nature of good and evil. "My son," he said, "there is fight between two wolves inside us all. One is Evil. It is anger, envy, jealousy, greed, arrogance, self-pity, resentment, inferiority, false pride, and ego. The other is Good. It is joy, peace, love, hope, humility, empathy, generosity, truth, compassion, and faith."

The grandson looked at his grandfather with fear in his eyes and asked, "Which wolf wins?"

"The one you feed."

Shortly after I joined the Liberal Party, a Liberal member of parliament died. The party had to elect another member to take his place. To my surprise, friends encouraged me to run.

It seemed like a ridiculous idea. I had only just joined the party and had no political experience. "Do you think I could win?" I disbelievingly asked one friend.

"Yes, of course," he said without a hint of doubt.

"Why?" I asked. "I have no experience."

"But people like you," he replied.

"It takes more than being liked—"

"They like you because you push for reforms," he said. Since joining the Liberal Party, I had worked with others who pushed to make the party more independent of the RPF. The current Liberal Party leaders easily acquiesced to the RPF's wishes. It frustrated me, and I knew it frustrated others. "Also," my friend continued, "no one has the credentials you have."

I laughed. "What credentials?"

"Your education, for one. Also your professional experience working with NGOs. And you've traveled a lot and lived in many countries—the United States, Canada, Burundi, Congo. You know more about the world than a lot of people. You should run."

"I'll think about it," I replied, but I didn't plan to actually do it. I didn't think I was qualified. In five years or so I might be, but not now.

Then the executive committee of the Liberal Party made the announcement that elections for the seat would be held on Sunday.

Again, friends encouraged me to run. This time, I agreed. I had little chance of winning, but I figured it would raise my visibility in the party. I submitted my candidacy, along with twelve other people. To my surprise, the executive committee selected my name as one of the three who were qualified enough to be put to a vote. My opponents were a pharmacist who had been a member of the party for many years and was a good friend of the member of parliament who had died, and Tharcisse Mutake, who had been removed from his position in the ministry of higher education because he expressed a view different from the RPF's about how to organize the commemoration of the genocide. Many in the party were angry at this injustice and thought he should win a seat in parliament as compensation. And then there was me: young (I was in my midthirties at the time), new to the party, and with no political experience. I knew my chances were slim.

The night before the election, I had dinner with two friends who were members of the Liberal Party. As we discussed the election, one friend, a doctor, told me frankly, "You cannot win this. Tharcise will." He quickly added, "Don't get me wrong, people like you. If you were running against someone else, you might be able to win. But everyone feels like Tharcise needs this."

I nodded. I understood his reasoning and thought he was right.

My other friend added, "But you're right to run. Even if you're not elected, it will put you in a good position to be elected next time."

I thought he was right, too. When I returned home that night, I prepared a brief summary of my ideas to present to the party the next day. I talked about the importance of the rule of law and the Liberal Party's independence. Although I didn't state it explicitly, I hoped that everyone would understand my meaning: The Liberal Party should not be subservient to the RPF, but a partner working toward the common goal of better government for the people.

The next day, I arrived at the meeting place for the election. Most of the Liberal Party's national council—about forty people—were there. The first round of ballots were cast and then each vote was read aloud. The pharmacist received the fewest votes, so his name was dropped. It was now a runoff between Tharcisse and me. The second round of voting ensued and once again, the names were read aloud. As they were read, I kept hearing my name. Again. And again. When the tally was complete, I had won! I couldn't believe it! I would be a member of parliament. It seemed impossible. A few weeks before I wasn't even sure if I wanted to join the party, and here I was being elected to parliament! I thought of my pastor's vision of me leading people and wondered if this was what he saw. *No one knows God's plan,* I thought. *This is my opportunity to make a difference.*

I was elected in October 1996 and anxiously awaited the swearing-in ceremony, when I would officially become a member of parliament and begin work.

I waited. And waited. The swearing-in kept getting delayed. One month. Two. Three. I was growing frustrated. *How can I help my country if I'm not an active member of parliament?* Four. Five. Then news began to spread: The current speaker of parliament, Juvenal Nkusi, was being forced out. The speaker was the third-most-powerful person in Rwanda, after the president and vice president. In fact, in some ways he was more powerful than the vice president, because he would assume the role of interim president if the president died or had to leave office. Rumors spread that Nkusi was being forced out because he was a collaborator with Hutu living in exile who wanted to overthrow the government. Yet no official accusations were made. It became clear that these were lies created for public consumption—a smear campaign to turn the people against him. The real reason he was being ousted was the same reason anyone in the government was forced out: Kagame didn't like him. Regardless of the reason, his departure would mean a significant shuffle of power in parliament. Not only would the speaker's role be vacant, but the deputy speaker's role would be vacant as well. Under the power-sharing rules of the transitional government, the Social Democrats and the Liberal Party could each nominate one candidate for speaker. Whatever party didn't win speaker would nominate two candidates for deputy speaker.

I was interested in the unfolding events, but thought little about their impact on me. Then one day in February I went to see Tito Rutaremara, a man I had come to know through my work with the NGO. Tito was considered by many in Rwanda to be a *mzee,* a wise man of great respect. At the time, I thought they were right. It wasn't until later that I would question his wisdom. Tito was the patriarch of the RPF. He was one of the party's founding members, majority leader of parliament, and chair of the parliament's political committee. All this meant that he was a yes man of Kagame, but I knew none of that on the afternoon in February when I met him at his house. "The speaker will most likely be voted out," he told me. "There could be a leadership position for you in parliament."

Leadership position? At this point I just wanted to get my seat in parliament. "Being an ordinary lawmaker is enough for me," I said. "I just want to be sworn in."

"We will see." A knowing smile spread across his face. "The RPF would like you to be deputy speaker."

This surprised me. Why would they want someone with no political or parliamentary experience to serve in such a high position? It didn't make sense. I protested, but again he smiled and said, "We will see."

A few days later the leaders of the Liberal Party heard that the RPF wanted me to be deputy speaker. They, too, thought it was an odd choice. They tried to nominate other, more experienced members, but the RPF said they would not support them. The RPF made clear that they wanted none other than me. *Why me?* I wondered. I figured it had something to do with my relationship with Tito and a couple other high-level officials in the RPF. The RPF's secretary general was from my area, he knew me in Burundi, and he admired me; and I had met in Canada the party's deputy chair, a man named Patrick Mazimhaka, and since then we remained in touch. *These men must be pushing for my nomination,* I thought. But there was more. I didn't know it at the time, but later came to believe that the RPF thought because I had once been a supporter of their party and because I was young and inexperienced, I would simply do whatever they asked of me.

While discussions swirled around who would be named deputy speaker, I was struck by how ridiculous it was that the RPF carried so much weight. The decision should have been at the sole discretion of the Liberal Party. But Liberals knew that without the support of the RPF, their candidate wouldn't win. Under the constitution, the four parties of parliament—the RPF, Liberals, Social Democrats, and Republican Democrats—were supposed to have equal power with thirteen seats each. But the RPF wasn't interested in equal power. To tip the scales in its favor, it orchestrated an amendment that allowed the military, which Kagame controlled, to be represented in parliament. While the military had played a critical role in establishing the new regime, it had no right to be represented in parliament. It was a blatant power grab to ensure more seats in parliament that supported the RPF.

The RPF had orchestrated the election this way: The Social Democrats would nominate Aaron Makuba, an experienced lawmaker, for speaker, and the Liberal Party would nominate me. The RPF would put their support behind Makuba, ensuring his election. My name, along with that of another from my party, would be submitted for the deputy speaker role as a formality.

The swearing-in was scheduled for the same day as the election of the leadership. All indications were that Makuba would be elected speaker and I would be elected his deputy. Then, about one week before the election was to be held, I got a phone call from a friend. "I heard the RPF has withdrawn its support of Makuba," he said.

"What?" We had all heard rumors for a while that this was going to happen. But still, I was surprised to hear the news. "Are you sure?"

"No, I don't know for sure. It's just what I heard."

"I'll talk to some people and find out what's going on."

I went to Tito's house that afternoon. I figured if anyone would know what was going on, it would be him.

"Yes, it's true," he told me when I asked him.

"Why?"

He told me that Makuba, who was Hutu, had been accused by other RPF members of persecuting Tutsi during the violence of 1973.

In particular, one member of parliament alleged that her husband had been persecuted at Makuba's command. "As you see, we cannot support him now," Tito said. Instead, the RPF would support a man by the name of Jean-Baptiste Habyarimana.[3] If the Social Democrats wanted a representative from their party to be speaker, they would have to nominate Jean-Baptiste.

As the days passed, we all waited, expecting Jean-Baptiste's name to be submitted. But the Social Democrats had grown tired of being bullied by the RPF. They nominated Makuba anyway. It was a huge slap in the face to the RPF. With its overwhelming political influence and sense of entitlement for winning the war, the RPF saw the Social Democratic Party's defiance as a provocation. Now it was only a few days until the election, and the RPF did not support any of the candidates for speaker.

In the midst of all this, my name somehow surfaced as an alternative. It was ridiculous! I didn't feel qualified to be deputy speaker, much less speaker. Yet my name kept coming up. Clearly, the men I knew in the RPF were behind it. Again, I went to see Tito. He confirmed the rumors: The RPF wanted me to be speaker. I told him I wasn't qualified. He shook his head. "You could be an excellent deputy speaker, and I know you can be an excellent speaker as well."

I began to wonder if he was right. After all, where had experience gotten the Rwandan government? Not very far. Besides, what I lacked in political experience I made up for in other qualities, namely my commitment to serve the people, to the rule of law, and to reconciliation—values that were enhanced by my newfound faith. I believed we were all created equal, and I wanted to work to make sure people were treated equally. I remembered what I had learned in church: God uses people to do His good works on Earth. *Maybe I could be speaker. Maybe this is God's plan for me.*

Not everyone supported my candidacy. One member of parliament plainly told me not to run. "You don't have high-level connections in the military. It won't be easy for you. You should just remain

---

[3] No relation to former president Juvénal Habyarimana.

a regular member of parliament." This member was trying to tell me
what I would soon find out: The government of Rwanda was a military regime, not a democracy. If I didn't have Godfatherlike protection from members of the military, I would pay the price. I brushed
off the warning. I was optimistic that good ideas and hard work could
put the government on track. I had no idea how hard it would be.

The day of my swearing-in—and the election—arrived. I stood in
front of the legislature holding the heavy pole that bore the Rwandan
flag in my left hand, with my right hand raised high in the air as I
took my oath:

> "I, Joseph Sebarenzi, in the name of the Almighty God, do hereby
> solemnly swear to the Nation . . ."

My seven-year-old son Respect and four-year-old son Pacifique
were sitting in the balcony along the back wall of the parliament
chamber, overlooking the assembly with Liberata, who was nine
months pregnant with our fourth child. Our one-year-old daughter
Esther, named after my mother, was being taken care of at home. My
brother Emmanuel was also there. I could feel the weight of their
presence in the same way I could feel the weight of the flag in my
hand.

> ". . . to discharge faithfully the duties entrusted to me, to remain
> loyal to the Republic of Rwanda, respect the head of state, the state
> institutions . . ."

I felt the weight of those missing, too. My father. My mother. John.
Beatrice. I thought of my father and the sacrifices he made for my
education. I remembered rowing the boat through the dangerous
waters of Lake Kivu to go to Congo to study. I remembered begging
to come home and my father's insistence that I stay. "If we die, you
will survive." I thought of my mother and her quiet encouragement.

She always told me I would go far in life. She believed in me before anyone else did—including myself.

"...and promote the interests of the Rwandan people, in accordance with the fundamental law and other laws."

And with those words, spoken on March 7, 1997, I was a member of Rwanda's parliament. Polite applause scattered among the seventy members seated in the assembly and the public seated in the balcony. I extended my hand to the prime minister, the chief justice, and President Pasteur Bizimungu. I then returned to my seat in the assembly with a soaring sense of confidence and anticipation. President Bizimungu turned to the public seated in the balcony and asked them to leave so the election of the new leadership could take place.

It was all but certain that I would be elected speaker. Deals had been made. Hands had been shaken. I had the support of representatives from the RPF and the military—and, of course, the Liberal Party. Still, I mentally tallied the votes as they were read. Twenty-eight votes for Makuba. Forty-two votes for me.

I was the new speaker of parliament.

More applause. Bizimungu invited the public to return to the chamber. As I again descended the steps of the assembly to take my place in the speaker's chair, I looked up and saw my wife and children. As my legs registered the steps one after another, I felt strangely calm. My heart didn't pound. My throat wasn't dry. I felt I was meant to be there. God had sent me there to make a difference, to make sure my family's deaths and the deaths of hundreds of thousands of other Rwandans weren't for nothing. I reached the front of the assembly and again shook hands with the president, the prime minister, and the chief justice. I then turned and came eye to eye with a sea of faces before me. I took my seat between the president and prime minister and pulled out my acceptance speech. Speaking our native language, Kinyarwanda, I made the customary greetings to the government leaders in attendance and then addressed my fellow lawmakers: "Honorable members of parliament, I am very thankful to you for your trust in electing me speaker of parliament. I am very happy and very thankful to you, but let us also be thankful to God." At this, applause broke out. It filled my heart with hope. God was rarely publicly invoked in Rwanda. I wasn't sure how this mention of Him would be received. In fact, a friend who had reviewed my speech encouraged me to remove it lest I be perceived as too religious. But I had faith that people would understand me. After all, I embraced religious freedom and tolerance, including individuals' right not to believe. But I could not deny God's importance in my own life, and what I believed was His role in rebuilding our country.

I continued by saying that parliament should enact laws that respected the people it governed, and that existing laws would be re-examined to ensure that they didn't hinder good governance. But I added a critical point: "However, as long as laws have not yet been amended or changed, it is crucial that they be implemented as they are, because infringing on laws—especially when it is done by authorities—leads to numerous and despicable evils." It was a statement I would make again and again throughout my tenure as speaker: the dire necessity for rule of law. The only way to have a civil and just society is to obey the laws that are established. We had seen the results during Habyarimana's government when rule of law was abandoned and vigilante justice took hold. We had a country full of mass graves to prove that point. Sadly, the leaders who had taken control after the genocide showed little respect for the law. They often behaved as if the military victory was a free ticket to absolute rule. I wanted to infuse a new way of governance.

I went on: "Let us continue working toward the goal of unity and reconciliation." I spoke about the need to address the crushing poverty under which most Rwandans lived, recalling the proverb, "A stomach that goes to bed hungry wakes up angry." I also called for education that stressed peaceful coexistence and reconciliation, but justice as well: "I believe that those who continue to engage in massacres should be severely punished so that potential criminals are discouraged." Although it was three years since the genocide had ended, atrocities were still being committed in Rwanda. In some areas, Tutsi and local officials were still being killed. Isolated assassinations of Hutu were still taking place. I couldn't mention the latter outright—howls of protest would have undoubtedly followed—but people understood my meaning. Peace was still elusive. Justice was essential to restoring peace and promoting reconciliation.

"The parliament will strive to work with other institutions in a trustful and complementary manner. But this should be done independently from each institution." The implicit message was not lost on those listening that day: Parliament had to act independently from the other branches of government, and no branch of government should be stronger than any other. "It is only that way that each institution will achieve its best, and that our common goal of promoting progress for our citizens will be achieved."

I finished my speech to applause. After the session ended, I walked out the doors of parliament. I stood in front of the building to have my picture taken with the president and other officials. Then I realized how dramatically my life was about to change: Soldiers who would serve as my bodyguards greeted me, my wife, and my two sons, and then escorted us to a chauffeured car. Public displays of affection are not generally acceptable in Rwanda, so Liberata waited until we were in the car to hug me. "It's impossible!" she said. "I can't believe this is happening!" We held hands as the car drove us to a reception.

My older son was giddy with excitement about riding in a new car and having bodyguards watching over us. "We're going to have escorts everywhere we go now?" he asked rhetorically with a melon-shaped smile stretched ear to ear. "And we get to ride in this beautiful car?"

My younger son was less impressed. "Where is our car? Why did we leave our car?" I had to smile at their innocence. My new position meant little more to them than a change in vehicles.

We arrived at the reception at Jali Club, the site of all government receptions, and were greeted by government officials and their spouses. While it was exciting to be around the country's leaders, the event paled in comparison to the party that awaited me at my house, where longtime friends from Kibuye, my brother Emmanuel, my sister Agnès, my two stepsisters Thérèse and Genevieve, my wife's family, and dozens of other friends and family had gathered to celebrate my new position. As I listened to the congratulations and watched the blur of people circulate through our home, my eyes kept falling on my wife. She would give birth any day and yet there she was, taking care of our guests and making sure they were comfortable. I could tell she was tired, but she never complained. The stereotype that wives of politicians take on an air of self-importance and grandiosity never applied to Liberata. My position would never change her. She remained the woman I met in college: kind, self-effacing, and gracious.

As the party wound down and guests trickled to the door, Liberata and I made our way to bed. Liberata immediately fell into a deep sleep, the gentle rhythm of her breathing quietly filling the room. Our youngest child, Esther, slept in a small bed on the floor near us. I lay in bed turning over the day's events in my mind. My speech had been well received, or so I thought. I didn't yet realize how many eyebrows my comments—particularly those about the independence of parliament—had raised. This statement, more than any other in my speech that day, made clear that I wasn't interested in the parliament's being a puppet of the RPF. I wanted a real government of checks and balances that enacted and enforced the laws that were best for the people of Rwanda, and a country that was ruled by law. I didn't know then that Kagame wasn't interested in a government with a powerful and independent legislature. He wanted total control and would stop at nothing to get it. Kagame wasn't there when I delivered my speech, but I'm sure he heard later about what I had said and wondered whether the RPF had made the right decision in supporting my candidacy.

But I was worried about none of this now. As far as I knew, people shared my vision. I was excited about the work that lay before me. As sleep began to overtake me, I thought of all that I wanted to do. I thought of my three children asleep under this roof and my fourth child, only days away from being born, who lay next to me, being rocked to sleep by the rise and fall of Liberata's breathing. I imagined a country where they could grow and prosper, living free of fear. I thought of my parents and how happy they would have been to have seen me that day. I thought of all of them and my heart filled with hope. I was ready to begin my journey.

Chapter 6

A Life on the Signature Line

—————∽ʍ∾—————

If men were angels, no government would be necessary. If angels were to govern men, neither external nor internal controls on government would be necessary.

—James Madison

THE CAR rolled to a stop in front of the parliament building on a crystal-clear day in March 1997. The National Assembly Building is one of the most beautiful in Kigali, a modern testament to democracy and freedom—everything Rwanda hoped to become. Situated on top of a hill, it overlooks the supreme court and the executive buildings. Farther in the distance downtown Kigali appears and beyond it, the mountains. As I stepped out of the car, I looked across the horizon to see the lush green of the earth reach up to meet an azure sky. A breeze whispered across my shoulder. The smell of trees and grass and life wrapped around me. It was a day when Rwanda's beauty eclipsed her history; a day that told visitors, "Nothing bad can ever happen here." But the building told a different story. It had been one of the first targets when genocide broke out. Pockmarks from bullets and grenades still dotted the façade. Bomb blasts had left holes like gaping wounds across its side.

But the walls of the National Assembly Building were not the only thing to carry the scars of genocide. I would occasionally see men, women, and children walking the streets of Kigali missing arms or legs or hands. Tent cities sprang up in the countryside, serving as makeshift homes of former refugees who were now returning to Rwanda to make a life for themselves. Tutsi returnees to Kigali and other cities occupied the homes of Hutu who had fled—a volatile situation that promised to explode when those Hutu inevitably returned. Poverty walked hand in hand with most Rwandans. Too little food. Too few homes. A debilitated infrastructure. A crippled justice system.

Sadly, no matter what the sky and mountains and breeze said, they could not drown out Rwanda's story.

My aide-de-camp, the chief of my bodyguards, exited the car first. I now had bodyguards—soldiers in the army's presidential guard— with me at every moment. The night of my election, they accompanied me to my home in the suburbs and set up operations within the walls of my yard. It was strange to have these men following my every move. If someone had to protect me, that meant someone else probably wanted me dead. It was an unsettling thought.

When I exited the car and approached the building, I began to walk up the path toward the public entrance. "Afande," my aide-de-camp said. Afande is a term used in the military to show respect to superior officers. I kept walking. "Afande," he said again. "That's the wrong way."

I realized he was talking to me and turned to see him walking up a different path. "That's the entrance for the public. Here is your entrance." He opened a separate door.

Afande? My own entrance? A car and driver? Bodyguards? I would never get used to all this. My life had fundamentally changed in the space of a few days. I was the same man I was before, but no one treated me the same. It was too much to think about. But that was no matter. I didn't have the time to think about it. I had too much work to do. I had an entire country to worry about.

And Rwanda had no shortage of crises. Parliament had essentially been gutted during the genocide. The previous members had fled. Every single member of parliament was new; no one had held a seat in parliament before 1994. In addition, human rights abuses persisted. I feared Rwanda would fall apart again. I could see the fear in Hutu's faces—the same fear that had followed me most of my life. Jean Baptiste Mberabahizi, a Hutu member of parliament, fled to Belgium just a few weeks after I took office. Many Tutsi thought he was overreacting, but I understood his fear. How much of this could people endure? Security is a fundamental human need. When people's lives are ruled by fear, they will do whatever it takes to make them feel safe, including killing those who threaten their security. That thought haunted me. If extremist Hutu organized again, another genocide seemed inevitable. I desperately wanted to prevent that—and for some reason I still don't understand, I had a quiet confidence that I *could* prevent it. I thought I could make a difference. I felt that I was meant to be there. I felt it was God's plan for me.

So I began work. And in a country recovering from war, the amount of work that needed to be done was staggering. After the genocide, the country was too chaotic to arrange for free and fair elections, so a five-year transitional government was put in place. Under the terms of the Arusha Peace Agreement, the RPF was the ruling political party. It shared equal representation in parliament with the three other major political parties: the Liberals, the Social Democrats, and the Republican Democrats.[1] The four parties also shared representation in the government leadership: The president and vice president were from the RPF; the prime minister was from the Republican Democratic Party; and the deputy speaker was from the Social Democratic Party. No one was elected by the people. Instead, they were elected by their political parties, as I had been. Popular elections were planned for 1999, two years away.

When I entered my office for the first time, I was taken aback by how sparse it was. A desk. A phone. A chair. It didn't look like the office of someone who held the third-highest position in government. I

---

[1] Other smaller political parties existed, but did not have equal representation in government.

had a private bathroom with a shower, but no running water. Much of the furniture had been looted during the genocide. Wooden furniture was particularly sought after because it could be used as firewood for cooking. Only the bare necessities occupied the office now. It was a sad reminder of all that Rwanda had lost. But as long as I could do my work, I didn't care what my office looked like.

I began talking with other members of parliament to hear their ideas and tell them mine. One day I invited a member of parliament to my home. My family and I had just moved from our house in the suburbs to an official government residence in the center of town. As we sat in my gazebo enjoying the warm afternoon air I told him, "I want to regularly meet with the press."

"How often?" he asked.

"Once a month."

He looked confused. "Once a month? Why?"

"I think the speaker of parliament should have good relations with the media. I'm going to set it up so once a month I meet with them and I answer their questions."

He nodded, but the bewildered look didn't leave his face.

Later, I spoke with my personal secretary. "I want to have an open-door policy once a week," I said.

"Open door for whom?"

"For everyone."

"Everyone?" he repeated.

"I want the public to have access to me one morning a week," I said. "We'll set a regular day and let people know that if they want to come talk to me and tell me what's on their minds, they can do it during that time. As long as I'm in town, I'll meet with them."

He smiled and nodded respectfully, but I could tell that he, like the member of parliament I spoke with at my house, wondered if I was half-crazy. I understood their shock. Leaders would occasionally have press conferences, and occasionally talk to the public, but both the media and the people were kept at arm's length. Sharing too much information could be dangerous. You could say something that could be misconstrued and anger the president or vice president. It was safer to keep as quiet as possible and hope you didn't get on anyone's bad side. But I didn't subscribe to this philosophy. I believed that one of the best ways I could serve the people was to hear directly from them what they wanted. And I believed that the media were a crucial part of that. If I kept them close—if they understood what I was doing and I could hear from them what they thought needed to be done—I could actually help people.

So I began meeting with both the press and the public. But meeting with them would only do so much. To really effect change, I had to create a strong parliament. I believed—and still do—that an independent and strong parliament is an indicator of good governance. Before I was elected speaker, the National Assembly passed an oversight bill giving parliament more powers to check the executive branch. It was an important law, and one specifically outlined in the constitution. It would allow parliament to summon any document or member of the executive branch, question him or her, and give a vote of no confidence if deemed necessary. Western countries with established constitutions take this system of checks and balances for granted. But for Rwanda, it was a groundbreaking piece of legislation. For the first time in its history, parliament would have the power to censure the government.

Parliament had adopted the bill and the supreme court had approved it. But President Pasteur Bizimungu kept sending it back unsigned. Undoubtedly, the executive branch worried it would take away too much of its power. It didn't want parliament looking over its shoulder.

In my mind, this law was the cornerstone of good government. Without parliamentary oversight, the executive branch essentially had free rein. If parliament—the representatives of the people—had the power to summon ministers and the prime minister and censure them if they failed to demonstrate good governance, the executive branch had no option but to strive for efficiency and honesty in running the country.

I met with Juvenal Nkusi, the outgoing speaker, to discuss it. "What should I do about this bill?" I asked.

"It's up to you," he said.

"What would you do if you were still in office?"

Again, he simply replied, "It's up to you."

I understood his reticence. If the president wasn't signing the bill, it meant the RPF was opposed to it. Nkusi was being forced out by a carefully orchestrated smear campaign that accused him of conspiring with Hutu insurgents to overthrow the government. He was already being targeted as a traitor. Advising me on this bill could further damage him.

Seeking more guidance, I held a meeting with all of parliament's committee chairmen and deputy chairmen. I got the same response: "It's up to you," they said. They wouldn't speak with me more about it, but I knew they supported it. Everyone in parliament did—but they were too afraid to say so.

I decided to meet with the chief justice of the supreme court. I thought perhaps there were legal issues surrounding the bill that was keeping the president from signing it. I had read their ruling and it was very clear, but I wanted to talk to him about it and make sure. I went to his home a few times, and each time he would tell me the same thing: "There are no legal issues with this bill. There's no question of its constitutionality."

About the second week of my tenure, I decided to meet with the president to discuss it. But I didn't want him to know the purpose of the meeting. I had never met with him before and I knew any mention of the bill would be contentious. I didn't want to put him on the defensive before we met. So I asked for a meeting as a courtesy visit to introduce myself and to hear from him what he thought were the pressing issues before parliament.

When I entered his office he greeted me warmly, but with some reserve. He didn't know me and I imagine he was unsure yet if he could trust me. He led me to a sitting area in his office, where we sat and exchanged pleasantries.

"Since I'm new to parliament and new in the speaker role, I thought it would be good if we could meet so you could give me some orientation," I said.

He seemed glad that I was making this effort and talked to me respectfully about minor issues facing the parliament.

Then I said, "I wanted to talk to you about the oversight bill."

Bizimungu's smile evaporated and his eyes narrowed.

I knew I would have to tread lightly. "This bill has been passed by parliament and approved by the supreme court; it would be good if you could sign it."

"We don't need this bill," he said.

"But this bill is called for in the constitution," I said. "I worry that, without it, the country could easily plunge into chaos again." I told him that one reason the genocide occurred was that there were no checks and balances among the branches of government. This law would ensure that ministers would be held accountable. It would show the people that no one is above the law and foster respect for the government.

He shook his head and folded his arms across his chest.

I continued, "Because this regime is new, we can stop corruption before it worsens—before we get to the point of no return. Individuals are too tempted by money and power. We need to make sure our institutions are stronger than individuals—"

"I know all this," he said with an exasperated tone that implied, *Don't lecture me.* "But we don't need this law. You can still control the executive branch without it. Besides, this law would just create confusion. Things are running smoothly now. If you introduce this law, it will create conflict between the branches of government."

I knew this was not true. How could a law that gives parliament oversight powers create conflict? "But without this law, the country cannot move forward."

He leaned toward me and asked me pointedly, "Under this law, leaders of the military could be called before parliament to answer questions, correct?"

"Yes, Your Excellency," I answered. "The ministry of defense is part of the executive branch. It should not be above the law."

"And military documents could be requested and reviewed?"

"Yes, Your Excellency," I said again, wondering why he was asking me such obvious questions.

He slapped his hand on the table as if what I said had validated his point. "That would compromise the country's security," Bizimungu said. "We can't have it."

He was concerned, of course, about Kagame, vice president and minister of defense. Although we would not be able to summon Kagame to speak before parliament, because he was the vice president, we could call his subordinates and request documents. I knew he was protecting Kagame. But he was protecting himself, as well. Bizimungu and Kagame were the only ones who had power over ministers, and now I was supporting a bill that would also give that power to parliament. Of course they were against it. Still, I agreed with him that we had to be careful about national security. The country was unstable. Hutu insurgents in Congo and in northwestern Rwanda were a real concern. I would not want Rwanda's security compromised. "I understand," I said. "But it would be good if you could think of how to resolve this issue."

"Okay," was all he said.

I could tell the conversation was over, so I politely thanked him for his time and left.

Over the course of a few days, I kept thinking about what he said and wondering how I could convince Bizimungu to sign the bill. I thought I had a solution, so I requested another meeting.

"I've been thinking about the oversight bill," I said.

"We don't need it," he said abruptly.

"I have a proposal that might resolve the issue," I said as I respectfully extended a written proposal with both hands.

He took it, thumbed through it dismissively, and then tossed it on the table. He leaned back in his chair and crossed his arms. "Talk."

"We can draft an amendment stating that if the ministry of defense cannot respond to parliament's inquiries for security reasons, the president would have the power to decide whether the issue warranted investigation."

He didn't respond.

"If you sign the bill," I continued, "parliament will amend it to include this."

"No," he said. "We don't need this bill."

And that was all he would say about it. I left his office frustrated at his unwillingness to discuss it. Was he not aware of the wise statement by James Madison, "If men were angels, no government would be necessary. If angels were to govern men, neither external nor internal controls on government would be necessary." But none of us were angels, so we had to use the tools we had to create a sound government. I thought politics was about compromise. How were we supposed to accomplish anything if the executive branch wasn't willing to compromise?

Over the next two weeks I called Bizimungu's office repeatedly asking to speak with him, hoping against hope that he would see reason and sign the bill. The president, who had been so willing to speak with me before, now would not return my calls. Desperate, I called Vice President Kagame's office requesting a meeting. Nothing. I would leave messages, but never hear back. I had been in parliament only a month and already I was being frozen out by the two most powerful men in the country. I worried that this bill would languish for years if action wasn't taken.

But there was a loophole. According to the constitution, the president has ten days to sign a bill into law after it is deemed constitutional. After that period of time, if the president doesn't sign it, the speaker can.

This was a risky move, particularly so early in my tenure. It would be an act of defiance on a grand scale that would most certainly enrage Bizimungu and Kagame. They could force me from my position. They had done it with the last speaker, the former prime minister, and other government officials. Why would it be any different for me? I considered my options: Sign it and risk my position, or leave it unsigned and become a puppet of the regime.

"What should I do?" I asked an influential member of parliament as we met in my office one day.

"Don't ever go against Kagame," he said. "If he's against it—which he clearly is—then you shouldn't do it."

"But this bill," I said, "it's critical."

He shook his head. "It's not a good idea to do something the president and vice president are against."

I also consulted a good friend and explained the situation to him.

"If I don't sign it, I worry that I'll lead a parliament that has no authority," I told him. "We won't be able to get anything done."

"You're right," he agreed.

"I think I have to sign it," I said.

He looked at me seriously. "If you do, be prepared. Anything can happen—more than just losing your job." I knew what he was implying. Paul Kagame was often referred to in hushed tones as Pontius Pilate because he didn't hesitate to get rid of his enemies. I was never convinced of that. When I heard about human rights abuses attributed to government soldiers, I didn't think Kagame was necessarily behind them. I tended to think these were rogue soldiers who, in the heat of fighting insurgents or in the postgenocide chaos, had acted on their own. I didn't really think Kagame would target me simply because I disagreed with his politics. Still, my friend's warning disquieted me.

During this time I repeatedly called Patrick Mazimhaka, a minister in the president's office, deputy chair of the RPF, and a close friend of the president. He was a wise and kind man, and a shrewd politician. He knew Bizimungu and Kagame held all the power and would never do anything to jeopardize his relationship with them. But he was a reasonable man and I hoped that maybe he would see how important this bill was and talk to Bizimungu on my behalf.

"Please ask the president to meet with me on this issue," I would ask him.

"Yes, *Afande*, of course," he would always say. But I would hear nothing.

I called Bizimungu's personal secretary. No response. I even went to his house several times to ask him to convince the president to meet with me. Everyone promised they would speak to him for me, but I never got a call back.

I talked to Liberata. "What should I do?" I asked her over dinner one night.

"It's too dangerous," she said, shaking her head. "Don't sign it. Wait and see what happens. Let them soften a little."

"But what if they don't soften?" I asked. "What if this bill just sits unsigned?"

"It's too dangerous," she said again. Liberata was no stranger to oppressive regimes. As refugees, her family, like millions of other Africans, had suffered many hardships because of politicians who worried more about power than people. In our eight years of marriage, she had fled alone with the children twice to other countries to escape violence. Now, finally, our life was stable. We were living in a nice government residence and had been blessed with four beautiful children, including our newborn daughter, Nicole. For the first time we were living a comfortable and secure life—all of us, as a family. We were safe. For Liberata, the idea that I could do something that might put that at risk was unthinkable.

Five weeks after I took office, I sat at my desk with my pen poised on the signature line of the bill. My job, my family, and possibly my life were on that line—but so was the future of my country.

I took a deep breath and signed it.

I didn't tell anyone, except one person. I called Mazimhaka and asked him to come to my office. I showed him the bill with my signature.

Mazimhaka had been in politics long enough to know never to reveal his hand. He was impressively adept at keeping his cards close to his chest. Yet I could still see a wave of shock register on his face.

"No one knows that I've signed it," I said.

"Okay, *Afande*," he matter-of-factly replied.

"If the public learns that I've signed it, they'll know that there is conflict in the government. It will send a bad message and embarrass the presidency. Tell the president if he wants to change his mind and sign it, he can, and no one will know otherwise."

"Yes, *Afande*," he said again and left.

I waited.

Hours passed and I heard nothing. Days passed. Finally, a week had gone by and still no word. *They think I'm bluffing,* I thought. They probably figured that I would lose my nerve and tear up the bill.

I called the prime minister. "I've signed the oversight bill," I told him. "I'll be sending it to you today to be published."[2]

He sighed heavily on the other end of the phone. "This is going to cause problems," he said wearily. I understood his reaction. He worried what publishing it would mean for his own future.

"You have to publish it," I told him. "It's in the constitution." I wanted him to know that he had no choice, that it was his constitutional duty. I hoped this would ease the burden for him somewhat.

I sent him the bill. I also made copies and sent them to the president, vice president, and members of parliament. I can only imagine the look of shock on Bizimungu's and Kagame's faces when they saw it. Immediately I heard from friends in parliament that the president and vice president were furious.

But members of parliament were elated. One member pulled me aside and whispered softly so no one else would hear, "Thank you for finally standing up to the government. It's about time. Now maybe the system will work."

He wasn't alone. Over and over again members of parliament would approach me. "Thank you," they would whisper. "Parliament will finally have some authority."

When I told my wife later that evening, her eyes widened. "Oh, my God," she said. "What will this mean for us?"

I told her not to worry—that everything would be okay. I held her hands and we prayed together, asking for God's protection.

A couple of days later, Mazimhaka and Joseph Nsengimana, chair of the Liberal Party, came to speak to me. I was expecting them. The cabinet had met the day before to discuss the bill so I knew they would want to propose a compromise. "The president would like to talk about the proposal you discussed earlier," Mazimhaka said, referring to the amendment that gave the ministry of defense some flexibility in dealing with parliamentary oversight. "He'd like to add the amendment to the bill," said Mazimhaka.

---

[2] For bills to become law, they had to be published in the official *Gazette*. It was the prime minister's responsibility to publish the laws.

I quickly agreed. I had no problem adopting the amendment, and I felt the fact that the president had sent them showed that he was at least willing to work with me. Pressing for the amendment allowed the government to save face, showing the public that parliament wasn't getting everything it wanted. In reality, I was less concerned with the ministry of defense; it was the other ministries' questionable practices that I wanted to investigate. Regardless, I knew enough to know that no matter what the law said, Kagame would not allow us to investigate him or the ministry of defense, especially with Rwandan troops in Congo. So a committee of parliament met with Mazimhaka and Nsengimana to draft the amendment, parliament voted on it, and the bill became law.

But this came at a price. Kagame refused to meet with me. I would call his office repeatedly and hear from his assistant, Yvonne, in a syrupy sweet voice, "He's not here. He's very busy. Oh, it's too bad he can't meet with you. You understand? I will remind him and let you know." I would never hear back. Again I would call, and again I would hear the same excuses. I would have had better luck scheduling a meeting with the pope than a meeting with Kagame.

I kept this fact to myself. Other members of parliament and government leaders didn't know that Kagame wouldn't speak with me. Another government official who was also being put off by Kagame asked me if I could help him get an appointment. I told him to keep trying, but that I would try, too, never revealing to him the reality of the situation. I worried that if people knew Kagame had frozen me out, members of parliament would be afraid to work with me.

But I could live with that. Literally, I could *live* with it. I had gone against the president and vice president, and the worst that happened was that I was ignored. I still held my position as speaker. I was still a member of parliament. I had the respect of my fellow parliamentarians. And above all, I had done what was right. That's all that mattered.

And we *did* do our work. After the bill was signed, one of the first things parliament did was call the minister of justice before the National Assembly to ask him why it was taking so long to bring those who had participated in the genocide to justice. Genocide suspects who had already been arrested were supposed to appear before a judge by the end of 1997. The year was coming to a close, and roughly 40 percent of those detained in prisons and 80 percent of those held in other detention facilities had no files establishing charges against them—which made it nearly impossible to reach the goal that the law had set. In addition, known masterminds of the genocide who had fled Rwanda had not been returned to the country for trial, and none was tried in absentia. While I understood the challenges of bringing so many people to justice, the fact that we were so far off our target was unacceptable, and bringing this minister before parliament was our chance to tell him that. In some ways, this was a "training" run for the new oversight law. I knew it was going to take a while for the government to become accustomed to it, because it was so revolutionary. As lawmakers, we were dipping our toes in the water—and getting ready to dive in.

In the midst of all of this, the government dropped a bombshell: It appointed Boniface Rucagu to be governor of the province of Ruhengeri in the northwest, where Hutu insurgents were the most active. Rucagu was a Hutu and believed by the RPF to be the only person who could help bring order to that turbulent part of the country and quell Hutu unrest. The only problem: Rucagu, a former member of parliament in Habyarimana's regime, was a suspected leader of the genocide. In fact, his name appeared on the government's list of genocide masterminds. He had even been arrested several times, although he was never brought to trial. And now the RPF, which said it was committed to bringing the killers to justice, had appointed one of the alleged masterminds to be governor.

Rumor was that the RPF had tortured Rucagu when he was detained. In exchange for not being brought to trial, he vowed his allegiance to the RPF. He would do as he was told by the RPF. He would look the other way when government soldiers exercised their version of justice. He would live a life of privilege and power while others suffered.

My family at my brother Samuel's wedding in 1980. Most of the people in this photo, including the children, were killed during the genocide: Samuel and his wife (center) were killed with their two daughters and son; my brother Gérard (front row, second from right); my sister Beatrice (front row, far left); my mother Esther (the first woman from the left wearing an *urugori*, a traditional headband); my stepbrother David (behind my mother); my stepmother Rose (with the *urugori* to the right of my mother); my other stepmother Helen (with the *urugori* standing behind Samuel's left shoulder); and my father (far right, the tall man in the white shirt and sports jacket). I am in the front row, third from the right. My brother Emmanuel, who returned to Rwanda after the genocide to find my family, is to my left.

Liberata in 1986, when I first met her.

Liberata and I on our wedding day, April 20, 1989,
at Lake Kivu in the Kibuye province of Rwanda, where I was born and raised.

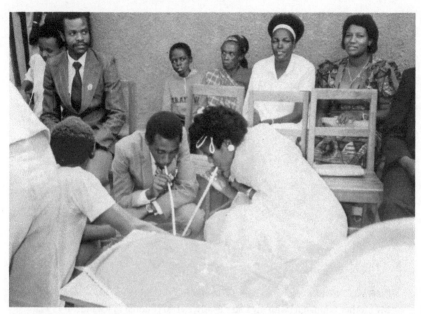

At my sister Beatrice's dowry celebration in my home village. Both Beatrice and her husband were killed in the genocide. My sister Agnes is seated behind them, second from the right. Today she lives in exile in the United States. My wife Liberata is in the far left corner.

My brother John Uwimbabazi holding my first son, Respect, when he was about seven months old.

My brother Emmanuel with my sister Beatrice's two children in Rwanda in 1994,
shortly after the genocide. They both witnessed the killing of their father. Their
mother was killed later, after the children were miraculously taken to safety.

My stepsister Brigitte with the Hutu woman who helped save her life.
Brigitte and her family were rescued by the French military during
Operation Turquoise, which took place toward the end of the genocide.

My sister Edith with two of her six children. Edith was killed in a church where she had gone to seek refuge. Her husband and all of her children, except for son Jean-Bosco Cyubahiro, who stands on the left, were killed in the genocide.

My sister Edith's husband, Amos Karera, and her three sons. Only Jean-Bosco (on the far right) survived the genocide. Amos was killed fighting in Bisesero.

The National Assembly in 1998. The holes in the side of the building are from mortar attacks during the genocide. I am standing in the front row, fourth from the right. Sixth from the right is President Pasteur Bizimungu. Next to him, standing with his hand across his chest and looking right, is Vice President and Minister of Defense Paul Kagame.

In front of the National Assembly Building. Vice President Paul Kagame stands second from the right. President Pasteur Bizimungu stands in the center. The soldier in the background is part of the presidential guard, the same group that served as my bodyguards.

Rwanda's King Kigeli V. Deposed in the early 1960s, after decolonization, he now lives in exile in the United States.

Government leaders at the Jali Club in Kigali in 1998. Of the eleven photographed, more than half are in exile or were imprisoned. The minister of transportation (far left) is in prison; the prime minister (third from left) lives in exile in the United States; the secretary of state (fourth from left) lives in exile in the Netherlands; President Pasteur Bizimungu (fourth from right) was imprisoned for five years; and the minister of justice (far right) lives in exile in Canada. I am standing third from the right.

The parliament complex in Kigali.

My family today. From left to right:
Respect, Pacifique, Esther, Liberata, Sandrine (in front of Liberata),
and Nicole (in front of me).

Liberata and I in 2007.

Word of his appointment spread like wildfire through parliament. Immediately a group of lawmakers requested that the matter be discussed before the assembly. Lawmakers thought he should be removed from his position and investigated. If he was found innocent, he could be reappointed. If not, he should be brought to justice. The list of genocide masterminds was an official government list that was circulated to other countries to ensure extradition of criminals. To appoint a person to a government position when his name appeared on this list marred Rwanda's international credibility. I agreed and put the matter on the agenda.

Soon after parliament began debating this issue, I received a phone call from Kagame's chief of staff, Major Emmanuel Ndahiro. "Boniface Rucagu would be very helpful in that part of the country," he told me.

"It is on the agenda," I said. "We're debating it."

"Yes, I know. You can do that. Just keep in mind that he will be very helpful." Ndahiro was polite and respectful, but I knew the implied message of his phone call. Members of the RPF had a way of talking in code. They spoke through innuendo and suggestion. They would never state directly what they wanted. I was slowly figuring this out and knew that when he said "You can do that" what he really meant was: "Stop. Take it off the agenda. Leave this alone."

"How can you possibly appoint someone to such a prominent position who is accused of leading the massacre of thousands of people?" I asked.

Again he replied, "He would be very helpful in Ruhengeri."

"Isn't there anyone else who can do that job? Someone who isn't accused of crimes like these?"

"Rucagu would be helpful," he said again.

He seemed to think that being speaker was like being a commander in the military, as if sole authority rested with me. But I had to lead by convincing and inspiring—not imposing. "We already have it on the agenda," I said. "I can't just remove it."

Once again he gave me the same response, "Rucagu would be helpful."

The more I dealt with the RPF, the more I felt that they were still behaving like rebels fighting a guerilla war in the bush. This wasn't the bush. Rules needed to be followed. Laws needed to be respected. I knew that the president and vice president would view parliament's objection to Rucagu's appointment as interference. But parliament could not, in good conscience, be silent about this.

I kept the issue on the agenda. Parliament summoned the minister of the interior to answer questions about the appointment of Rucagu. When the minister appeared before the National Assembly, they pelted him with questions. "If Boniface Rucagu is innocent of the charges, then why is he still on the list?" "How can you appoint someone governor who is on the government's official list of criminals?" "If he is innocent, his name should be taken off the list!"

Because the oversight bill had not yet been published, parliament had no power to censure the minister. They could only ask him questions to make sure his statements were on public record. In the end, parliament approved a nonbinding resolution calling for Rucagu's removal and investigation. The government ignored it. A supposed mastermind of the genocide was now a governor.[3]

Despite this setback, parliament began to gain momentum. The new authority granted to us by the oversight law emboldened lawmakers. I could feel a shift in their attitudes. No longer were members waiting to be told what to do. They began taking initiative; setting legislative priorities; looking beyond the present and thinking of the country's future. The newspapers heralded our achievements. When constituents came to my office during my open-door sessions, they would tell me how happy they were that parliament was finally making changes. We still had a lot of work to do, but I could feel us moving forward with more certainty, more speed, more purpose.

---

[3] In 2005, Rucagu was summoned before a community court in Rwanda to answer charges about his role in the genocide. Rucagu remained governor until 2009. He was the longest-serving governor in Rwanda's history.

The contempt the executive branch had for our progress remained, by and large, veiled. Every move we made was met with resistance, but they would never condemn us outright. That changed in November 1997, on the third anniversary of the new parliament. It was a big celebration. President Bizimungu was invited to speak before the assembly. I greeted his car and escorted him to the floor of parliament, where I gave the first speech: ". . . The parliament, the executive branch, and the judiciary were put in place in accordance with the democratic principle of the separation of powers. Our country has adopted this principle with respect to checks and balances among the branches of government. To achieve true separation of powers, which is the rule of law and progress for its people, it is essential to have relationships between the institutions that are based on trust and that complement each other. . . . Let me remind you that the oversight of the executive branch's actions does not mean parliament mistrusts the government. Rather, it is intended to help the executive and cabinet members properly fulfill the duties our country has entrusted to them . . . Parliament will continue to strive—along with other institutions—to lead Rwanda to a future of rule of law, reconciliation among Rwandans, and lasting development. . . ."

President Bizimungu's response shocked me: "We congratulate you—but sometimes your efforts are wasted. Most Rwandans think that parliament's role now is to simply contradict or oppose the executive branch. In fact, the executive branch and parliament have the same goals. . . . Therefore, when the executive branch takes the initiative to transmit a proposal to parliament . . . it should be embraced rather than opposed. That is not the mandate of parliament."

Although I knew before he spoke that this was how the executive branch felt about the legislature, I was surprised that he had stated it so directly on a day that was supposed to celebrate the parliament's accomplishments. It was a slap in the face. But at least we knew for certain where the president and vice president stood. No more innuendo.

A couple of months later, I was sitting at my desk when my secretary entered with a look of excitement on his face. "There's a call for you," he said. "It's the vice president's office."

I was stunned! It had been nearly a year since I took office and for the first time I was getting a call from the vice president. I dropped everything and said as calmly as I could, "Send the call through."

It was Kagame's secretary, Yvonne. "The vice president would like to meet with you. Could you come to his office at eleven o'clock tomorrow morning?"

"Sure," I replied evenly, when in fact I wanted to shout, "Yes! I've been trying to meet with him for ten months! Of course I will meet with him!"

This was a good sign, I thought. He was reaching out to me. I figured he had finally realized that ignoring me for almost a year had done nothing to stem the flow of parliament's work. Perhaps he had finally decided that we could be more successful if we worked together. As I prepared for our meeting, I felt boundless confidence that this would be the beginning of a new era of government. But simultaneously, I couldn't help but wonder how Kagame would treat me. It was clear that he had opposed many of the measures I had initiated. Would he confront me? Yell at me?

The next morning I called for my driver and was taken from my office at the National Assembly to his office in the ministry of defense in Kiyovu, another section of Kigali that was near my government residence. His secretary ushered me into his office, where he sat behind his desk. He stood to greet me, smiled, and extended his hand. "Welcome," he said.

I crossed the room with my own hand outstretched. "Thank you very much for taking the time to meet with me," I said. As he escorted me to the sitting area of his office I was caught off-guard by something: I noticed that from his window, I could see directly over the walls that surrounded my home! His office building sat on a small rise, giving Kagame literally a bird's-eye view of where I lived. If he wanted, he could watch my comings and goings; he could see who visited me and for how long; he could see my wife and children greet me when I came home from work. Although I didn't think he had the time to watch who came and went, it was unsettling to see how little privacy I had.

"I'm sorry it took me so long to meet with you," he said as he sat down. "I've been extremely busy. I wanted to make sure I had enough time to talk with you. I didn't want to rush our first meeting." He smiled kindly.

I sat with him and began to tell him everything I had wanted to articulate since I took office. I explained to him why I signed the bill giving parliament the power to oversee government activities. Although I knew Kagame and Bizimungu were furious with me for doing this, when I mentioned it now, he seemed unfazed.

"The only way we can grow stronger is if there is integrity at all levels of government," I said. He didn't look at me as I spoke. "The only way any regime can succeed and be strong is to instill a culture that respects human rights and enforces good governance. If we do this, people will trust the government."

"Sure," he said, nodding in agreement. I was surprised at how different his demeanor was from Bizimungu's. Bizimungu seemed annoyed when I told him my ideas, whereas Kagame seemed genuinely interested.

His willingness to listen emboldened me. As I spoke I became more passionate. I felt this was my chance to get the executive branch to embrace my vision for the country. "Without strong institutions and checks and balances, sooner or later, more massacres will occur," I said. "But if we build rule of law, it will by itself protect our children and grandchildren. And parliamentary oversight of government is a powerful tool toward that goal."

"Yes, that's true," he said agreeably.

I continued, telling him the same things I had told Bizimungu and members of parliament; the same things I had been talking and dreaming about since I took office almost a year before.

He agreed with everything I had to say. Then he said, "I want to ask you something." He proceeded to inquire about a Tutsi member of parliament who was suspected of ordering the torture of three people, including a woman. I realized then that this was why Kagame had agreed to meet with me. Both the secretary-general of the ministry of justice and a prosecutor had come to me a few weeks before asking me to remove this lawmaker. While I was horrified by the allegations, I didn't have the power to remove members of parliament based on accusations. I told them that if they wanted him to be removed, they had to officially charge him and bring him to trial.

"We need to remove this man from parliament," Kagame now said to me. He reminded me that it had been done before. Before I became speaker, three members of parliament had been removed after they were accused of crimes.[4]

"Yes, but it was illegal to remove them in that way," I said. I told him that our constitution clearly states that any member of parliament can be brought to justice, but a member cannot be removed unless convicted of a crime.

Kagame said nothing.

"If he is brought to justice and loses the case, then it is not parliament who is removing him—it's the supreme court," I said. "It would be good if we could follow the law."

"Yes," he said, again nodding in agreement. "If that is the law, then we need to follow it. You're right."

And that was it. There was no screaming. No fists pounding on desks. No accusations of insubordination. In fact, Kagame said very little. He seemed to agree with my vision for the government. He had responded affirmatively to everything I suggested. I thought of what everyone had told me about Kagame—to be careful, that he destroys his enemies—and had to laugh. My instincts had been right. This was not a bad man. He seemed like a completely different person from the man I had heard whispered about. He was willing to work with me. I thought that finally I would have the working relationship with the executive branch that I had hoped for. I thought of all that parliament had accomplished without Kagame's support. *With his support we could achieve so much more. This is a turning point,* I thought. *The lines of communication are now open. We agree on the vision for the government. We can begin to work together.* As I left his office, my step felt lighter.

---

[4] Although these three members of parliament were removed, they were never charged with a crime, fueling speculation that their removal had been politically motivated.

Chapter 7

Clinton's and Annan's Healing Missions

---∿---

The failure to try to stop Rwanda's tragedies became one of
the greatest regrets of my presidency.

—BILL CLINTON

PRESIDENT BILL Clinton and his wife, Hillary, entered the small meeting room at the airport through a back door. They, along with Secretary of State Madeleine Albright and other U.S. dignitaries, had arrived at the Kigali airport a few short hours before as part of a planned visit to honor those who were killed during the genocide. Clinton's visit was originally supposed to be a two-day trip that would include a tour of some genocide sites. But a few days before his arrival, those plans were scuttled due to security concerns. Instead, he would spend only a few hours at the Kigali airport, where he would meet with genocide survivors and deliver a speech. Since news of his impending visit had hit Kigali, the Rwandan government had been tripping over itself trying to prepare. The visit became the dominant topic of conversation in political circles. A U.S. president had never before come to Rwanda. For the leader of the world's most powerful country to visit one of Africa's smallest nations was very big news. To genocide survivors, Clinton's decision to visit was an apology in and of itself, or at the very least, an acknowledgment that he should have done things differently. To Kagame, Bizimungu, and other leaders—including myself—it legitimized Rwanda's new government. It was an important visit, and everyone had worked feverishly to make sure it was as perfect as possible. Yet I couldn't help but feel that the excitement over Clinton's visit eclipsed the sad reality of what his administration had done—or rather, what it had *not* done—during the genocide.

In January 1994, four months before the genocide erupted, Major General Roméo Dallaire, the Canadian commander of the United Nations mission in Rwanda, sent a fax to U.N. headquarters in New York recounting an informant's claim that Hutu extremists were planning the extermination of Tutsi. The informant, who was referred to by the code name Jean-Pierre, was allegedly a cell commander of the *Interahamwe*. He said that he and other cell commanders were ordered to compile the names of Tutsi who lived in their areas. No one doubted their purpose: These were death lists. There was more: Jean-Pierre said that when violence broke out, the *Interahamwe* would begin by killing Belgian peacekeepers to ensure the withdrawal of Belgian troops. He also said that he could identify arms caches hidden throughout the country.[1]

Dallaire informed his superiors of what he had learned and told them that he planned to raid the weapons caches. The United Nations responded by telling him he had no authority to do so and ordered him to suspend the operation immediately. Dallaire pleaded with Kofi Annan, then U.N. assistant secretary-general for peacekeeping operations, warning of the imminent threat of violence, but Annan

---

[1] In recent years, many have disputed whom Jean-Pierre worked for. Some suspect he was on the payroll of the RPF or the then ruling party. Yet regardless of his motivation, the information he provided was accurate, and if the United Nations had allowed Dallaire to act on that information, the genocide might have been prevented.

told him in no uncertain terms that he did not have the authority to raid the caches. Throughout the month of January, Dallaire continued to implore the United Nations for support. "You've got to let me do this," Dallaire begged. "If we don't stop these weapons, some day those weapons will be used against us."[2] Again and again, he was denied. Dallaire's hands were tied, and the fate of the country's Tutsi was sealed.

Jean-Pierre's claims proved all too accurate. Shortly after President Habyarimana's plane was shot down, ten Belgian peacekeepers were killed. It was an evil—and strategic—act. The killers knew that just six months before, the United States had withdrawn its troops from Somalia after eighteen of its soldiers were killed. They thought that if they killed the peacekeepers of Rwanda's former colonizer, Belgium would do the same. They were right. Not only did their action scare Belgium away, but it scared the rest of the world as well. Believing that the American public would not tolerate another risky mission to another volatile African country, the United States and, by extension, the United Nations, did nothing.

In fact, they did worse than nothing. When the genocide began, the United Nations had approximately 2,600 peacekeepers in Rwanda. Dallaire estimated that a force of only 5,500 would be enough to stop the killings and restore order. Not only did the United Nations reject the request, but on April 19, the U.N. Security Council withdrew all but 500 of its troops. According to Dallaire, "The U.S. said not only are we not getting involved, we are not going to support anyone else getting involved."[3]

The United States rejected other measures as well. The United Nations requested, at Dallaire's urging, that the U.S. military jam the airwaves to stop the broadcasts of Radio Mille Collines (RTLM), the hate-filled radio station of the *Interahamwe*. RTLM was instrumental in promoting the genocide. It blatantly encouraged citizens to kill,

---

[2] Power, Samantha. *"A Problem from Hell": America and the Age of Genocide*. New York: Harper Perennial, 2003, pp. 344–45.

[3] Quoted in Amanpour, Christiane. "Looking back at Rwanda genocide." CNN. April 6, 2004.

even broadcasting the names and addresses of Tutsi over the airwaves. In Kigali, killers would roam the streets with radios in hand, listening to their orders about whom to kill, where they were hiding, where they were last seen. Jamming the radio waves was a low-risk involvement that could have, at the very least, made communications difficult and perhaps impaired the efficiency of the slaughter, but the Pentagon refused, citing the cost ($8,500 an hour for keeping a jamming aircraft over the country) and questioning the legality of the action.[4]

Many of the world's powerful countries chose not to help. We had no exports that they needed; no natural resources to mine; no port to protect; no strategic importance. All we had were people. Apparently that was not enough. Bob Dole, who was Senate majority leader at the time, said after the American diplomats in Rwanda were evacuated in early April, "I don't think we have any national interest there. The Americans are out, and as far as I'm concerned, in Rwanda, that ought to be the end of it."[5] Sadly, it was. Approximately twenty thousand Rwandans were killed over the three days it took to evacuate four thousand foreigners. Of course, the foreign governments were right to evacuate their nationals, but the military forces that were used to shepherd them to safety could have easily helped protect the lives of innocent Rwandans as well. Instead, they rescued their own and turned their backs on other human beings.

Years later, in her autobiography, Madeleine Albright would write about the role the United States should have played: "Reinforcing [U.N. troops in Rwanda] would have been far better than nothing, if we could have found the right troops. Truly effective action would have required a heavily armed, almost certainly U.S.-led, coalition able to deploy quickly, intimidate extremists, arrest leaders, and establish security. I deeply regret not advocating this course. Many people would have thought I was crazy and it would never have won support from Congress, but I would have been right, and possibly my

---

[4] Dallaire, Roméo. *Shake Hands with the Devil.* New York: Carroll & Graf, 2004, p. 375.
[5] *Face the Nation*, CBS, April 10, 1994. Quoted in *A Problem from Hell* by Samantha Power.

voice would have been heard."[6] But in reality the United States could have done a great deal without ever sending troops. If President Clinton had strongly spoken out against the genocide and threatened the Rwandan government with action if they persisted, I firmly believe those perpetrating the genocide would have stopped. A country like Rwanda would never stand a chance against a force as strong as that of the United States. The threat of force alone would have made the leaders of the genocide call for an end to the killing, and because of Rwandans' strong obedience to authority, their followers would have listened. Just as the beating of the drum had saved my life as a child, a similar nationwide call for peace would have saved the lives of hundreds of thousands during those dark months in 1994. All that was required was for Bill Clinton to say: "Stop the killing or else . . ."

I have no doubt Bill Clinton continues to regret his inaction. Years later he would write about it in his autobiography: "We were so pre-occupied with opposition in Congress to military deployments in faraway places not vital to our national interests that neither I nor anyone on my foreign policy team adequately focused on sending troops to stop the slaughter . . . we could have saved lives. The failure to try to stop Rwanda's tragedies became one of the greatest regrets of my presidency."[7]

I also believe it is a regret of the American people. I've traveled throughout the United States and worked with many Americans, and have been continuously amazed by their compassion and willingness to help others. The NGOs that operate in impoverished countries all over the world are largely funded by the generosity of Americans. But American politicians too often underestimate their people, claiming that a humanitarian effort abroad would not have support at home. I've seen too much evidence to the contrary. It is the politicians who are afraid, not the American public. Yet, sadly, the United States' image is often tarnished because of its leaders' foreign policy

---

[6] Albright, Madeleine. 2005. *Madam Secretary: A Memoir.* New York: Hyperion, 2003, p. 195.

[7] Clinton, Bill. *My Life.* New York: Random House, 2004, p. 593.

decisions. If Americans had been accurately informed of what was happening, I have no doubt that they would have been willing to help.

I thought of all this as I watched Bill Clinton enter the airport meeting room and take his place on the podium to begin his speech. Looking at him, I realized that even I could not help but be a bit starstruck. I was immediately impressed by Clinton's physical presence, his youth, and his good looks. The charisma that he was so famous for was evident as he stood before us. I looked at his wife and Secretary Albright, who were seated next to him. Hillary Clinton seemed small compared to her husband, and very humble and kind. It wasn't as I had pictured the wife of a U.S. president to be. I expected a woman with an air of self-importance. But her manner was gracious and welcoming.

Clinton began to speak. Thoughts of my family forced their way into my mind, along with the painful realization that always surfaced when I thought of them and of the international community's failure to respond: *If someone had acted, my family would be alive today.* But part of my journey toward forgiveness included forgiving those who were bystanders during the genocide. So I quieted my thoughts and listened intently to what he had to say.

"I have come today to pay the respects of my nation to all who suffered and all who perished in the Rwandan genocide," he said. "It is my hope that through this trip, in every corner of the world today and tomorrow, their story will be told; that four years ago in this beautiful, green, lovely land, a clear and conscious decision was made by those then in power that the peoples of this country would not live side by side in peace."[8]

He spoke of the horror of the genocide, how people were hunted down like animals and killed. Then he said, "The international community, together with nations in Africa, must bear its share of respon-

---

[8] Office of the Press Secretary, the White House. "Speech by President Clinton to Survivors Rwanda." March 25, 1998.

sibility for this tragedy, as well." Applause broke out. "We did not act quickly enough after the killing began. . . . We did not immediately call these crimes by their rightful name: genocide." He was referring to the fact that, during the three months of killing in 1994, his administration performed an excruciating linguistic dance to avoid use of the term "genocide," because doing so would have required them to intervene under the terms of the 1948 Genocide Convention. Or, if they labeled it genocide and then chose not to act, it would reflect poorly on the government. A paper prepared by the Office of the Secretary of Defense during the genocide stated it clearly: "Be careful. Legal at State was worried about this yesterday—Genocide finding could commit [the U.S. government] to actually 'do something.' "[9] So while an entire ethnic population was being decimated, no one in the Clinton administration would refer to what was happening as genocide. A now-infamous press conference held by Christine Shelly, the State Department's spokesperson, in the midst of the genocide painfully demonstrated the U.S. government's fear of the word. After describing what was happening in Rwanda as "acts of genocide," a reporter asked her to define the difference between "genocide" and "acts of genocide." She stammered, "Well, I think the—as you know, there's a legal definition of this. . . . Clearly not all of the killings that have taken place in Rwanda are killings to which you might apply that label. . . . But as to the distinctions between the words, we're trying to call what we have seen so far as best as we can; and based, again, on the evidence we have every reason to believe that acts of genocide have occurred." The reporter retorted, "How many acts of genocide does it take to make genocide?" She replied, "That's just not a question I'm in a position to answer."[10] And one White House National Security Council staffer, Susan Rice, who is now the U.S. ambassador to the United Nations, reportedly asked in a teleconference during

---

[9] Office of the Secretary of Defense, "Secret Discussion Paper: Rwanda," May 1, 1994. Quoted in *A Problem from Hell* by Samantha Power.

[10] State Department briefing, Federal News service, June 10, 1994. Quoted in *A Problem from Hell* by Samantha Power.

the killings, "If we use the word 'genocide' and are seen as doing nothing, what will be the effect on the November [congressional] election?"[11]

At the podium, Clinton continued: "It may seem strange to you here, especially the many of you who lost members of your family, but all over the world there were people like me sitting in offices who did not fully appreciate the depth and the speed with which you were being engulfed by this unimaginable terror." This assertion frustrated me. He could not claim that he didn't know what was going on. No one could. The murders were carried out in broad daylight. Footage of people being hacked to death was broadcast on television. It was reported in newspapers. It was told in gruesome detail by those fleeing the violence. Whatever excuse anyone could give about the decision not to act, lack of awareness was not one. Again, I thought of my family. *If someone had acted, they would be alive today.*

"The United States has provided assistance to Rwanda to settle the uprooted and restart its economy, but we must do more," he said. "I am pleased that America will become the first nation to contribute to the new Genocide Survivors Fund. We will contribute this year $2 million, continue our support in the years to come, and urge other nations to do the same." This was met with applause.

Clinton finished his twenty-minute speech to more applause and handshakes. I applauded, too, but felt unsatisfied. The speech had done little to help me understand why the international community hadn't responded to the crisis. I couldn't get past his comment that he "didn't fully appreciate" what was happening during the genocide. Still, I applauded. Rwanda has always been known for its hospitality and kindness toward visitors, and I was, above all else, Rwandan.

I only wish the same hospitality had been shown to Kofi Annan when he visited two months later. Many blamed Annan for his lack of re-

---

[11] Power, Samantha. *"A Problem from Hell": America and the Age of Genocide.* New York: Harper Perennial, 2003, p. 359.

sponse to requests to intervene on behalf of Tutsi when the genocide began. After all, he had been the one to respond to Dallaire's requests to raid the arms caches with an emphatic "no." Others defended him, saying he did all he could amid opposition from the United States.

As his visit was planned, it was decided that he would address parliament, which meant that I, as speaker, would give the speech to introduce him. I was excited about the idea of introducing such an important world figure—he was, after all, now secretary-general of the United Nations—and I eagerly began to prepare.

Then I received word from the administration: Anastase Gasana, the minister of foreign affairs, would also deliver a speech. It seemed odd. I wondered why we needed two introductions. But I soon learned the answer: Rumors began to circulate that Gasana's speech would be critical of Annan. Bizimungu and Kagame, it was said, wanted to deliver a message to Annan. They knew I would not deliver a diatribe, so they told the minister of foreign affairs to do it instead. The idea of a guest of honor being publicly chastised made me cringe.

Annan arrived in parliament on May 7, 1998, and Gasana delivered his speech. The rumors were right. It was more an inquisition than a welcome. He listed point by point how the United Nations had failed Rwanda, beginning in 1922 when the League of Nations put the country under Belgian control. The massacres of Tutsi since the 1960s "were carried out under the watchful eyes of the U.N. and its human rights organizations," Gasana said. The tension in the room as he spoke was palpable.

After the diatribe ended, it was my turn. As I began, I wondered if evidence of my embarrassment at Gasana's speech showed on my face. I spent the next ten minutes kindly welcoming Annan to Rwanda and parliament, and talked about our goals for reconstruction and moving the nation forward. As I spoke, I hoped that my words would break the tension and put Annan more at ease.

Next Annan spoke. "I have come to Rwanda today on a mission of healing," he said. "The international community and the United Nations could not muster the political will to confront [the genocide]. The world must deeply repent for this failure. . . . Looking back now, we see the signs which then were not recognized. Now we know that what we did was not nearly enough." Just like Clinton's statement claiming that he did not realize the gravity of the situation in Rwanda, Annan's comment that the signs "were not recognized" rang hollow. Annan, like Clinton, was not accepting personal blame for what happened, but faulting the international community as a whole. *Is not the United Nations the international community?* I thought. It seemed that "international community" had become a smokescreen for politicians to hide behind.

Annan continued, talking about how the United Nations was committed to helping Rwanda bring the perpetrators of the genocide to justice and rebuild the country. As he closed his speech he said, "You and only you can put an end to the violence. You and only you can find the spirit and greatness of heart to embrace your neighbors once again."

When he finished, reserved applause scattered throughout the National Assembly. Then members of parliament stood and asked Annan accusatory questions about his role in preventing peacekeeping troops from being sent to Rwanda. It was an uncomfortable exchange. The reaction to his speech compared to the reaction to Clinton's was stark. Clinton had been warmly welcomed with applause throughout his talk. When Bizimungu introduced Clinton he had said, "Your decision to visit Rwanda is an eloquent statement of your condemnation of genocide, a show of solidarity with the victims, and a challenge to the international community to work together to stem the recurrence of genocide." How was his visit any different from Annan's? Didn't both men share equal blame? In fact, I believe Clinton bore a larger share of the blame. As president of the United States, if he had committed troops to Rwanda, other countries would have followed. Annan didn't have that kind of power. He was not a commander in chief. All he could do was entreat the Security Council for support. Yet Clinton was given a hero's welcome and Annan was being attacked. Neither deserved to be attacked.

After his speech I was chauffered to the Jali Club for Annan's reception. I was one of the first to arrive. As I waited outside the doors of the reception hall, Kagame approached me. We were politely talking about nothing in particular when Kagame's aide walked up and told him there was a call from the president. Kagame excused himself. When he returned, he said, "I just spoke with the president. He was unhappy with the speech." Neither Kagame nor Bizimungu were in parliament when Annan spoke; they had both listened to it on the radio. "It was very bad," he added.

His comment surprised me. I was not fluent in English, but what I had understood sounded good to me. Although I was frustrated with his claim of ignorance about what was happening, I appreciated his comments about the importance of healing and moving forward. "Really?" I said. "I thought it was a good speech."

"No, it wasn't," Kagame replied. Apparently the administration was angry that Annan did not accept more personal blame. (Yet none in the RPF had accepted personal responsibility for rejecting foreign intervention.) And they took issue with his assertion that "only you can put an end to the violence." Many thought this was a case of blaming the victim. I, for one, agreed with Annan. I thought Rwanda had to look inside itself to put an end to the violence. After all, the genocide was Rwandans killing Rwandans. That the international community didn't respond was a great wrong, but so was the violence itself.

"We are boycotting the reception," Kagame said.

I was stunned. "No," I said emphatically. "We can't do that. It would be very rude." I thought again of Clinton's warm welcome and Rwanda's tradition of hospitality and grace. How could we not offer the same to Annan?

"We're boycotting it," Kagame said again. "It won't be a problem," he added, trying to mollify me. "Everything will be fine."

"Let the president boycott it if he wants," I countered. "But you, the prime minister, and I should stay. It's the right thing to do."

"No," Kagame said. "We're leaving."

"I think it would be good if I stayed," I told him.

Kagame nodded. "Stay if you want." With that, he and the prime minister left.

My heart sank. Annan was going to arrive any minute. How was I going to explain Bizimungu's and Kagame's absence? I was embarrassed—embarrassed for our leaders, for myself, for the country as a whole. I was not alone. Other Rwandan officials at the reception heard the news and were equally shocked. This was not the Rwanda we knew. We didn't shun visitors. I then thought of the speech given by the minister of foreign affairs and realized that the reaction to Annan was not really a reaction, but a well-coordinated, premeditated plan. Before Annan even said a word, the administration had decided that he would be the scapegoat. He would be the one to shoulder the blame for the failure of the international community to intervene in the genocide. Of course it made sense. The undersecretary-general of the United Nations was relatively powerless in terms of what he could do to help Rwanda. This man from Ghana could do little other than enlist other countries' support. Clinton, on the other hand, could help Rwanda a great deal. Blaming him would have only alienated the United States and put millions of dollars of aid at risk. No one could fault him. It all made sense to me now, and I was further ashamed by it.

When Annan arrived I greeted him and made small talk. He is a very kind man with a genuine warmth about him. After a few minutes, Annan asked me, "When is the president coming?"

I swallowed and gave a half-smile. "Unfortunately, he's not coming."

Annan looked up at me, shocked. "Why?"

"He's busy," I said. "He had some last-minute obligations to attend to."

"What about the vice president?"

"He won't be able to make it either," I said.

The look in Annan's eyes told me that was all I had to say. He knew what was going on. He was an experienced diplomat who understood when he was being snubbed.

He left me and returned to his delegation, who began earnestly whispering—no doubt trying to figure out what was going on. Quickly word spread about the administration's boycott. People huddled together around the room, whispering to each other while they cast furtive glances over their shoulders. I clenched a drink in my hand and smiled awkwardly at the other guests.

After about twenty minutes, Annan returned, shook my hand, thanked me, and left. I had never been more relieved to see a party end.

Annan's snubbing made international headlines. "Annan given cold shoulder by officials in Rwanda," read the *New York Times*. *Le Monde's* headline declared, "*Le Rwanda refuse la main tendue de Kofi Annan*" ("Rwanda refuses Kofi Annan's outstretched hand"). As I listened to the reports on the radio, my embarrassment deepened. *At least it's over,* I thought. *Now we can move on.* But memory of it persisted. Months later I visited the United Nations in New York and met with Kieran Prendergast, undersecretary-general for the department of political affairs, who surprised me when he asked, "So why did your government boycott the secretary-general's reception?"

When I heard this, I inwardly cringed. But I had no choice but to maintain the position of the government. "People were expecting him to apologize for his personal failure in Rwanda," I said. "When he didn't do that, people were upset. It was unfortunate that it happened, but it was a reaction. You can understand that people react differently to situations?"

"Yes, I know," he said. "But you did not have that reaction. You received him warmly. He told me that you were very kind toward him."

Although I was glad to hear those kind words, I still felt ashamed that my country could not have received him more graciously. Yes, Annan was wrong for not doing more to stop the genocide, but he deserved to be treated with respect. Reproach and grace are not mutually exclusive. It would have been possible to condemn his actions without embarrassing him.

When I look back at the international community's failure to act in Rwanda, the mystery that confounds me is how good people can make decisions that are so harmful. How can we allow political and other calculations to deflect us from the noble course of action and lead us to yield to evil? It is a mystery as old as humankind. As Edmund Burke wisely observed, "All that is necessary for the triumph of evil is that good men do nothing." I have no doubt that Bill Clinton and Kofi Annan are good men who want to do what's best for the world. I'm sure Madeleine Albright, Bob Dole, and Susan Rice are also good people. Yet they failed to help at a time when their help was desperately needed. After the Holocaust, people marveled at how otherwise kind-hearted Germans could ignore the concentration camps that bordered their towns. How could they go about their daily lives while systematic killings were taking place virtually next door? Sadly, fifty years later, we were asking ourselves the same question. It's even more baffling when we must ask that question of our leaders. As it says in the Book of Luke, "To whom much is given, much is required." The more power one has, the greater the obligation to protect those who are less powerful. Until we, as part of the human race, can take that truth to heart and live as one human family, we are doomed to live in a world where evil will prosper.

Chapter 8

A Creeping Autocracy

Injustice anywhere is a threat to justice everywhere.
—MARTIN LUTHER KING, JR.

S OME THINGS you know without ever being told. Other things
you learn slowly. You learn them despite what you want to
believe. That is how I learned about the authoritarianism that
was taking hold in Rwanda. When the RPF signed the Arusha Peace
Agreement in 1993 to end the civil war, I believed that the RPF wanted
to build a democracy. When, in the wake of genocide, it didn't take
advantage of its military victory and throw out the peace agreement,
I believed the RPF was seriously committed to building a country
based on rule of law. I believed that they wanted what was best for
Rwanda. I believed in Paul Kagame. Most everyone did. So when he
slowly started weakening the parliament, the executive branch, the
judiciary, we didn't fully realize what was happening. Like the gazelle
who doesn't know the rustle in the grass is a leopard, we didn't know
what hit us until it was too late.

• • •

In March 1999, a member of parliament arrived at my house. He had called earlier asking to meet with me, with a wiry urgency in his voice. When he arrived, I could tell his news was serious.

"Your Excellency, I've heard that the RPF is creating a Forum of Political Parties that will have the power to remove members of parliament."

"What?" I asked, trying to contain my shock.

He explained that the Forum of Political Parties would include representatives from the four major political parties of parliament—the RPF, the Liberal Party, the Social Democratic Party, and the Republican Democratic Party—and the four smaller parties.[1] This forum would have the power to remove any member of parliament at any time. The RPF would chair the forum, and the secretary-general of the RPF would serve as spokesperson.

"Are you serious?" I asked. This seemed impossible. It was blatantly unconstitutional. I couldn't believe they would propose something like this.

"Yes," he said gravely.

"This is clearly an attempt to control the parliament," I said.

He nodded. "But they've been working toward that for a long time," he said. "Really, it's been going on since after the genocide."

I asked him what he meant. He told me how the RPF took advantage of its military victory in 1994 and disregarded key elements of the power-sharing provided for in the peace agreement. "As you know, the RPF took the presidency, the vice presidency, the deputy prime minister, and the key ministries."

"Yes," I said. "But that in itself isn't bad. If they used those positions to rebuild the country, to build rule of law, to promote reconciliation—"

"You're right," my friend interrupted, "but the tricky part is that there was no vice presidential role in the peace agreement. Kagame

---

[1] The four other smaller parties were the Islamic Democratic Party, the Democratic Christian Party, the Rwandan Socialist Party, and the Rwandese People's Democratic Union.

created that role so he could take it, and then work behind President Bizimungu. So he took the position of vice president and he also took the position of minister of defense. He became the power behind the throne."

I nodded. By that time, it was no secret that Kagame held the reins of government and that Bizimungu had little power. The media openly referred to Kagame as Rwanda's "strongman." Because Bizimungu was a Hutu and member of the RPF, his presidency gave the government a diverse face and made the international community think it was inclusive, not a Tutsi-dominated government. In reality, Bizimungu's presidency was window-dressing, not a commitment to reconciliation. I often thought of how difficult it must have been for Bizimungu to play that role. Who would ever want to be in that position? The same political trick had been played during Habyarimana's rule: A Tutsi was named minister of institutional relations to make the cabinet look inclusive. But it was just for show—then and now.

My friend continued, "And Kagame imposed representation of the military in parliament." This had often bothered me. Having members of parliament in military uniform was a form of intimidation. Although some military lawmakers were very effective, it was clear that they were there to ensure that Kagame's views were adopted in parliament. Like all soldiers, the military lawmakers would follow the orders of their military superiors; Kagame was the most powerful man in the military and had been their commander during a four-year war. They knew how harsh he was. They knew what happened to soldiers who did not obey his orders.

"The RPF also gave the president the power to remove the prime minister, which the peace agreement didn't call for," my friend said. Under the Arusha Peace Agreement, cabinet ministers were chosen by the prime minister. But the RPF imposed a change so that the prime minister couldn't appoint cabinet ministers without the approval of the president. "So Kagame is essentially appointing the ministers, including the prime minister," he said.

He was right. In 1995, Prime Minister Faustin Twagiramungu,

a Hutu, was forced out of office after disagreeing with Kagame and
Bizimungu on a number of issues. The straw that broke the camel's
back came when the prime minister asked why the ministry of
defense had not done more to stop human rights violations that had
been committed by a number of soldiers. He was forced to resign and
fled to Belgium. Three ministers who supported him were also fired;[2]
two went into exile. When Twagiramungu left, Rwanda lost one of
its most vocal critics of a nascent dictatorship. He had opposed the
dictatorship under Habyarimana and he was one of the rare politicians who openly opposed Kagame's rising power. He understood
that the concentration of power in the hands of one person threatened the rule of law. He understood that when power is moved away
from state institutions and into the hands of political parties and
individuals, dictatorship is not far behind. Twagiramungu's demise
as prime minister was the beginning of the end of the power that
office had.

It also brought to mind the fate of Valens Kajeguhakwas, a very
wealthy Tutsi who was a respected member of parliament and a
major supporter of the RPF financially and politically during the
war. But by 1997 he had grown disappointed in the party. That
year, he made a statement in parliament that the country was on
the wrong course. He was reacting to a report issued by a delegation that had traveled to remote parts of the country to assess
how Rwandans were recovering from the genocide. Their report
highlighted continued suffering and the government's insufficient
response. After his statement, he was forced out of office. Years
later he fled to the United States, leaving behind a very successful
bank that the RPF government sold. The Rwandan government
sought his deportation, telling the U.S. government that he was
a criminal. The U.S. government denied the request but arrested
him nonetheless. He spent two years in an American jail until a

---

[2]The three ministers who were fired along with the prime minister were Alphonse
Nkubito, who died a natural death in Rwanda; Seth Sendashonga, who was allegedly
assassinated by RPF operatives in Kenya; and Jean Baptiste Nkuliyingoma, who still
lives in exile in Belgium.

judge finally cleared him of all charges. He has suffered greatly because of the RPF's vendetta against him.

"But it's not just what's happening in government," my friend continued. "Look at what's happening within the RPF. Kagame is now chair of the party, which gives him even *more* power." I had also thought of this before. In 1998, Kagame had engineered his election as chair of the RPF and the election of Bizimungu as deputy chairman. So, basically, the vice president was acting as the president's boss. This blurred the lines of authority and put Kagame in a very powerful position.

"And have you ever noticed that he appoints people to positions regardless of their party affiliations?" he asked me.

"Yes." I nodded. The power-sharing agreement during the transition period called for executive positions to be filled based on political party affiliation and only after consultation with party leaders. But with time, I noticed that these positions were filled by the RPF without the input of the political parties. This shifted appointees' allegiance from their political parties to the RPF. After all, if the RPF put them in office, keeping the RPF happy would be their priority.

As I processed all this, I couldn't help but wonder how it had gotten this far. "Why didn't you stop it?" I asked. "In those early years after the genocide, when it was just starting to take hold, why didn't you stop it?"

He shook his head and sat back in his chair. I could tell it was not the first time he had thought about this. No doubt he had asked himself the same question a number of times. "In 1994, everyone was so traumatized after the genocide, we so badly wanted peace, we trusted that the RPF would do what was right," he said. "Some of the changes the RPF pushed for were so vague that we didn't bother to ask questions. And I don't have to tell you that we were afraid of questioning the RPF's intentions."

I nodded. On the one hand, they trusted the RPF too much, and on the other hand, they feared Kagame too much to say anything. "And now we are paying the price," I said.

I thanked him for coming and escorted him to the door. After he left, my mind reeled. I thought of all that he had said. Although I had known of everything he mentioned, I had never really thought of it as a concerted effort by Kagame to grab power and create an authoritarian regime. I guess I had been like the others, thinking that Kagame and the RPF were doing their best to govern a country still in crisis and build something out of the ashes of genocide. But now I thought of all that had happened in the last few months and began to seriously worry where the country was heading.

A year earlier, I was listening to the radio when I heard that the government had removed Supreme Court Deputy Justice Augustin Cyiza from office. I listened to the news in disbelief. The constitution didn't give the government the power to remove a justice. The government could only suggest to parliament justices it wanted removed. The final decision belonged to parliament.

I knew the government was unhappy with Cyiza because of a recent ruling he had made. A Rwandan beverage company had taken the government to court because it had seized the company's raw materials in a tax dispute. The lower court ruled in favor of the company, and the government appealed. The appeals court ruled in favor of the government, and the company appealed. When the case reached Deputy Justice Cyiza's courtroom, he ruled in favor of the company. His decision was final. So in disregard for the constitution, the government simply decided to remove him from office. It was a blatant attack on the judiciary's independence.[3]

A few days after the news broke, Cyiza came to my office. He smiled when I greeted him, but the smile was empty. His eyes were tired. Worried creases lined his forehead. I welcomed him as he sat in the chair across from my desk.

"I have written a letter," he said, taking it from his briefcase and

---

[3] In July 2008, Rwanda's constitution was amended to institute term limits on all judges, including the supreme court justices. This is another step backward, as it weakens the judiciary even more.

handing it across the desk to me. "It tells my side of the story." He was obviously shaken by what had happened—he had lost his job and he feared for his future. And although he didn't say so, I suspected that he feared for his life, too. A year before, in 1997, another deputy chief justice, Vincent Nsanzabaganwa, had been killed at his house in Kigali. His killers were never caught, but most everyone guessed it wasn't random.

I took the letter and started reading it as he spoke.

"Would you circulate this to other members of parliament for me?"

"Yes, of course," I said. I respected Cyiza. He was a Hutu who had served in Habyarimana's regime, but he acted independently and with integrity, which could not have been easy. He was a major in the army and had protected a number of Tutsi during the genocide. In addition, after the war ended, he convinced about eight hundred former soldiers to join the new government, preventing them from fleeing the country, and undoubtedly saving lives. Plus he was competent and dedicated to country unity. I knew I had to do what I could to ensure his voice was heard, even if it meant angering the RPF. I still held out hope that Kagame would see the mistake he had made and change his mind.

After Cyiza left my office, I asked my staff to make copies of the letter and distribute it to members of parliament. As word spread of the government's actions, criticism grew. Foreign embassies, parliament, and the public were enraged that the government would overstep its bounds like this. Yet, like all outrage at the RPF-dominated government, it was muted. Outright protest would never have been tolerated. Still, whispers persisted: The RPF had gone too far this time. Soon after this, I received a call from the president's chief of staff, Colonel Frank Mugambage, asking to meet with me.

When he arrived, he began explaining to me the government's side of the story. "We had to remove Augustin," he told me. "It was for the good of the country." I knew he was speaking in code: *Don't argue*, was what he was really telling me. *Don't make waves.*

"It's unconstitutional," I said. "Only the National Assembly has the power to remove a justice of the supreme court—and then only with two-thirds majority vote. You can't just remove a justice because you disagree with his decision."

He shook his head. "We didn't remove him because we disagreed with him," he argued. "We took action because he was making decisions alone. He wasn't following procedures."

The irony of his statement was not lost on me. "Even if that is the case," I said, "you don't have the right to remove him. You should have documented the case and made a request to parliament to remove him. If you had proof of this, then parliament would have voted on it. You would have respected the constitution and there wouldn't be this outcry against the government."

"There is no outcry," he said. "What outcry?"

I knew I was pushing too hard. I softened a little. "This can be fixed," I said.

"The government has made its decision," he said with finality.

"You can still correct it," I said. "Make the case to parliament and we will vote on it."

"The government has made its decision," he said again.

I sighed. This was going nowhere. I knew that the RPF's stonewalling was, in fact, a demonstration of force. It signaled that the RPF could strike any judge at any time. *Well*, I thought, *if they will not reverse their decision, at the very least they can tell me honestly why they want him removed.* "Just between you and me," I said, "tell me what's really going on, so at least I know."

"What are you implying?" he shot back defensively. "The RPF is transparent. We have nothing to hide. We do what we do for the good of the country!"

His reaction surprised me. I again softened my tone, "I wasn't implying anything. I was just wondering." Later I heard that the RPF was involved in a smuggling operation that allegedly brought a beer similar to that produced by the plantiff's company into Rwanda. This made sense to me because today, the RPF controls many business interests in Rwanda across several industries. When I heard this, I thought back to my conversation with Frank and wondered about his defensiveness. Did he think I knew something about it and was accusing the RPF of driving a legal company out of business to promote the illegal business of the party? But I knew none of this when we spoke.

With our conversation at a dead end, I thanked Frank for coming and he left my office. I could tell he was unhappy with me and knew he would report back to RPF's leaders what I had said.

My conversation with Mugambage reminded me of an earlier conversation I had with the former secretary-general of the RPF during which I had advocated the rule of law. "We will not be prisoner to Habyarimana's laws," was his response. It was as if the laws should not be followed if they were the same laws that had existed under the previous regime. It made no sense. Not everything that Habyarimana did was evil. Some good laws had existed under that regime. I had made the argument then, as I had many times before and would many more after, that as long as a law is not amended, it should be followed. If the law was unfair or outdated, it should be amended, not simply disregarded. But Kagame wanted to show everyone that they could strike at any time regardless of what the law said. They wanted to show everyone that their power reigned supreme.

I knew I had to talk to Kagame about this to get anywhere, but I also knew that Kagame would resist meeting with me. So I waited until circumstances threw us together to talk to him about it. As luck would have it, I was scheduled to attend a Labor Day celebration on May 1 in Rwanda's national stadium. I knew Kagame would be there, too, and that I would likely be seated next to him because of my rank. That would be my chance.

The day of the celebration, I was led to the VIP seats in the packed stadium. Looking at the crowd of people gathered there, my pride in my country swelled. Dancers dressed in traditional Rwandan costumes performed on the soccer field below. Flags waved. Colors saturated the stands. I took it all in and had soaring hope that this was what our country *could* be: United. Peaceful. Happy. Was it too much to wish for?

I was seated next to Kagame, as I had expected. As we watched the festivities below, we chatted about the large turnout and the dancing.

After a few minutes of pleasantries, I said as casually as I could, "This situation with Cyiza has created an outcry."

He looked at me and nodded.

I wanted to tell him the same thing I had told Frank Mugambage: that what he had done was unconstitutional; that he should reinstate Cyiza to his supreme court position. But there was no point. Mugambage had undoubtedly already recounted to him our conversation. He knew how I felt. Besides, Kagame almost never changed his mind; it would show weakness. So instead of pushing Kagame to reinstate Cyiza, I would encourage a compromise. "You could at least give Cyiza another job," I told him. In Rwanda, if you are forced from a high-level position like Cyiza's, your career is over. Good jobs are scarce to begin with, and when the government is against you, no one will hire you. By pushing Cyiza out of office and tarnishing his name, Kagame had doomed him to a life on the fringes of society. If Kagame gave him another job, it would at least provide some protection for him and his family. I was sure Kagame didn't care about this, but I knew the public outcry about Cyiza's ousting—particularly from foreign embassies—must have been bothering him. I hoped by presenting an option that seemed to address that fact, I would have more luck.

Kagame nodded. "Yes, you're right," he said. "Tell Cyiza that I will meet with him."

Good, I thought, relieved. *At least Cyiza will have a job. He will have some safety and security.* And I hoped that appointing Cyiza to another position would allow the public and parliament to focus on the issues confronting the country. But I had no idea what was coming.

In the year before the creation of the Forum of Political Parties, parliament had been steadily gaining momentum. We were creating laws and summoning ministers to explain their actions. Of course Kagame wanted to stop that. He wanted a parliament that he could control. He already controlled members of parliament who belonged to the RPF and the military; now he wanted to wield power over the rest. Creating the Forum of Political Parties was a way for Kagame to remove members of parliament who stood in his way. And the political parties supported the idea of the forum because it would give them the opportunity to get rid of representatives who weren't toeing the party line. The constitution stipulated that each lawmaker had the right to act independently of his party's wishes. The forum would put an end to that. It would squelch any independence lawmakers had.

Of course, those who supported the forum did not present it this way. Instead, they told the public on national radio broadcasts and through newspaper articles that no provisions existed to hold members of parliament accountable for their actions. The forum, they said, would be a mechanism to do that. But what they didn't tell the public was that mechanisms already existed to keep members of parliament accountable. They were not above the law. The judiciary had the power to legally remove lawmakers who were found guilty of a criminal offense, and parliament had an internal disciplinary committee. The RPF knew this, but the public did not. So the idea of the forum was sold as a just and fair system of checks and balances on parliament. In reality, it was neither.

I was disheartened—not only because the forum was unconstitutional and contrary to the principle of separation of powers, but because it would counter the momentum that parliament had been building for the last two years. For the first time in our nation's history, we had built a legislative branch with a backbone. Now they were threatening to take it away.

I tried to schedule a meeting with Kagame to discuss the forum, but, as usual, he was unreachable. Instead I tried to meet with the secretary-general of the RPF. Not surprisingly, he would not discuss it with me either. So I decided to write a letter to the president asking him to stop the creation of the forum. Meanwhile, I spoke with some leaders of the other political parties, telling them the forum was a bad idea, but they all adamantly supported it. Even my own party supported it! It demonstrated how greatly the RPF had weakened the political parties. Also, most of the parties' leaders—including the prime minister—were cabinet ministers, which would mean that the forum would allow them to exert power over members of parliament who could investigate and censure them. Only one party leader had the guts to oppose creation of the forum: Hamidou Omar, who chaired the Islamic Democratic Party. It was a small party, but because of the power-sharing system, he was the third-most-powerful member of parliament. He and I had always worked well together. The fact that he opposed the forum reinforced my respect for him.

My letter to the president created an outcry within RPF's inner circle. One afternoon I heard Charles Muligande, secretary-general of the RPF, attacking me on national radio. Muligande had been a friend of mine and we shared a mutual respect, so I was surprised to hear what he had to say: After a string of unfounded accusations against me, he said I didn't have the authority to write such a letter to the president without the approval of all lawmakers. Further, he said I was just a spokesperson for parliament, not the speaker. It was, of course, untrue. Everyone understood that as the head of the legislature, duly elected by my colleagues, I had right to write to the president protesting policy. In fact, I regularly wrote to the president on a number of issues.

Muligande's words shocked me. How could this man who had been my friend attack me in this way? I was accustomed to random attacks from Tito Rutaremara, the RPF's leader in parliament, but to hear Muligande say these words was a fresh cut. What bothered me the most was that he must have known he was not telling the truth. Yet I had to remind myself: It was not him talking—it was his boss, Kagame. If he wanted to keep his job, he had no choice but to do as he was told.

Despite the RPF's public condemnation of me, I received a letter from President Bizimungu a few days letter saying that he was willing to see if we could come up with a compromise. He recommended that I get together with party leaders to find a solution. His response surprised me. When I wrote the letter, I had little hope he would help. But I thought that if he did not, it would be on record that I was fighting this. As deputy chairman of the RPF, he could have responded by telling me that I was wrong and that the forum should be created. This was one of the rare times Bizimungu indicated that he disagreed with Kagame. Over the last few months, rumors had been spreading that Bizimungu was increasingly at odds with Kagame. Now I was beginning to see it. It made me happy to see him exercise some independence on such a sensitive issue.

I followed his recommendation and wrote letters to all political parties calling for a meeting. On the day of the meeting, about ten political party leaders showed up, including Charles Muligande. I knew my chances of changing their minds were slim, but I had to try. I felt like a mouse in a den of lions.

"We cannot move forward with this," I told them. "The forum is unconstitutional and unjust. It also works against the very principle of separation of powers, and it will weaken parliament's momentum. You need to give up the idea."

They immediately protested, stating that political parties should have authority over their members. They said that because lawmakers represent their political parties, the parties should have the right to remove them.

"But once elected, lawmakers are no longer under their political parties' power," I reminded them. "It says so in the constitution. Lawmakers are there to serve the people. They're accountable to the law and procedures. If members of parliament do something wrong, there are constitutional procedures for removing them."

But they did not want to discuss existing constitutional procedures. Instead, they insisted that members of parliament are elected by their parties, and thus, their parties had the right to discipline them.

What I wanted to say was that the forum would not strengthen their parties; it would only strengthen the RPF. But it was no use. They knew that Kagame supported the creation of the forum. And if Kagame supported it, then it would happen. They cared little for the constitution, little for rule of law. They wanted power over lawmakers. Plus, they feared Kagame.

Once it became clear that they were not budging, I proposed a compromise: "If the forum is created, it should at least be created legally," I said. "An amendment to the constitution should be drafted and voted on. Then you can explain your rationale and procedures to parliament and to the public." My hope was that it would be rejected. But if not, it would at least have legal boundaries, rather than be a renegade organization exerting control over legal, established institutions.

But they never initiated an amendment. They created the forum on their own, with full support from the political parties. The forum immediately began removing members of parliament as if the meeting had never taken place. Those who had been active in government oversight or had criticized the government, directly or indirectly, were among those targeted. In the space of about a month, eight lawmakers were gone. Few met happy endings: Eustache Nkerinka fled to Germany; Jean Leonard Bizimana and Leonald Kavutse were eventually imprisoned; Jean Mbanda was also later imprisoned for three years without ever being brought to trial and eventually fled to Canada; Donatien Rugema fled to Denmark, where he died; Deus Kagiraneza, a member of the RPF, fled to Belgium; and Major Alphonse Furuma, a former member of RPF's executive committee, eventually fled to the United States. Only one—Jacques Maniraguha—remained in Rwanda and out of prison.

The forum's procedures were eerily systematic: Leaders of the political parties drew up lists of lawmakers they wanted removed. The forum would discuss them and Charles Muligande would go on national radio to read the list of parliamentarians who would be ousted. "They have two weeks to resign," he would say. "If they don't resign, their parties' leaders will expel them from the party." Once they were expelled from the party, they would lose their seats in parliament.

If there was any doubt who was in control, the forum did not vote out members of parliament who belonged to the RPF or the military—those members were simply told to leave by RPF officials. Also, if one of the other parties wanted someone out whom the RPF supported, the RPF always won. For example, the Liberal Party tried very hard to remove Eugenie Kabageni from her seat in parliament, but the RPF supported her, so she remained. It was clear that the forum served the RPF, not the other parties.

Our nightmare had begun. Morale in the National Assembly was low. Everyone was whispering about who would be the next to go. I could feel the stress eating away at all of us. We knew something bad was happening, but we didn't know the extent of it. We didn't fully realize that our country was veering toward autocracy.

The judiciary was next. It began in 1998, with Deputy Justice Cyiza's dismissal. Also in 1998, the justice of the lower court, Jean-Bosco Iyakaremye, who had presided over the same case as Cyiza and also ruled in favor of the company, was forced to resign and fled to Canada. In March 1999, the minister of justice, Faustin Ntezirayo, could no longer bear the pressure the RPF was placing on the judiciary. He, too, fled to Canada. Then, in July 1999, Chief Justice Jean Mutsinzi and two of his deputies, Paul Ruyenzi and Paul Rutayisire, were ordered to resign. No reason was given. These men were all Tutsi and members of the RPF who had lived in exile for many years, but they were not insiders. The justices did as they were told and submitted letters of resignation. This time, the government attempted to follow the law: It sent a formal request to parliament asking lawmakers to approve the resignation of these three judges, attaching their letters of resignation that cited "personal reasons" for leaving.

As part of the same request, the government also asked for the removal of another deputy justice, Alype Nkundiyaremye, who eventually fled to Belgium and died there. They also belatedly submitted Cyiza's name—essentially asking us to legalize his removal. Looking back, we should have debated this. We should have questioned the government. But I think parliament was still shell-shocked from the creation of the forum. The government knew this. It was no accident that they presented these resignations to parliament so soon after the forum had ousted eight lawmakers.

The government sent the names of a new chief justice and four new deputy justices to parliament for approval. In the space of twelve

months, five of the six members of the supreme court were replaced
by justices hand-picked by the RPF. The final nail had been driven
into the supreme court's coffin.

The timing of the introduction of the Forum of Political Parties
and the ousting of the supreme court justices was not random. It
coincided with the end of the transitional government that had
been established after the genocide. The constitution stated that by
July 1999, the transitional government would come to an end. By
that time, free and fair elections to choose a new government and
president were supposed to have taken place. But free and fair elections were not in Kagame's plans. Both Hutu and Tutsi alike were
dissatisfied with RPF's leaders. Under free elections, there was no
way the RPF would have won. It was in their best interest to extend
the transitional government.

I, too, thought that the country was not yet ready for presidential and legislative elections, but for entirely different reasons. My
greatest concern was how divided Rwanda remained and how the
government had not designed a formula to ensure fair power-sharing
between the minority and the majority. Hutu accounted for at least 80
percent of the population. Tutsi accounted for less than 20 percent.[4]
The concern was that elections would fall along ethnic lines, as was
often the case in divided societies. It had happened in Rwanda in
the early 1960s. But even worse, in situations like this, extremists,
not progressives, almost always won elections. A formula had to be
established that would ensure that Tutsi were not once again deprived
of a voice in government. I advocated, and still do, that Rwanda adopt
a consensus democracy where the majority and minority can share
power to ensure that every ethnic group in the country feels represented and safe. Although it is an imperfect solution, I believe it
would help put an end to the succession of Hutu-dominated or Tutsi-

---

[4]Because of unreliable census gathering in Rwanda, the exact percentages are unknown. These are estimates.

dominated governments that had historically run the country and caused so much divisiveness.

I once shared this idea in a meeting with Kagame in 1998. I suggested that the four major political parties that shared power (two of which were Hutu-dominated and two of which were Tutsi-dominated) continue to do so beyond the transition so they would continue to have equal representation in parliament. Keeping these parties, I believed, would ensure an ethnically balanced representation in parliament. I told him that these parties should be open to all Rwandans who wanted to join. I also suggested that the constitution give each political party the chance to serve as president on a five-year rotation. "This would allow each ethnic group to feel part of the political arena," I said, quickly adding, "Because of the RPF's role in ending the genocide, I'm sure everyone would agree that the RPF should be the first party in the rotation." I believed this to be true, and I also hoped it would quell any uncertainty Kagame might have that the RPF would lose power by adopting this plan.

I continued, "If we do this, I think the people will focus on the issues that confront all of us—both Hutu and Tutsi—instead of being consumed with this violent competition for power."

Kagame nodded eagerly as I spoke. "Sure," he said. "That's a good idea. We should consider it."

I left his office thinking, once again, that he was on my side. It was meetings like this that would derail my concerns that he was masterminding the creation of a dictatorship. *See,* I would say to myself, *he's receptive to new ideas. He wants what's best for the country.* Of course, I was fooled. I later learned through others close to him that he didn't like my idea. Further, he said that I was ambitious; that I was proposing this form of democracy because it would eventually allow me to become president, given my influence in the Liberal Party. It was preposterous! I was just interested in a win-win solution that would put an end to the violent competition for power between Hutu and Tutsi that had plagued our country for nearly a half-century. But I never got the chance to tell him. I never heard from him about the issue again.

In addition to my concerns about elections falling along ethnic lines, I thought the transitional government should be extended because I disliked the way the RPF conducted elections. The RPF's election method for local officials was the queuing method, in which citizens voted by lining up behind their candidate of choice. It completely disregarded the principle of secret ballot. Everyone could see who voted for whom. Government soldiers and local officials would "monitor" these elections under the pretense of ensuring safety—but I didn't believe it, and I don't think most citizens believed it either. Hutu and Tutsi alike would feel bullied into supporting the RPF candidates. In addition, in many instances, RPF operatives would order candidates it did not support to withdraw from the race.

For these reasons, when the government proposed an extension of the transitional government for another five years, we agreed. I hoped that the changes I advocated could be made during the second phase of the transition. It was wishful thinking. Instead the RPF continued to consolidate its power—and excluded independent-minded politicians. Kagame had us right where he wanted us.

I fought this growing autocracy the only way I knew how—through work. Every day, I went to my job as speaker and continued to work as if the forum had not been created. I encouraged other members to do the same. "We work for the people, not the Forum of Political Parties," I would tell them. "We need to keep doing our work. That is our best defense." And in almost every case, that's what we did. It made me immensely proud to see my fellow members of parliament pressing forward despite the shakeup. We continued to create laws. We continued to scrutinize bills presented to us by the government and insist on accountability. And most important, we continued to investigate accusations of corruption and mismanagement by government officials.

In October 1999, after committee investigations, parliament voted out of office two ministers: Anastase Gasana and Charles Ntakirutinka. In a separate investigation, lawmakers called all four of Rwanda's former ministers of education before parliament to answer questions about embezzlement charges related to a $26 million World Bank project to reconstruct schools after the genocide. Two were found to have some responsibility. One, Laurien Ngirabanzi, resigned. Parliament recommended that the other, Colonel Joseph Karemera, who was ambassador to South Africa at the time and therefore out of parliament's disciplinary reach, be sanctioned together with the staff who were responsible. It never happened.

In addition, parliament investigated mismanagement in the ministry of rehabilitation and repatriation of refugees. Several officials were found to have had responsibility in the mismanagement of funds, including Christine Umutoni, the former second in command of that ministry. Parliament also found the minister, Patrick Mazimhaka, negligent and therefore subject to parliamentary censure.[5] Our message was clear: The Forum of Political Parties would not keep us from doing our jobs. We kept moving forward. And in doing so, we were accomplishing something that had never been done before in Rwanda.

Throughout all of this, Kagame seemed to support parliament. When I spoke with him, he told me he thought parliament's censure of corrupt officials was the right thing to do and that we should continue our good work. I thought that Kagame had finally understood that we needed accountability if we wanted to build rule of law. Again, I was mistaken. I later learned that Kagame supported our investigation of these ministers because he wanted many of them out of office himself. His support was tactical, not principled.

As all of this unfolded, I thought of all the people who had been forced out of office by the RPF: a prime minister, other members of the cabinet, numerous members of parliament, and five supreme

---

[5] Christine Umutoni was later appointed ambassador to the European Union and Patrick Mazimhaka served as vice president of the African Union for five years. Both were appointed to their respective positions by Kagame's government.

court justices, to name only a few. It seemed that almost every month I would hear of another casualty.

Through it all I had kept in contact with Cyiza, the deputy justice who was one of the first to be pushed out. Kagame had given him a job as he had promised me at that Labor Day celebration, but in title only. The position was in the ministry of defense, which meant Kagame was Cyiza's boss. He was given a car reserved for high officers in the army, but no salary. "I have no office," he told me one day when I met with him. "I have no responsibilities. It is a phantom job." He had become a born-again Christian and spent his time going to church, preaching, and lecturing at private universities. But he lived in fear. "I worry I might one day get hurt," he told me. He did not have to say any more; I knew what he meant. Years later, in April 2003, I learned that he had disappeared. No one ever heard from him again.[6]

Bit by bit, Kagame was consolidating his power. And still, we didn't see the whole picture. Those who did see it feared the RPF too much to speak out. They knew that severe consequences would follow. So people complained in private but applauded in public. But at what cost? As journalist Frank Kent once said, "The evils of government are directly proportional to the tolerance of the people." Our tolerance abetted the growing dictatorship. The international community also kept silent, trading Rwanda's seeming stability for democracy, not realizing that the economic recovery and stability rested on shaky ground.

Every time a person chose to keep quiet, someone was wrongfully removed from office, or threatened, or forced into exile, or killed. There is a Rwandan proverb: *Inkoni ikubise mukeba uyirenza urugo—* throw away the stick that beats your rival, because that same stick can be used to beat you. We failed to apply this wisdom. As a result, we were watching a dictatorship take hold before our eyes.

It reminded me of the famous poem by Pastor Martin Niemöller, the Lutheran minister who was imprisoned by the Nazis during the Holocaust:

---

[6]In 2007, his wife and children fled Rwanda, finding refuge in Kenya.

When the Nazis came for the communists,
I did not speak out;
I was not a communist.

When they came for the social democrats,
I did not speak out;
I was not a social democrat.

When they came for the trade unionists,
I did not speak out;
I was not a trade unionist.

When they came for me,
there was no one left to speak out.

I worried that Rwanda was slowly becoming a country where no one would be left to speak out.

Chapter 9

Betrayal

———ɷ———

> What others say and what I sign to is not the same. . . . It
> is my name! . . . I cannot have another in my life! . . . How
> may I live without my name?
> — *The Crucible*, Arthur Miller

T HE RUMORS began mildly at first: "President Bizimungu
rarely goes to his office," people would whisper to each other
over drinks or in meetings. "He really doesn't do any work."
Then they became weightier: "He's more concerned with his business ventures than running the country." Heads would shake pite-
ously. "It's a shame, really." Then the attacks became more vicious:
"Bizimungu has psychiatric problems," people would say. "He has
affairs with other women." And finally: "He's become an extremist.
He can't be trusted."

It was 1999, and although President Bizimungu had just begun his
second five-year term in the extended transitional government, it was
clear that his career was coming to an end. Bizimungu was increasingly at odds with Vice President Kagame. It didn't surprise anyone
when the rumors started. "It is not a matter of *if* Bizimungu is forced
out," people would whisper, "but *when*."

I feared they were right. The pattern was all too familiar by this point: When Kagame decided that he didn't like someone, they weren't just removed from power, they were ruined. Smear campaigns would begin from which the victims hardly ever recovered. "Everyone ignores a dead dog in the road until it begins to smell— then they want it gone," Kagame was supposedly fond of saying. And his operatives made sure his opponents smelled like dead dogs.

Everyone murmured that this would be Bizimungu's fate. It saddened me. I knew Bizimungu wasn't perfect. He and I had come into conflict many times over the course of the three years that we worked together. But he was a good man and a hard worker. Now, his job was at risk.

As rumors about Bizimungu swirled, my party prepared to elect a new leadership. We had tirelessly worked over the course of the last year to reorganize the party and draft a new charter and bylaws, and now we were ready elect a new executive committee. As election day approached, a friend said to me, "You should run for chairman."

"I have no interest in being chairman," I told him.

"Why not?"

"You know what happened in 1997," I replied, referring to our last party elections, when we elected the governor of rural Kigali to be the new chairman. The RPF didn't like him. Soon after the election he was fired from his governor post; he eventually fled to the Netherlands. Ultimately, Pie Mugabo, a friend of Kagame, was named chairman. It was clear that the RPF wanted its rival parties to be headed by weak leaders that they could dominate.

"But you're now friends with Kagame," my friend countered.

"Not really," I said. It was true that Kagame and I had developed a good working relationship over the last eight months. He had begun meeting with me regularly and was receptive to my ideas. But I wouldn't describe us as friends.

"Well, you're very popular in the party and with the public," he continued. "Being chairman would put our party in a good position for the presidential and legislative elections in a few years."

"That's exactly what I worry about," I said. "The RPF doesn't want the Liberal Party in a good position for elections. That's why this is dangerous." I was doubly concerned because of the rumors about Bizimungu. According to the constitution, if the presidency is vacated, the speaker of parliament—not the vice president—becomes president until special elections can be organized. Everyone was whispering that I would be the interim president, which led to more whispers that I should become the permanent president. People were growing increasingly disillusioned with Kagame. Like me, they had had high expectations when he toppled the genocidal regime in 1994, and like me, they had been disappointed. People were beginning to think of an alternative, and my name kept coming up.

"You can't deny that you're in a good position for it," my friend said. "You're more popular than Kagame. You grew up in Rwanda. You haven't been involved in any scandals or corruption. You're a genocide survivor who's lived in Burundi and Congo. A lot of people identify with you—even Hutu. They know you're committed to reconciliation."

"I have no interest in being president," I told him. "Besides, the constitution says that a president would have to be a member of the ruling party. I'm not." Although I didn't say so, I knew that even if I wanted the job and the constitution allowed for it, Kagame would never let it happen. If Bizimungu was on the way out, it's because Kagame wanted total control. He clearly wanted to be president. Someone like Kagame, for whom laws were only roadblocks to power, would never trust that an interim president would voluntarily give up the position even though it's written into the constitution. He would never take that chance.

Besides, I wanted to focus on my work in parliament. I was proud of all that we had accomplished in the last two and a half years. Finally the National Assembly had become a strong body that held the executive branch accountable for its actions. We had established a public account committee—and an auditor general's office—to scrutinize the use of public funds; we called ministers before committees to justify their budgets, something that had never been done in Rwanda; we passed laws to establish a national tender board to oversee the procurement process of big government contracts to stave off corruption; an independent commission for human rights to investigate accusations of abuse; and a commission for national unity and reconciliation. But perhaps most important, under the oversight bill that I signed into law in 1997, we had summoned ten ministers and censured two.

Increasingly, parliament was earning a reputation as the only institution in the government doing any real work. In November, a Belgian newspaper published an article about how the Rwandan National Assembly was no longer "a simple rubber stamp" and the "peaceful revolution" that had ensued: "It happened smoothly, almost discreetly. One morning in early October, Rwanda awoke to find, for the first time, a real executive oversight body: the parliament had just forced two ministers accused of embezzlement to step down. . . . Today, the mechanism [of checks and balances]—and doubtlessly Mr. Sebarenzi's unusual courage in a society where one does not contradict the government—prevented the RPF from paralyzing the system."[1]

It seemed as if we were finally developing a real government that adhered to the rule of law. I wanted to continue to build on that momentum. And although Kagame and I were at this point working relatively well together, I worried that my becoming chairman, which would mean increased power and visibility, might not sit well with him.

Still, my fellow party members continued to press me to run. When I told them I wanted to focus on my work in parliament, I would hear, "But the party needs you." "You're abandoning the party to protect your own interests." Besides, they would say, Kagame was the chairman of his party; the prime minister was the chairman of his party; why couldn't the speaker also be chair? Even some friends within the RPF told me I should run.

I began to think maybe they were right. But if I was going to be the leader of the Liberal Party, I wanted to make sure Kagame wasn't opposed to the idea. Too much was at stake. Although I thought it was ridiculous that the ruling party should have any say in the other

[1]*La Libre Belgique.* November 6 and 7, 1999. By Marie France Cross. Translated by Christopher V. Scala.

parties' elections, I wasn't going to jeopardize the work I was doing in parliament over this. I decided to talk to Kagame.

"I need some advice," I said when I met him at his home office.

"Yes, of course," he said affably. "What do you need?"

"Many people in my party want me to run for chairman," I said. "But I thought it would be a good idea to talk to you first and make sure it doesn't interfere with my job in parliament."

"Not at all!" Kagame said.

"It won't be a problem?"

"I don't see any problem. I'm the chairman of my party and it's no problem," he said.

I left his house feeling as if a weight had been lifted off my shoulders. I would be able to satisfy my colleagues in the Liberal Party who wanted me to be chair, and Kagame was not opposed to it. I called a few close friends and told them what Kagame had said. They, too, were relieved. We thought finally we could elect a party leadership that Kagame did not oppose, but that wasn't a puppet of the RPF. This would be our chance to really move forward as a party.

Soon after, a member of parliament, Gatete Polycarpe, called me. Although a member of the Liberal Party, Gatete was closely tied to the RPF—many believed he was an informant for Kagame. "You should postpone elections," he said. "The RPF is against it."

I didn't believe him. I had talked to Kagame myself just a couple days before. If the RPF was against the election, he would have told me. *Gatete is just pursuing his own agenda,* I thought. He was a successful businessman who actively pursued his business interests, to the detriment, I thought, of his work in parliament. Perhaps he was worried that if I became chair of the party, I would come down on him. I thanked him for his call but told him that we would proceed with elections as planned.

But as the days passed and elections grew closer, I began hearing the same thing from a few other people who would say to me, "The RPF is against these elections." I decided that I should talk to Kagame again to be sure.

This time when I met with Kagame, I was more direct. "Many

people are saying that the RPF is against these elections," I said. "What's going on?"

Kagame was taken aback. "That's ridiculous," he said. "The RPF has nothing to do with the Liberal Party's elections. Why would we be against it?"

"So we should go ahead with our elections?" I asked, wanting to make sure there was no confusion.

"Sure," Kagame replied. "Of course, go ahead."

I left his office feeling very confident. Now when I heard rumors that the RPF was against elections I would ignore them. "I've talked with Kagame and the RPF is fine with it," I would say. Yet not only did the rumors persist, they grew more intense. Gatete was now telling other Liberal Party members that the RPF asked him to tell them that the RPF was against elections and that elections should be postponed.

I decided to see Kagame for a third time. "Your Excellency," I began, "I keep hearing that the RPF is against these elections."

"They're just rumors," he said. "Ignore them."

"But I heard from Gatete that the RPF is against it," I said. I knew he was close to Gatete, so if they were lies, maybe Kagame could shut him up.

Kagame shook his head and leaned back in his chair. "It has been a long time since I met or spoke with this man. What you're hearing are lies. Go ahead with your elections."

I left his office not knowing what to think. Other members of the party had told me that these rumors couldn't come solely from Gatete. He was being too aggressive and talking to too many people. "The RPF is behind this," they would say. "Be careful." But on three occasions I had asked Kagame if he was against the elections, and all three times he had told me no. Why would he lie to me? I had no choice but to believe him.

Elections were scheduled for December 19, only two days away. The rumors had not abated. I still shrugged them off, but I was having a harder time doing it convincingly. People had started saying that it was no longer the RPF, but Kagame specifically who was against elections—and not only was he against the elections, but he specifically didn't want me to be chairman. In addition, Gatete and Pie Mugabo, the current chair, had begun campaigning hard against me.

"I have a feeling something bad is going to happen," I told Liberata one evening after I returned from work. "These rumors aren't going away." We prayed together, asking God for guidance and protection, but I still felt an uneasiness in my gut.

The day before elections, I got a call from Dennis Polisi, a lawmaker and member of RPF's executive committee. "Protais and I need to meet with you," he said, referring to Protais Musoni, another member of the RPF executive committee and secretary-general of the ministry of security.

"What about?" I asked him.

"It's related to elections in your party."

What now? I thought. Protais was very close to Kagame. I knew something was wrong if he wanted to talk to me. I told him to meet me at my home in the afternoon.

When they arrived I greeted them and invited them to sit.

"We're bringing you a message from the vice president," said Protais.

"What message is that?" I asked.

"You need to postpone the elections."

I couldn't believe it! "Why?" I asked.

"For security reasons," he said.

"What security reasons?"

"Some people are against this election," he said. "You never know what could happen. People might riot."

This was ridiculous. Voting was restricted to members of the Liberal Party's national council—about fifty people in all. How could they worry about riots? "Well, you're in charge of security," I said. "Make sure nothing happens."

"No, we don't want to take the chance."

I was tired of this. If the RPF didn't want me to be chairman of the party, why didn't Kagame just tell me that when I met with him?

"This just confirms the rumors that the RPF is opposed to the Liberal Party's elections," I said.

He vigorously shook his head. "No, no," he said adamantly. "We have nothing to do with it."

"Okay," I said. "If the vice president wants to postpone elections, that's fine with me. But you need to talk to the chairman." I knew this would mean that elections would be delayed. Chairman Mugabo would gladly do as the RPF told him. But I also knew that protesting their postponement wasn't going to change anything. The hands of the party were tied. All of the preparations we had done in the previous months—electing representatives at the provincial level and adopting a new charter and bylaws—were for nothing. The RPF was firmly in control.

After they left, I called a friend to tell him about the conversation. "Excellency," he said, "they announced on the radio a half-hour ago that elections were going to be postponed."

"What?" I shouted more than asked. "I was meeting with them a half-hour ago!"

"Well, they've already made the announcement."

"When did they say elections would be held?" I asked.

"They said they were postponed to another date." I knew this meant that elections would be postponed indefinitely.

I knew then that things were worse than I thought. They must have already talked to Mugabo and made the decision before they came to talk to me. I felt like a rabbit who had been snared without feeling the trap snap across its leg.

I immediately called Kagame on his personal cell phone. The call was answered by his aide-de-camp. "I'm sorry, he's busy," he said. "He'll call you back." I wondered if he had taken lessons from Yvonne on how to deflect unwanted calls. I never heard back.

The next day I called again and again I heard, "I'm sorry. He's very busy. I'll remind him again. I'm sure he'll be calling you back soon." No word.

The next day: another call, another excuse. Kagame had frozen me out.

I thought of a conversation I had had with my mother-in-law a few months earlier when I had opposed the removal of a member of parliament. She was worried about the frequent disagreements between the government and parliament.

I was surprised she knew, although I shouldn't have been. Liberata's mother is a very smart woman. "These conflicts are normal," I said, trying to put her at ease.

She shook her head. "Don't you worry it might cause you problems?" she kindly asked.

I smiled. "Unfortunately, there are things I have to speak out against and try my best to change the course of events."

Now it was she who smiled. *"Aho kuba intumbi waba imva,"* she said. *It's better to be dead than to live like a dead person.*

About a week later, I received a call from a trusted friend in parliament. "I need to talk to you," he said, his voice etched with urgency. "It's important."

"Then talk," I said.

"Not on the phone. We need to meet."

When he arrived at my office later that day, he wasted no time with pleasantries. "They're trying to remove you," he told me bluntly.

"Remove me?"

"They don't want you to be speaker anymore," he said. "They want you out."

"What?" I asked. "Why?"

"They're saying you're a threat to security, that you're working with the king's army to make preparations to overthrow the government."

"What?!" I almost laughed. The deposed king of Rwanda has lived in exile for close to fifty years, residing in the United States in a modest apartment outside Washington, D.C. He had no power and little money. The idea that I was working with him to build up a military was almost comical. But my friend wasn't laughing.

"I just wanted to warn you. They want you out."

I thanked him for coming and walked him to the door. As I closed the door behind him I thought of my last meetings with Kagame and how sincere he had seemed. Now this? I couldn't make sense of it.

That night when I arrived home, I told Liberata what I had heard. "That's impossible," she said, shaking her head in disbelief. "Maybe Kagame doesn't want you to be chairman, but why not speaker? You have a good relationship with him. Why would he want to do this?"

"I don't know why," I said. "I don't even know if it's true."

"Please, call Kagame and see if you can resolve this," she said. "Find out what's going on."

I decided she was right. Kagame was at a meeting outside Kigali with a group of genocide survivors nicknamed "Fourteen"—the number of their membership. They were all Tutsi business people who had fled to Kenya before the genocide and strongly supported the RPF during the war. Kagame would be meeting with them for a few days, so I decided to call his personal cell phone to try to reach him. Again his aide-de-camp answered, and again I left a message asking for Kagame to call me back. He didn't.

A few hours later I received a call from a close friend who was also a member of Fourteen. "Excellency," my friend said in a voice barely above a whisper, "Kagame is saying a lot of bad things about you. He's saying that you're causing trouble for the government."

"Okay," I said warily.

His voice became gravely serious. "Don't be fooled into thinking this issue will be resolved. It will not," he said. "Everything that is happening, he is behind it. Don't trust him."

"Okay, I understand," I said. "Thank you for calling."

"Be careful."

"Yes, thank you," I said again.

I hung up the phone and put my head in my hands. I couldn't believe this was happening. The Fourteen group knew me well and liked me. Undoubtedly, Kagame knew this and realized he had to win them over. The smear campaign against me had begun. *This is the beginning of the end,* I said to myself. Pretty soon, I would be the dead dog on the side of the road that everyone wanted gone.

I decided that I needed to find out what was going on from someone inside the RPF. I called Bizimungu. He was still president and deputy chairman of the RPF. Surely he would know something, and if anyone would talk to me, Bizimungu would.

I asked if I could meet with him, telling him it was urgent. "Absolutely," he said. "Come now."

When I arrived at his office, he greeted me kindly, "How are you?"

"I am not fine," I answered bluntly.

He looked shocked. "What happened?" he asked.

"I heard that the RPF is in the process of removing me from my role as speaker," I said. I decided the time for innuendo was over. I was tired of tiptoeing around the RPF. I needed to know what was going on. "And I would appreciate it if you could tell me why you want me out."

He raised his eyebrows and jerked his head back in surprise. "What?!" he asked, alarmed. "I've heard nothing about this!"

At first I didn't believe him. *He's deputy chair of the RPF,* I thought. *How could he not know?* But then I thought of the swirling rumors about Bizimungu and his deteriorating relations with Kagame. Then I realized that he, too, was being frozen out. It was clear that he wouldn't be president much longer.

I told him what I had heard and he shook his head in consolation. "To tell you the truth," he said, "I'm surprised you made it as far as you did." I knew what he meant. Since I took office I had disagreed with Kagame repeatedly and come through relatively unscathed. I thought of what I was told by a member of parliament when I first decided to run for speaker back in 1996: "You shouldn't do it," she said. "You don't have high-level connections in the army or the RPF. It won't be easy for you. You should just remain a regular member of parliament." I did not believe her then, but now I knew she was right.

As I sat across from Bizimungu I thought of how far our relationship had come. I remembered our early meetings when he would pound on his desk and shout at me because I disagreed with him. I thought of his speech before parliament saying that we were wasting our time by opposing the executive branch. I thought of the times when he would treat me like a disruptive schoolboy in front of other members of parliament. Yet I always knew where I stood with Pasteur Bizimungu. By contrast, I never knew where I stood with Kagame. He was always pleasant with me and seemingly supportive. Whenever I met with him he would say, "Sure! Sure!" to my requests. But his promises were empty. Kagame controlled people through secrecy. No one ever knew what he really thought about anything until it was too late.

I looked at Bizimungu and thought of how intertwined our fates had become. I wondered what our futures held. A pit sat heavily in my stomach.

"I'll see what I can find out," Bizimungu said. "I'll let you know what I hear." He gave me a sympathetic smile and although he didn't say so, I knew he was thinking, *I'm next.*

I shook his hand, thanked him, and left.

As I rode in my car back to my office, I realized that I wouldn't hear anything from Bizimungu. He was as much at risk as I was. It would be too dangerous for him to fish around for information. When I got back to my office I called a close friend who was also a high-ranking government official and asked him to meet me at my home that evening.

When he arrived I escorted him to the gazebo so we were out of earshot of my bodyguards. I told him what was going on. "Can you find out if it's true?" I asked. "What their plans are?"

"Of course," he said. "I'll find out what I can. I'll call you."

"No," I said hastily. "It's too dangerous. Kagame can't know that we're talking to each other." My phones were likely tapped. Kagame could see who came to my house from his office. The bodyguards who followed my every move were most certainly giving Kagame daily reports. These men were soldiers; Kagame was the minister of defense. I knew they were no longer protecting me.

So we made a plan. When he found out what was happening, he would tell someone who had no ties to the government and would not be watched. This person would call me and give me a message.

I waited for the phone call. I knew in my gut what I would hear. Hadn't I heard it already? From my friend in the Fourteen group who was brave enough to call me. From the countless whispers. Still, it seemed impossible that I would be targeted like this. Why would Kagame do this to me? To make sense of it, I first had to understand the man I was dealing with . . .

Kagame was born to a middle-class family in Rwanda in 1957. His family fled to Uganda when he was only three years old to escape the massacres—the same massacres that sent my mother into hiding in the bush when I was a baby. Whatever wealth his family had in Rwanda was lost when they snuck across the border into Uganda. Kagame grew up fighting off hunger and disease in a refugee camp, where his father ultimately died. Kagame and his family were treated as second-class citizens in Uganda, but couldn't return to their homeland because of continuing violence against Tutsi. When he was in his twenties, he found himself unemployed. Unable to find any other opportunities, he joined a rebel force to overthrow the Ugandan government, fighting in the bush along-side Uganda's current president, Yoweri Museveni. He showed great promise in the rebellion for both his keen intelligence and his ruthlessness, and was appointed to a prominent position in intelligence. Later, when the rebels had won and Museveni came to power, he was appointed deputy chief of military intelligence, reportedly committing grave human rights abuses to further the cause of the new government. But Rwanda was the true aim of his ambitions, and in the late 1980s, he joined the newly formed RPF. When the war started, Kagame was participating in a military training program in the United States. Just a few days into the fighting, the RPF's commander in chief was killed, so Museveni asked Kagame to take his place. He got the position over officers who outranked him, breeding resentment in the ranks. Supposedly he used the skills he had learned training in Castro's Cuba and honed as deputy chief of intelligence against dissenting Tutsi soldiers to ensure obedience.

Knowing all this, it was easy to understand why Kagame became the man he did. He was raised in a world where human rights were trampled upon, and in turn, he trampled upon human rights. This doesn't excuse his behavior. People all over the world suffer innumerable injustices and choose not to perpetuate them. Still, I could understand how someone who is driven out of his homeland and raised amid violence and resentment would resort to those same tactics to gain some measure of security. It is why we must protect our children against violence and hatred—so they don't perpetuate that aggression as adults. No matter what has happened to us, we must learn to forgive and teach our children to forgive so our children don't grow up thinking one injustice can be avenged by another injustice.

The ring of the phone startled me. I picked up the receiver with trepidation. "What you've heard is true," the woman's voice on the other end of the line said. Then she hung up.

A few days later, the secretariat of the RPF drew up a petition for my removal as speaker. The list of allegations against me had grown. No longer was I accused only of working with the deposed king to overthrow the RPF regime, I was also accused of misusing public funds to pay for a sculpture of a dove that sat in the parliament building's garden. In truth, the government of Rwanda didn't pay a dime for the sculpture. It was a gift from the artist, who saw it as an opportunity to get some free publicity for her work. When the parliament's secretary-general asked me if the artist could display it, I immediately agreed. I thought the dove—the symbol of peace— would be an appropriate display in the garden, where all our official ceremonies were held. But now I was being accused of spending a small fortune of the country's money to purchase it—a waste of government funds when so much of the country was in disrepair.

They would have been right, if it had been true. But like the other allegations, this was baseless.

The secretary-general of the RPF called a meeting of RPF representatives in parliament and those representing the military—nineteen people in all. He circulated the petition and told the members to sign it. When they asked why, he answered, "Vice President Kagame said that the speaker is a threat to the nation's security."

All nineteen signed it.

Then the petition was circulated to the other parties. Again, people objected and again they were told I was a threat to the nation's security. When the petition was presented to members of the Social Democratic Party, one member asked, "Why do they want the speaker to be removed?"

The chairman didn't even explain. "Sign it, or don't," was his only response. The implication was clear: Sign it or suffer the consequences. In the end, every member of parliament who was in Kigali at the time signed the petition.

After it was signed, one member of parliament came to me and said, "Don't think I am against you." He shook his head sadly. "We have accepted to be dogs and we have signed it."

"I understand," I said. And I did. I knew how Kagame operated. If the RPF and the military signed a petition, other members of parliament really had no choice but to do the same. Still, I felt betrayed. These were the lawmakers I had worked so closely with over the last three years to make parliament what it was today. I had fought for pay raises for them. I had fought to get them out from under the heel of the RPF. Now I felt that it was all being snatched away.

I called my driver and asked him to take me home. I didn't look behind me as I left my office. I didn't look as I exited the doors and climbed into the car. I stared straight ahead as the wheels of the car gripped the asphalt and we pulled away. I thought of the day I first arrived and how inspired and confident I had been. I thought of all the plans I had for the future of parliament and the future of the country. The car rolled quietly out of the gate that surrounded the

National Assembly. I glanced over my shoulder and watched the building as it grew smaller in the distance. The holes from the bomb blasts still gaped open on the façade, like mouths frozen in a silent scream. I couldn't take my eyes off them.

In the days that followed, members of parliament and others in the government who had been my friends stopped coming to see me. They didn't talk to me when our paths crossed in the hallways. If they saw me at a distance they looked the other way. It was as if I had the plague. Anyone who talked to me knew he was putting himself at risk. In times of trouble a man learns who his real friends are. A handful of close friends continued to visit me and pray with me. Their friendship meant more to me than I could ever express. It was immensely comforting to know I wasn't alone.

The others who talked to me were members of the RPF who wanted to make sure I left my position quietly. Repeatedly I would be approached and told, "Don't worry. There will be other opportunities for you. I heard Kagame wants to appoint you to be a minister."

The reason they were worried was that, according to the constitution, I had seven days after the petition was signed to call a meeting of parliament to argue my case. Doing this would be an embarrassment to Kagame and the RPF. The public would see that I was being forced out under false pretenses. But still, I wasn't sure if I wanted to debate the petition—I didn't think it would do much good.

I decided to go see Bizimungu. He was one of the few people who had been kind to me through all this and I wanted to let him know my plan before I did anything. "I'm going to call a meeting to discuss the petition," I said. "I think I'm going to resign."

"Okay," he said. He shook his head sympathetically. "It's your decision."

A few hours after my meeting with Bizimungu, my phone rang. It was Kagame's secretary asking that I meet Kagame at his home office that evening. I knew Bizimungu must have told him my plans to call a meeting to discuss the petition. I'm sure Kagame worried that I was going to debate it. But the fact that Kagame wanted to speak with me was promising. *Maybe he's going to change his mind*, I thought. I knew the chances were slim, but I held out hope. I thought of how sour my relationship with Kagame had been when I first started in parliament. We had managed to get past that. Maybe we could get past this. That optimism walked hand in hand with me as my car pulled up to his compound.

It was already dark when I arrived. Kagame lived in the presidential compound—a collection of small houses behind a high wall ringed with soldiers. Of course, the presidential compound was supposed to be Bizimungu's residence. But a couple of years earlier, Kagame decided he should live there. The symbolism was not lost on anyone.

The soldiers standing sentry saluted when they saw my car and the gates swung open, as they always had. When I exited the car, Kagame's aide-de-camp greeted me and escorted me to the sitting area in Kagame's office. Then Kagame entered with James Musoni,[2] a close associate of his. Kagame shook my hand. "I got your message that you wanted to see me, but I was very busy," he said apologetically. "But now I have time. So tell me why you wanted to meet with me."

I looked at Musoni and then back to Kagame. "Thank you very much for your time, but I would like to meet with you alone." I didn't want a third person listening to our conversation. I worried that Musoni would gossip about what he heard and a distorted version would make its way to Kagame, who would then blame me for the lies. It was too risky. I wanted to know that everything we said stayed within those four walls.

"Yes, of course," Kagame said and asked Musoni to leave.

Once we were alone, I sat across from him. As I had at every other meeting with him, I felt supremely confident. I knew I was right; I knew the rumors being spread about me were lies; I knew members of parliament signed the petition only because they felt they had no

---

[2] James Musoni is no relation to Protais Musoni.

other choice; I knew that no matter what he said, I still had my honor and dignity. "I'm going to call a meeting to discuss the petition calling for my resignation," I said.

He didn't reply.

I continued, "But first, I would like to know what problem you have with me."

"I have no problem with you at all," he protested. "I'm as surprised as you are by all of this. There's no basis for the charges against you."

I knew he was lying. "Then how did the petition for my resignation get this far? Who is behind it?"

"It's your own people in the Liberal Party," he answered.

Another lie. The leaders of my party had no power. The year before they had tried to remove a member of parliament but failed because the RPF was against it. If they were unable to remove a regular member of parliament, then clearly they could not remove the speaker.

"Besides, there could be other opportunities for you," he said, echoing what other members of the RPF had told me. "Go ahead and resign. You'll still be a member of parliament. You can still do your work."

I thought of how many times Kagame had lied to me and how many times I had given him the benefit of the doubt. I thought of all the times he had told me, "Sure!" and I had believed him. I was tired of it. If Kagame was lying to me like this, there was no chance that I could save my position as speaker. I knew then that I would not call the meeting to defend myself. I was as good as gone. But perhaps I could still save my name.

"May I ask you a favor then?" I asked.

"Sure."

"I don't want to leave my position in this way," I said. "I don't want to leave being called a threat to national security." I thought of all the work I had done in parliament and how all of it would be tainted if this treason charge followed me. "I can go quietly. Let me resign my post in a proper way."

Kagame looked at me evenly. We had been speaking in Kinyarwanda this whole time, but now he said to me in English, "It's too late."

His words shot through me. "But it's not too late!" I objected. "You can change this." Kagame was all-powerful. No matter what had been started, it would take only a word from Kagame to stop it. "I still have a couple days before I need to call a meeting, you can—"

He abruptly cut me off. "I was not involved in this," he said. And then the entire expression on his face changed. His eyebrows narrowed threateningly and deep lines etched his forehead. This was a different man from the one I had seen the last three years. He leaned forward and pointed a finger at me, "But if you don't resign, I *will* get involved."

For the first time throughout this entire ordeal, my heart skipped a beat. This was the commander in chief of the army. If he was telling me that he would get involved, I knew what it meant. I thought of everything I had ever heard about Kagame—how he couldn't be trusted, how he didn't hesitate to have his enemies killed. I remembered all the warnings I had dismissed over the years. Now they reeled through my mind in rapid-fire succession and I knew that more than my role as speaker was threatened.

I smiled politely and nodded. "Then I will resign," I said. I thanked him for his time, said good night, and turned to leave.

I walked out of his house and into the night. An even blackness stretched across the sky. The hum of the city was quieter. Insects were beginning their shrill serenade. A cool wind made the hairs on the back of my neck stand on end, as when a dog senses danger. They brushed across the collar of my shirt with a pricking alertness. I heeded their warning.

By the time I arrived at my house, my children were in bed. Liberata was in the dining room, where she had been anxiously awaiting my return. As soon as she saw me she jumped to her feet, "How did it go?" she asked. I could see her face searching mine for some clue.

I shook my head. "Not good," I said. "I have no choice. I have to resign."

Her shoulders collapsed. "What happened?" she asked.

As I recounted the conversation she shook her head wearily.

"If you could have seen his face," I told her. "He was a changed man. I feel like for the first time I really saw who this man is."

"It's terrible," she said.

"I know," I said. But then I offered a weak smile. "It's not all bad. In some ways this will be better. I can do my work without all the pressure of being speaker and without having to tiptoe around Kagame."

She mirrored my smile. "We can get our life back," she said.

"You realize we'll have to move?" I said. "If I'm no longer speaker, we can't live here. The new speaker will move in. We'll have to rent a house."

"I'm not worried about that," she said. "Moving is nothing compared to what we've been through the last three years. I want our life back. Where we live doesn't matter."

I embraced her.

That night I called the national radio station asking them to announce a meeting of the National Assembly at three o'clock the next afternoon, January 7, 2000.

I arrived at parliament that morning as I did every morning. But I could tell by the looks on people's faces that they knew what was happening. I would smile and nod in their direction, but their eyes would not meet mine. Throughout the morning, employees filtered into my office with tears in their eyes. "I'll miss you, Your Excellency," they would say. "Thank you for everything." I forced back my own tears.

At three o'clock I took my seat in parliament. I was still officially the speaker, but because the meeting was about me, I could not chair it. So I sat in my regular seat among the other lawmakers while the deputy speaker moderated. As we waited to convene, I chatted pleasantly with the member of parliament seated next to me, as if it was any other day, not the day that I was being pushed out of office because of a petition he and everyone else around me had signed.

As the other lawmakers took their seats, one member of parliament, Major Rose Kabuye, crossed the assembly to talk to me. She was a good parliamentarian and I respected her. When she approached me, she said, "Excellency, don't engage in a debate today. Just resign quietly." Even at the eleventh hour, the RPF was doing all it could to make sure I wouldn't cause a scene.

"Don't worry," I told her kindly. But it felt like another betrayal on an already long list of betrayals. It wasn't enough that she and the others had "accepted to be dogs," as my friend said, and called for my resignation. She still had to fulfill her duty to Kagame and ask me to keep my mouth shut.

From my seat, I addressed my fellow lawmakers for the last time. I thanked them for their hard work and applauded all that we had accomplished together. "Since the day I was sworn in, I've used all my energy and conscience to help the National Assembly of our country move forward as a strong and independent institution," I said. "What we have achieved was achieved by all of us." I continued, "I don't want to make any comments today about the petition. . . . But in the end I want to say that for anything wrong I may have done to any of you, I apologize. Please accept my resignation."

I finished my speech to silence. My colleagues looked at their desks or straight ahead. No one looked at me. I smiled outwardly, but inside I felt hollow. Kagame had won.

Next, a handful of lawmakers took turns addressing the assembly. Most talked about procedures for moving forward, but two people took the opportunity to further attack me. It reminded me of a Rwandan proverb: *Umugabo mbwa aseka imbohe*—"Unwise individuals laugh at those who suffer." One Liberal Party member—who had been promised the speaker position once I was gone—said members of parliament should accept my resignation because I fought the creation of the Forum of Political Parties. Another member talked about how I had wasted the government's money paying for the dove sculpture, a sculpture that, in fact, cost the government nothing.

After they were done with me, they turned to attack another law-maker, Hamidou Omar, who was being pushed out of his position as the third-most-powerful member of parliament. Tito Rutaremara, the influential RPF member who helped get me elected speaker but had since turned against me, insisted that Hamidou be voted out because he, too, opposed the creation of the Forum of Political Parties. But the major accusation against Hamidou was that he didn't distance himself from me. Omar shot back, "Why should I distance myself from the speaker? He has made no mistakes. Besides, who among you has distanced yourself from him?" Applause in the public gallery erupted. The deputy chair silenced them.

Those were the only words spoken in my defense that day. As I sat listening to the accusations and attacks, I thought of how many lawmakers had pulled me aside during the last week and privately told me how unfair it was that I was being pushed out like this—but none of them said a word in my defense. My career was the second casualty that day. Integrity was the first.

But at least it was over. I could take my seat as a regular member of parliament and do my work. I might not be able to get as much accomplished, but I could still do a lot. I could still make a difference.

"I need to meet with you." It was Pie Mugabo, chair of the Liberal Party, on the other end of the line. "I have a message to deliver."

Whatever it was, I knew it wouldn't be good. Since I had resigned my post as speaker a few days before, gossip had been circulating that I was going to be pushed out of parliament. This time, I didn't second-guess it. Nothing surprised me anymore. I agreed to meet him at the house of a friend, a businessman from my area.

When I arrived, Mugabo greeted me and invited me to sit. Then he said, "I have a message for you."

"Yes," I said. "What's the message?"

"If you write a letter and admit to conspiring against the government and apologize, everything will be okay. You can keep your seat in parliament," Mugabo said. "If you don't write the letter, you'll lose your seat in parliament."

So this is how it will happen, I thought. *I'm being blackmailed.* Of course, it all made perfect sense: In the media and diplomatic circles in Rwanda, my resignation was hotly debated. People were not convinced that I was guilty of the charges against me. Everyone suspected that I was being forced out for political reasons. People were asking why, if I was guilty, I had not been arrested. If I had really done all they accused me of, wouldn't they do more than simply ask me to resign my position as speaker? This threatened to ruin Kagame's credibility, not just in Rwanda, but internationally as well. If I wrote a letter confessing to these allegations, they could bandy it about to radio and newspapers, telling people, "See! He's confessed! He's guilty!"

"This is ridiculous!" I said to Mugabo. "I can't confess to something I haven't done. They're lies."

"Be reasonable," he replied. "Write the letter and you can continue like nothing happened. Think of your wife and family."

I leveled my eyes at him. "Do you believe that what is being said about me is true?" I asked.

"Of course not," he said.

Once again, I was being betrayed by someone who wanted to save his own skin. "I cannot do it," I said. "I can't."

He paused for a moment and looked at me, waiting for me to see reason and change my mind.

"I can't," I said again.

We went around and around like this for nearly an hour. Mugabo is a good drinker. As we talked, he drank and drank. "Please, just write the letter," he practically begged me. "People are waiting for me! I have to give them an answer. Please write it. Please."

It was clear that he was on a mission from Kagame, and if he failed, he would suffer the consequences. No one was above Kagame's wrath.

I told him no for the final time and left.

The next day we met again. Again we talked for an hour. Again he drank. Again he pleaded with me to write the letter so he could tell his superiors it was settled. And again I told him no.

The following day he sent me a letter telling me I had twenty-four hours to write the letter. If he didn't have it by then, I would lose my position in parliament.

I wrote him back telling him once again that I couldn't apologize for something I had never done and that I would not write the letter.

Two days later, a meeting was called of the RPF-dominated Forum of Political Parties to discuss my fate.

After the meeting ended, Hamidou Omar, who was also a member of the forum, came to my office to see me. "I'm sorry to tell you this, Your Excellency," he said, "but the forum has voted to remove you from parliament."

Hamidou was a good colleague who, although a member of the forum, had argued fiercely against it when it was established. He was also the one who defended me in parliament when I resigned. He looked genuinely sad to tell me the news. "I'm sorry," he said again and left.

I stood for a while staring at my desk. I wasn't surprised. I knew this was coming. Still, it seemed unreal. Less than a month after rumors first surfaced about me and nearly three years after I took office, I was no longer a member of parliament.

I left my office and went home for the afternoon. Although I had been voted out, I would still return to handle the transition of my work to someone else.

When I got home, Liberata stood waiting for me. I went to her and kissed her. I didn't have to say a word. She knew what had happened.

We turned on the radio to listen to the news. The Forum of Political Parties' decision to remove me was the lead story. As we listened, Liberata shook her head. "No!" she said. "No! It's not possible."

"It's done," I told her.

"What's next? They eliminate you from your speaker position; they eliminate you from parliament. What's next?"

"It's done now," I said. I held her arm reassuringly. "It's over."

"But they make you sound like a traitor—like you're going to overthrow the government," she protested. I could tell she was scared.

"We can lose everything, but we can't lose our hope," I said. "They can't take that from us. We have to know that there is a reason for this. We don't know what it is yet, but there's a reason." I reminded her of a biblical verse from the Book of Romans: "In all things God works for the good of those who love Him."

"But what will happen?" she asked again.

I quieted her. "It will be okay," I said gently. "I promise we will be okay." It was a promise I worried that I couldn't keep.

Chapter 10

Escape into Exile

———〜〜〜———

Be strong and courageous. Do not be terrified; do not be
discouraged, for the Lord your God will be with you wherever you go.

—JOSHUA 1:9

A T FIRST I didn't believe people when they told me that
Kagame wanted me dead. *They're overreacting,* I would think
when friends came to my home or called me, telling me that
Kagame would not let me stay in the country and live. "I am not the
first high-level official to be forced out of government, nor will I be
the last," I would say. Most officials who were forced out of one position were given another, less prominent position in government or
marginalized, but they were left alone. Why would it be any different
for me?

"You are not like the others," a friend said to me one day in January 2000. "Too many people are talking about this. There's a lot of
support for you."

We sat in the gazebo within the walls of the speaker's compound,
where I was still living. It was a few days after the RPF-dominated
Forum of Political Parties had forced me out and I had not yet moved

into the house that we would be renting in Kigali. My friend sat facing me, leaning toward me and talking in sharp words barely above a whisper. "The public opposition to your resignation is making the administration look bad," he said. "And you know Kagame does not like that."

"But he is the one who caused it!" I shot back. But I knew what he meant. My dismissal had caused an uproar in Rwanda and in the international press. Although Rwandans were not free to take to the streets in protest, they objected to the decision in their quiet way, talking about it in bars and on buses in town, or in the hills or on the roads of the rural villages. I was receiving a lot of attention, most of it supportive, and I knew my friend was right: Kagame would not tolerate it. But still, why have me killed? Wouldn't that just make Kagame look worse?

I thanked him for coming, as I had thanked the others, and said I would keep in mind what he said. And I did, but still, I didn't really believe it, until a couple of days later, when a relative of mine came to my house and told me she had a message for me.

"Yes, what is it?"

"I've heard that an assassination is being planned."

I didn't have to ask, but I did anyway, almost as a reflex. "Assassinate who?"

She lowered her eyes. "You."

"Who wants to assassinate me?" Again, I knew the answer, but felt that I had to ask.

"Someone who has the power to do it." I knew she meant Kagame, but she could not say it. Even in private conversations, people would not say Kagame's name in any negative way. Everyone fears Kagame, from ordinary villagers to generals.

"How do you know this?"

She told me the message came from a friend of hers who worked in intelligence. I knew the man and knew that he thought highly of my work as speaker. This was different from the other warnings I had received. This man would have access to that kind of information. If he said there was a plot to assassinate me, I had better believe it.

I looked at the woman who had just told me the news. Her eyes pleaded with me. "Please," she said, "you and your wife have to get out of Rwanda. This is real, my friend. If you stay, you will be killed."

I thought of the bodyguards who still patrolled the compound under the guise of protecting me. I thought of my aide-de-camp, chief of the bodyguards, who still escorted me everywhere. I had wondered why I still had bodyguards when I was no longer speaker. Now it was clear. These soldiers worked for Kagame, not me. Their guns, meant to protect me, could just as easily be used to kill me. I thought of other high-level officials who had been ousted from their positions and fled the country—Prime Minister Faustin Twagiramungu, Minister of the Interior Seth Sendashonga, Minister of Information Jean Baptiste Nkuliyingoma—and wondered if they had left because they were threatened. Why else would they have gone into exile?

After the woman left, I borrowed another friend's cell phone and called the man who had supposedly given her the message. I spoke in code: "Did you send me something?"

"Yes."

"Is this something I should be careful with?"

"Yes," he answered. "There are many *abagizi ba nabi* out there." *Abagizi ba nabi* was the phrase in Kinyarwanda for malevolent people. Whenever someone was killed under suspicious circumstances in Rwanda, the official story was that it was a random act of violence committed by *abagizi ba nabi*. I knew then what my fate would be. I knew then that I would be killed on the way to church one day, or on my way to work. I would be gunned down in my car or on the street, and government officials would shake their heads and say, "So many *abagizi ba nabi* out there. What a shame." It was an all-too-familiar story.

"Thank you," I said.

"Of course." And then he hung up.

That night as Liberata and I got ready for bed, I took her hands and led her to the edge of the bed and told her to sit. I sat beside her. She, too, had heard the rumors. I suspected she knew what was coming. Still, I dreaded actually saying it.

"Kagame is planning to have me killed," I said as gently as I could, simultaneously realizing there was no gentle way to break this kind of news.

She looked at me, disbelieving. "How do you know this?"

"I've heard it from a lot of friends, but today, I got credible information from someone who knows these things. I think we need to believe it."

"Which someone? Who?" she asked, her eyes searching me.

"I can tell you the name, but only if you can keep it secret under any circumstances," I said. I didn't say so directly, but I worried that if things went badly and Liberata were tortured, she would reveal everything.

I think she had the same thought, because she immediately replied, "No, don't tell me. I trust you." But then she added, "But I cannot believe that he would take your life, Papa Respect! Why would he do that? Kagame is a Tutsi like us. If you were Hutu, your life might be at risk. But as a Tutsi? No."

Many Rwandans believed this, but I always thought it was a flawed belief. Anyone who could kill another human being, regardless of their ethnicity, has the potential to kill you. "If you can harm a stranger, you can harm a brother," I said to her. "I am not safe because I am Tutsi."

She sat looking at me, bewilderedly shaking her head.

"I know, I didn't believe it either," I said, grabbing her hands. "But think of all that's happened to us. We never believed that they would force me to resign as speaker. We never believed they would force me from parliament. But they have. They've taken everything from us—why not my life, too?" I looked at her evenly. "We have to leave Rwanda. We have to go into exile. It's not safe for us here."

Liberata's already worried face was now crestfallen. "Exile? Again? How many times will we go into exile? It seems our entire life has been spent running from something. I don't want to run anymore."

"I know, neither do I." And I didn't. The prospect of leaving and starting over again made me weary. People from stable countries who have never had to flee their homeland don't appreciate just how difficult it is to live in exile, to live as a refugee. Going into exile tears you from your roots. You must leave everything behind, all of your belongings, all of your friends and family, to go to a strange country. You have no idea when you leave where you will end up or how you will make a living. I thought of all the Rwandans who had fled the country with literally nothing but the clothes on their backs, to start life over again in a foreign land. Liberata's family had done it in the 1960s; Liberata and I had done it in the early 1990s and again in 1994. We thought when we returned to Rwanda after the genocide that we were done running. We were wrong.

I had fled many times in my life, but I had never had to escape a country that wanted to hold me hostage. It was surreal. *How has my life come to this?* I thought the next day as I sought out my brother Emmanuel to devise a plan. There's no guidebook for this kind of thing—at least none that I knew of. I was not a criminal whose life had been spent on the lam from the law, nor was my brother. Yet the two of us sat down and began plotting like criminals preparing to dig out of our cells. It had the makings of a farce, but neither of us was laughing.

First, we had to decide where we would go. "What about the American embassy?" my brother offered. The American embassy was close to the speaker's compound, less than a half-mile away. It would be the easiest place to go, but I was skeptical it would work.

I shook my head. "No, I don't think that would be a good idea. The embassy will negotiate with the government. I will be given up."

"But you don't know that—"

"It's too risky," I replied. "If I go to the embassy, in one way or another I'll end up back in Kagame's hands. Even if he let me live, it would only be for a while. If he wants me dead, he will find a way to kill me eventually." As I spoke, I thought of the fate of a governor and deputy justice. The governor of Butare, Pierre-Claver Rwangabo, was shot dead in his car on his way back from a meeting in 1995. Deputy Justice Vincent Nsanzabaganwa was killed in his home in 1997. In both cases, *abagizi ba nabi* were blamed for the deaths. But many people suspected that these were not random murders; these men must have been targets. And now so was I.

"So where will you go?" Emmanuel asked.

Rwanda was bordered by Tanzania in the east, Burundi in the south, Uganda in the north, and the Democratic Republic of Congo in the west. I had never been to Tanzania, so that was not an option. Eastern Congo was unstable due to fighting between Congolese and Rwanda, so I couldn't go there either. The choice was between Burundi and Uganda. Burundi was the most logical choice. We had lived there and I knew it well. We still had friends who lived there. I had even met the president of Burundi, Pierre Buyoya, while I was speaker. Maybe he would help me. But I knew that the government of Burundi had become friendly with Rwanda. When Kagame found out where I had fled—and he would most certainly find out—he would ask the government of Burundi to extradite me. And that would be it. The president of Uganda, Yoweri Museveni, on the other hand, was an enemy of Kagame. Kagame had fought for Museveni when he lived in Uganda, but since then relations had soured. Surely Museveni wouldn't send me back to Kagame. We agreed that I should cross into Uganda. But how? How would I get out of the compound without raising suspicion among the bodyguards? How would I drive all the way to the Ugandan border, nearly a hundred miles, passing through checkpoints, without being caught?

"Let me talk to Benjamin," Emmanuel offered. Benjamin was our cousin and a brave man. He was a successful musician in Rwanda, but had formerly been a member of the military. "He could help us."

I agreed that Benjamin would be a good person to consult, but emphasized that no one else could know. "We can only tell people who will help us. The more people who know, the greater risk there is of getting caught," I said. "We have to keep this secret. And no phone calls." Everyone in Rwanda assumes their phones are monitored, and mine most certainly was. Suddenly, government officials who worked closely with Kagame had begun calling me, telling me not to go into exile. "Don't worry," they would tell me. "You'll be given another position. This is just politics. Everything will be okay." I knew enough to know there was no such thing as "just politics" in Rwanda.

With that, Emmanuel and I went our separate ways, the weight of our secret heavy on us, thinking about how our lives were about to change, and how no one we loved could know about it.

This was our plan: On Sunday morning, I would take the older children to church. Liberata would stay behind at the compound with the younger ones. Then I would leave the children at church and come home under the pretense of not feeling well. I would tell my bodyguards that I was going to rest. This would put them off-guard—we hoped. We were in the process of moving from the speaker's residence to a rental house in another part of Kigali. Emmanuel would spend the morning at the compound, loading furniture into a pickup truck and driving it to the rental house. After Emmanuel had gone back and forth a few times to make it look routine, I would sneak into the back of the truck and hide amid the furniture. We would drive to the other house undetected—we hoped. At the rental house, Benjamin and two other men would be waiting for me. There I would take Emmanuel's ID card. We were full brothers and looked alike, but we had different last names. Although people knew my name, few of them knew what I looked like. We would leave the house in a car and meet another man on a motorcycle on the outskirts of town. When we neared checkpoints, I would get out of the car and onto the back of the motorcycle. Since motorcycles had no trunks or backseats to search, they were waved through checkpoints faster than cars. I would flash my brother's ID and we would pass through without raising suspicion. We would drive to an isolated spot along the river that divides Uganda from Rwanda (I could not go through the official port of entry). Once there, I would cross the river into safety—we hoped.

Liberata would take a different route. After Emmanuel dropped me at the rental house, he would return to the compound and drive Liberata and our baby Sandrine on different roads that led to the official Ugandan border crossing. Assuming I could make it across the river without being caught, she would be able to cross into Uganda legally and without incident. Our other children would stay behind—this was the part of the plan that felt like a vise grip on my heart. But we could not take them with us. It would put all of us at risk. Respect was now ten years old; Pacifique was eight; Esther was four; and Nicole was three. We knew no one would hurt them (even Kagame would know well enough to leave my children alone), and my brother Emmanuel would be there to take care of them until we could send for them to join us in Uganda. I imagined their faces when they returned from church to find that their father and mother and Sandrine were gone. And, worse, I couldn't help but wonder if I would ever see them again. We had a good plan, but so much could go wrong. I could easily be killed. As I prepared to escape, it was faith that buoyed me—and hope.

Sunday mornings are quiet in Rwanda. Those who go to church are at church. Those who do not are generally resting after a night of drinking. Life moves slower Sunday mornings in Rwanda, and we hoped that this would work in our favor.

So one cloud-covered Sunday morning in January, just three days after I had first heard of the assassination plot, my older children and I piled into the car with my aide-de-camp and headed to church as planned. I told my aide-de-camp that I was not feeling well and would return home after dropping the children off at church. "The pastor will drive the children home after church," I said. "I need to lie down for a while."

Once the children were settled at church, I drove back to the compound. We pulled into the compound around ten o'clock. "I'm not going anywhere today," I said casually, "and I don't expect any visitors. Just my brother and brother-in-law will be moving things." The words came easily, but I wondered if my face revealed the lie. "You and the others can relax. It should be an easy day."

He nodded. I tried to read his face for any hint of suspicion, but saw none. As I exited the car, I saw my brother Emmanuel and my brother-in-law, also named Emmanuel, loading our belongings into a pickup truck that had a metal grate canopying the bed. As I walked to the dining room, I called the two Emmanuels to come with me. I thought of the name Emmanuel, which means "God with us." I felt blessed that two Emmanuels were helping me this day.

We quickly reviewed the plan while I changed clothes. I took off my suit and put on sweatpants, sandals, a T-shirt, and a cowboy hat. I no longer looked like the speaker of parliament. I looked like any other Rwandan man.

As my brother and brother-in-law left the room, Liberata walked in. We looked at each other but said nothing. Then I took her in my arms. "It's time for me to go." She held on to me tighter than she ever had in all the many times we had said good-bye.

"Maybe this is a mistake," she said. "Maybe everything will be okay here." The tremor in her voice made it clear she was choking back tears.

"We can't, you know that. We have to trust in God that He will watch over us." I pulled her away from me and looked at her face. "We have to leave. We have a good plan and God will play his part."

She nodded with little conviction.

"Let's pray together," I said.

We knelt and prayed once again—a prayer we had said so many times, for God to protect us from harm, to watch over our family and bring us all together again safely.

After we ended our prayers, I said, "We should go talk to your mother."

Liberata's mother had become like my own. The idea of leaving her made a fresh break in my heart. She did not know about our plan, but now we had to tell her. She was old and would help Emmanuel take care of the children. It was only fair to let her know we would be leaving.

Liberata and I entered her room. Liberata sat on her bed and I squatted beside her. We explained to her that we would be leaving, that we had no choice. We didn't tell her where we were going, only that once we were settled the children would join us.

Her Rwandan stoicism kept the tears at bay, but her face betrayed her. "What about the children?" she said with pity. "They will be so sad without you both."

Liberata comforted her. "They will be okay. They will be safe here. Papa Respect's brother will take care of them. We will send for them soon. It won't be long." Hearing her speak those words made me realize how much Liberata had suffered—and how much she was suffering now at the thought of leaving four of her children. We had never spoken about it, but I knew that she, too, wondered if she would see them again. It all seemed too much to bear.

"I have to go," I said to both Liberata and my mother-in-law. "We will see you again soon."

I left the room and Liberata followed. We kissed. As I turned away, she grabbed my arm, not wanting to let go. I pulled her arms away. "It will all be fine," I said as I walked away. "It will be okay." Neither of us was sure we could believe it.

I climbed into the back of the pickup truck, which was parked inside the walls of the compound. The bodyguards were all outside the wall. My brother was outside with them, chatting to distract them. No one could see me get in. Still, I did it quickly. I thought of how Kagame's office looked down into the compound. Could his security guards be watching us from there?

I wedged myself between chairs and a mattress. It was cramped, but it was a short drive to the rental house. After I had climbed in, my brother-in-law arranged the belongings to make sure I was well hidden and that I would not get hurt. Then, for good measure, he climbed on top of the grate that arched above the truck and called to my brother that he was ready. My brother excused himself from the company of the guards and climbed into the driver's seat. As we drove through the gates of the compound, the guards noticed only my brother-in-law sitting high atop the pile of furniture. They did not even look to see that I was part of that pile.

My brother drove mercifully slowly, which kept the shifting and bouncing to a minimum. We arrived at the house only a few miles away. I climbed out of the truck quickly, relieved that the first part of our plan had been executed without incident. *This will work,* I thought. *I'm going to make it!* As I stepped out of the truck, I saw my cousin Benjamin waiting for us in a car with two other men: one was a Rwandan named Emmanuel (another Emmanuel!) who would cross with me into Uganda; the other was a Ugandan who knew the back roads of the country. He would also cross with me and help Emmanuel and me get to Kampala, the nation's capital. The Ugandan didn't know who I was or why I was crossing illegally into the country. Benjamin had told him I was a businessman and needed to smuggle something. He did not need to know the truth.

My brother and the other Emmanuel followed me into the house. There, we hastily reviewed our plan. I took my brother's ID card. Then I turned to say good-bye to my brother and brother-in-law. I tried to convey in a glance my appreciation for what they had done for me, and what they had yet to do. My brother would now go pick up Liberata and drive her to Uganda. He was risking so much for me. No words could thank him enough. We shook hands and gave each other a very businesslike good-bye. None of us could afford to let our emotions take hold now. I climbed into the car with Benjamin, the Ugandan, and the other Emmanuel. We were gone.

As we drove I thought of Liberata and prayed that her departure would go smoothly. I would not know until I was in Uganda whether she had made it safely across. She would be taking a different road. We agreed that this was best, so if either of us ran into trouble, the other could still make it to Uganda. But it meant that I would know nothing about her journey until I got to

Kampala. Once there, I would go to the government and ask for protection. Liberata would do the same when she arrived. It was only then that, God willing, we would be reunited and each would know that the other was safe. So as we drove, I could do nothing but pray and wonder and worry. I did not know what happened. I did not know that my brother returned to the compound and picked up Liberata and Sandrine without any problems. I did not know that after driving about ten miles toward the Ugandan border, Liberata realized that she had forgotten her passport. She would be unable to drive into Uganda without it, and she could not cross on foot using back roads with a baby swaddled to her back. It would have been too dangerous. So my brother turned the car around and drove back to Kigali, dropping her and Sandrine off at a medical clinic, where she would be able to wait while he returned to the compound to retrieve her passport. I did not know that by the time he reached the compound, the bodyguards had discovered that I was gone. I did not know that my brother was arrested and taken to the headquarters of military intelligence, where my brother-in-law had already been taken, and where they would both be grilled for information, while Liberata waited and waited at the clinic with Sandrine wondering what had happened to Emmanuel. I did not know that Liberata, frustrated at not knowing what was going on and then finally deciding she had no choice, took a taxi back to the compound. She rushed into the compound, falling and hurting her knee in her frenzy to get inside and find out what had happened. She arrived to hear that the two Emmanuels had been arrested. Not long after, the head of military intelligence, Lieutenant Colonel Jackson Nziza, and Kagame's chief of staff, Major Emmanuel Ndahiro, arrived. Major Ndahiro was also a high-ranking official in the ministry of defense, as well as Kagame's personal physician. There was no doubt who had sent them.

"Where is your husband?" they asked.

"He has left," Liberata replied.

"Yes, we can see that. Where has he gone?"

"I don't know."

"Did he go to an embassy?"

"I don't know."

"Burundi?"

"I don't know."

"Uganda?"

"I don't know."

"Why did he leave?"

At this, Liberata flared. "Why should he stay here with all the terrible things you're saying about him? You say he is a traitor. You say he wants to overthrow the government. You say on your TV and the radio that he is a bad person. Why would he stay in a country that accuses him of these things?"

"No, no, you misunderstand," the men's voices softened. "No one has said that he has done anything wrong. He is safe here. He needs to come back."

Liberata was silent.

I did not know that as one continued to question her, the other searched every part of the compound, looking for me. I did not know the terror that gripped Liberata. The children were still at church, but would be home any minute. What would happen to all of them?

Lieutenant Colonel Nziza and Major Ndahiro did not give up. "You need to call your husband and tell him to come back." The forced kindness in their voices was starting to fade. "Call him now and tell him. Nothing will happen to him."

She picked up the home phone and dialed my cell. But I didn't have my cell phone. My brother had it, but when he returned to the compound and saw the soldiers coming, he hastily hid it, along with my passport. But one of the soldiers found both and kept them. It was this soldier who answered my phone. "It is not him," she told her interrogators. "I can't reach him."

The men knew there was nothing more they could do, at least not now. At that moment, the children arrived home from church. The men departed with a final dictate to Liberata, shrouded in the cloak of a favor. "Please, find a way to get hold of your husband and tell him to come home. He is safe here."

But I did not know any of this as our car made its way through Kigali, past the National Assembly, standing proud against the gray sky. I watched it slide past from under the visor of my hat. I thought of all that had happened in that building. Of all the work we had done, of all the things we had accomplished, of all the hope we had for the future, and how it was all snatched away. For the second time that day I forced back tears.

Our car reached the edge of Kigali and a motorcycle waited for us. I exited the car and climbed onto the back of it, behind a man I had never met before, in whose hands I now placed my life. We rode to the first checkpoint. But as we approached, we realized that no guards were manning it. We drove on to where the next checkpoint would be. Again, no guards were there. No other checkpoints would be on our route, so the man on the motorcycle returned to Kigali, as we drove as fast as we could on the road leading north, leading to the river that would deliver me to freedom.

As we neared the border, we saw a police car driving toward us. None of us in the car said a word. We all tried to look casually ahead of us and not meet the policeman's eyes. After it passed, we turned cautiously to look over our shoulder. The police car had stopped and the driver had climbed out of it to place a stop sign facing south— the direction from which we had just come. He was setting up a roadblock. Had we been just two minutes later, we would have been stopped.

"They must have found out I'm gone," I said. Immediately I thought of Liberata. I wondered if they were setting up roadblocks on the road she was traveling.

"We're almost to the border," Benjamin said. "Let's hope there are no more improvised roadblocks."

There weren't. We arrived at the end of a small road, and in front of us was a river. This was where I would cross.

• • •

But we were not alone at this river's edge. Another car was parked a short distance away. Standing beside it were two men who looked as if they were of some importance—local officials, perhaps—and a bodyguard.

"Do you think they know?" I asked Benjamin.

"I don't think so," he said, shaking his head. "They look too relaxed. Let me go talk to them and see what I can find out."

Benjamin climbed out of the car and casually walked over to theirs. Emmanuel, the Ugandan, and I stayed put, I with my head turned away. Again, I prayed silently to myself. After a few minutes, Benjamin returned to the car.

"It's okay," he said. "They don't know anything."

"What did you say to them? Didn't they wonder why you were here?"

Benjamin smiled, "They recognized me." Benjamin was a famous musician in Rwanda. When these men saw him, they were too star-struck to notice me and the other men sitting in the car a few yards away. "I told them I was here scouting out a location to shoot pictures for my next album cover. They don't suspect a thing." We all smiled.

Then we heard the turnover of a car's engine and turned to watch our riverside companions drive away, waving enthusiastically out the window to Benjamin, surely going home to tell their friends about the famous singer they had just met.

Now we were alone, except for a few boys swimming in the river upstream. But they would not notice us. It was common for smugglers to cross here. Surely they were used to seeing men wade across the river. We were safe to cross. Benjamin bade us farewell—quickly, efficiently—then waited by the car for us to cross. Emmanuel, the Ugandan, and I stood on the banks of the river. It was narrow—only about twenty feet wide—and shallow enough that we could walk across. We took off our pants and shoes and clutched them to our chests as we took our first, tentative steps into the river. The water was cool on my toes, but pleasant. It reminded me of the water in Lake Kivu that I swam in as a boy. Had I ever dreamed when I was young that I would be here now? Running for my life? Illegally crossing a river into another country? I'm sure my younger self would never have believed it. I hardly believed it now, even as I lived it. The water quickly reached the top of my thighs. The river's bottom was soft sand and gravel. Small stones pushed their way between my toes with each step. The current was swift, but not too strong. It pulled my legs, but did not threaten to upend me. We reached the other side and scrambled up the bank. We were in Uganda! We had done it! All of us smiled broadly and patted one another on the shoulder. We would be in Kampala by nightfall and I would be reunited with Liberata. I would be safe. We were going to survive.

We quickly put on our pants and shoes again. I checked my pocket, where I had stowed away cash worth about twenty-five hundred U.S. dollars. It was still there, safe and dry. We began walking. It was around noon now. We knew we had to get away from the border. The closer we were to the border, the greater risk we had of being captured and taken back. So we walked, fast but not fast enough to be noticed. Almost immediately we found ourselves in a small village dotted with straw-roofed huts and banana plants. As it was a Sunday, no one was working. Children played while men and women sat talking. Not much was going on to occupy them—until we arrived. As we walked, we could feel everyone's eyes turn to stare at us. We tried to look casual and unthreatening, but still, they stared. Uganda's conflict with Rwanda had intensified recently. Being so close to the Rwandan border and so obviously Tutsi, we were immediately suspect.

We had been in the village only a few minutes when we heard a man shout behind us. "Hey! Stop!"

We did as he said. We stopped. We turned to face him—a man with a gun, joined by about a dozen other men with sticks. They were not police officers or soldiers, that was clear. They wore everyday clothes and they carried their weapons too cavalierly. This was the local militia. Untrained men with guns always scared me. They were too trigger-happy, too impressed with their own power.

"Who are you?" the leader of the ragtag force asked. "Where are you going?" As he spoke, the men encircled us. The other villagers encircled them.

"Kampala," I said. "We're going there for business."

The man regarded me suspiciously. "Let me see your IDs."

We each dutifully retrieved ours and presented them to him.

"You are from Rwanda?"

We all nodded. I kept a steady eye on the mob, who regarded us as lions regard zebra.

"You are spies." He did not ask us, he stated it. Of course, his assumption made sense: Rwanda and Uganda were, after all, enemies.

"No, no!" we all protested. "We are not spies!"

"You come here from Rwanda? To this small village? If you were businessmen you would have driven to Kampala." The crowd that had gathered around us started to step closer. "We are arresting you," the leader of the militia said. "Sit." He gestured to a bench with his gun.

"Please, believe us," I pleaded, even as I followed his direction to sit. "We are not spies. We're just on our way to Kampala to conduct some business." As I spoke I mentally calculated how far we were from the Rwandan border. Not far enough. Only a quarter-mile, maybe less. It would be too easy for them to send me back, where I would inevitably be captured and where I would inevitably be killed.

Just then, Emmanuel told them he had to use the toilet. They led him to an outhouse a few yards from where we sat. He went in alone and a few moments later, returned to where the Ugandan and I were sitting. Moments later, shouts rose up near the outhouse. "It's a gun!" Apparently when Emmanuel went into the outhouse, he threw a pistol he had been carrying into the toilet, afraid that they would find it on him and punish us for it. But those who were standing near the outhouse had heard a strange noise and got suspicious. They searched the outhouse after he left and found the gun. "It's a gun," came the shouts again. They pulled us to our feet. Then men appeared with a long cord, which they wound tightly around our wrists. Pain shot through me as they tightened it. "You *are* spies!" they shouted, as if they had doubted it before but now the gun was proof. "Why would you have a gun if you were businessmen?"

The leader of the group searched my pockets and found my money. He took it—all of it. I had nothing now. The shouts grew louder. "Spies! You are Kagame's spies!"

"No!" I shouted back, but they didn't hear me. *Here I am trying to escape Kagame, and I am being called his spy,* I thought.

"We are taking you to the police," the militia leader said.

Thank God, I thought. The police could help me get in touch with the government and get protection. *Maybe this will turn out okay after all.* But before I could even complete the thought, I felt the sharp blow of a stick across my shoulders. Then my back. A mob of about thirty men descended on us, beating us while they pushed us down the road toward the police station—herding us like cattle.

Emmanuel and I cried out for them to stop, but our pleas only made their beatings more intense. Again and again, the sharp crack of the stick fell on me. I tried to lower my head and raise my hands, but they were impotently tied in front of me. *This is not going to end well,* I thought. A few weeks earlier I had been the third-most-powerful man in Rwanda, and now I was bound like a common criminal and being beaten by a mob. I knew that I had to tell them the truth. Even if it meant that they would send me back to Rwanda, I had to take my chances. My choice was to die in Rwanda or be beaten to death here.

"Stop!" I yelled again. "I will tell you the truth! I will tell you who we are!" My voice rose above the din and the leader of the militia shouted at the others to stop.

I looked up and watched the crowd back away. Their faces shone with victory.

"Tell us," the leader of the militia said.

I approached him. "Please, can I talk to you alone for a minute?"

The man regarded me with the same suspicious stare he had watched me with since our arrival. "Okay," he said, taking me aside.

So I told him. I whispered the whole story, rapidly, matter-of-factly. I didn't want the others to hear. I still believed that the fewer people who knew the truth, the better chance I had of surviving. "I can't go back to Rwanda," I said to him. "I, too, am an enemy of Kagame. He will have me killed if I return."

"Oh, I see," he said. For whatever reason, he believed me. Maybe he thought the story was too far-fetched to be fiction, or maybe he had heard news about me on the radio. "I'm sorry all of this happened," he said, gesturing toward the crowd.

Inwardly, I sighed with relief. We would now be free. "It is okay. Can we please go?"

He shook his head. "No, I still have to take you to the police station."

"Why?"

"It is my duty," he said simply.

I could tell it was no use arguing. So we continued our walk to the police station. The militiamen escorted us, and a few villagers came along to see how it all turned out. About twenty people in all trudged along the two-mile path to the station. As we walked, I asked the leader where exactly we were going.

"To the customs office, right near the border."

I stopped. "But that will be right across the river from the Rwandan customs office!" I knew that the two offices would sit just opposite each other on the river. A bridge would be nearby. Rwandan police would be literally only a few yards away. "They're looking for me! They'll see me and come across to take me back!" Kagame would not hesitate to order his soldiers to violate the soil of another country to take me back.

"That is the closest station," he said a little incredulously. "We must take you there."

"Please," I pleaded. "Take me somewhere else! You don't understand, I can't go back there!"

He looked at me with pity, but still he answered, "No, I'm sorry. This is where we have to take you."

I thought of all of us arriving at the checkpoint. The Rwandan officers on the other side of the river would see the crowd and come over to investigate. I turned to Emmanuel. "Pray, Emmanuel," I said to him quietly. "Pray inside yourself. Only God can deliver us now."

I, too, prayed. God had brought us this far, surely He could bring us just a little farther. Then I remembered something: A few months earlier, when I was still speaker of parliament, an evangelist came to my office and prayed with me. He told me that God had told him to remind me of what it says in Joshua 1:9, "Be strong and courageous. Do not be terrified; do not be discouraged, for the Lord your God will be with you wherever you go." I thanked him for sharing the passage, but didn't see its relevance to my life at the time. Things were going well, what did I need God's protection for? Now I knew. I thought of those words and again prayed, *God, you promised you would be with me everywhere I went, but please* kora igitangaza—*make a miracle.*

We were only a few hundred feet from the police station when the miracle came. Rain. A hard, driving rain. The clouds that had hovered over us all day burst open and rain came down in opaque sheets. By the time we reached the customs office, everyone had retreated indoors, including the Rwandan police on the other side. *Thank you, God.* Emmanuel, the Ugandan, and I were hurried indoors, where we stood dripping water onto the floor. They untied our wrists, which were badly scratched from the rough cord. Our bodies were bruised from the beatings. The rest of the mob waited outside, trying to huddle against the rain.

The Ugandan police officers were surprised to get such a large number of visitors on this rainy Sunday. "Tell them who you are," the militia leader instructed.

So I did. "I am Joseph Sebarenzi. I was the speaker of the Rwandan parliament. I was forced out of office and now Kagame wants to kill me." I was at their mercy.

The police officers' faces softened as I spoke. I could tell they were sympathetic. They knew how harsh Kagame could be. After all, he had been a high-level official in Ugandan intelligence. His reputation was well known. "Don't worry, you're safe here," said one of the officers.

Thank you, God, I now prayed.

"But not for long," he added. He looked outside and saw the crowd. We all knew that as soon as the rain stopped, the Rwandan officers would come out of their office and see the crowd. Then they would amble across the bridge to find out what the fuss was about.

"We have to get you out of here," he said. But then, with an apologetic look on his face, as if he was confessing a sin, he said, "It's just that—we have no car. I don't know how we can get you out of here without the Rwandans' seeing you." As he spoke, the rain began to lighten. I was stuck. These outlying offices had no phone, no way of calling someone for help.

Please, God, another miracle! The rain continued to abate.

The officers consulted among themselves, trying to figure out a way to sneak me out. While they talked, the rain stopped.

We watched through the windows as the Rwandan customs officers emerged from their station and walked across the bridge. We heard them approach and ask others in the crowd what was going on. "Your spies are inside!" they shot back. (The villagers, fortunately, had not heard the true story.) "You sent Kagame's spies to us and we have captured them!"

We are dead, I thought. *This is it.* Just then, a Ugandan man walked in and was greeted by the other officers. He was a member of the Ugandan military and these men knew him. "What's going on here?" he asked, in a voice both accusatory and curious. He was driving back from Rwanda, where he had visited relatives for the weekend, and had seen the crowd outside. I didn't care about any of this. All that mattered to me was *driving.* He had a car.

Immediately the Ugandan officers explained who I was. "We have to get him out of here," they said. "Now!"

He turned to me and smiled. "Oh, I've heard of you!" he said. "You were the speaker? You're so young!" I was grateful for his kindness, but this was no time to chat about my political career. I had never wanted to leave a place so badly in my life.

The officers began pushing him out the door. "You have to leave now. The Rwandan officers are here."

"Yes, you are right!" he said. "Let's go. Now!"

We rushed out the door and into his car. As we exited, the Rwandan officers walked in, oblivious to who I was. Before we had even closed the doors to the car, the driver had pushed the pedal to the floor and we were speeding away. To safety. I hoped.

• • •

There is a French proverb, *L'homme propose et Dieu dispose*. Man makes plans and God decides. We made our plan, and God decided how it would be. God decided that day that I should live, and that Liberata should live. He also decided that our children should not be left in Rwanda without their mother—so He sent her back to the compound. When the children returned home from church, they learned that I was gone, but she was there. I can only imagine the grief and fear they would have felt if they had returned to find both of us gone. So Liberata stayed with the children. She moved into the rental house with them and remained in Kigali. She was most certainly followed, but she was left alone. God protected her.

He also protected me. The Ugandan military officer drove well into the night. As he drove, I sat in the back seat with Emmanuel and the Ugandan who had crossed with me. Our clothes were soaked through with rain. We were exhausted and hungry. Our bodies ached from the beatings we had suffered. We had no idea where this man was taking us. I trusted him, yet I couldn't keep negative thoughts from popping into my head: *What if he was only pretending to be an ally? He could be a supporter of Kagame. He could be driving me back to Rwanda to turn me over. He could kill me himself.* It wasn't until we reached a military base at Mbarara later that night, until I overheard him call an official in Kampala and tell him that he had the former speaker of Rwanda's parliament and that I needed protection—it wasn't until all of this that I felt completely safe.

That night, the Ugandan officer told me I would be taken to Kampala the next day. The government, I was assured, would protect me. I thanked him, but was unable to find the words to tell him how grateful I was for what he had done, to tell him that he saved my life, to tell him that I would never forget him. I never have.

When I went to bed, I lay awake thinking of Liberata, wondering if she had made it to Kampala. Tomorrow I would know. But tonight, I needed sleep. I desperately needed sleep. I closed my eyes and drifted off.

The next morning, before I left for Kampala, I decided to call the speaker's compound to let my mother-in-law know that I was safe and to ask if she had heard news from Liberata.

"Hello?" I heard the voice on the other end of the line say.

My heart skipped a beat. It was Liberata. "Mama Respect?" I asked.

I heard a catch in her throat. "Yes, Papa Respect."

"What are you doing there? What happened? I thought you would be in Kampala by now." I knew the lines were monitored, but hiding my whereabouts now was pointless. I had protection. I was safe.

"You should come home, Papa Respect," was all she said.

"What?"

"You should come home. It is safe now. Nothing bad will happen." I could tell from her voice that she didn't mean it. I knew someone had told her to say that. I knew she was saying it for the sake of those who were listening to our conversation.

"No, I cannot come back," I said. "I got to Uganda. I am safe here."

That was all she needed to hear, that I was safe. Finally. Yoweri Museveni's government was protecting me. I had guards with me at all times. So I was safe, but I didn't feel safe. The very fact that I needed protection made me feel at risk. How could I live like this? The Ugandan government began working with the United States embassy and the United Nations' High Commission for Refugees to find a safe place for me to live. Meanwhile, the Ugandan government kept my whereabouts a secret. When the Rwandan government asked them to extradite me, Ugandan officials would reply that they didn't know where I was. Soon I would go to the United States, where I would be resettled. I would start over again. How could I express my gratitude to Museveni's government, and the United States, and the United Nations for all that they did to ensure my protection? Without their help, my life would have been jeopardized.

Of course, Kagame and his people knew I was in Uganda. I would call Liberata regularly, using a cell phone so they could not trace my calls and discover my exact whereabouts, but no doubt these calls were monitored. During each conversation she would tell me the same thing, "Come home. It is safe now." I knew she had to say that to protect herself, but it was not true. The political situation in Rwanda was proof enough that things were unraveling.

Regularly I would hear from friends or on the radio that someone else in Rwanda was being targeted. There was Pierre Celestin Rwigema, the prime minister. He was forced to resign. While I was speaker, we had investigated him for mismanagement and embezzlement. The RPF wanted him out and hoped we would censure him. But our investigation could not prove that he had done anything wrong, so we cleared him. I knew that the RPF would not let that stand. So when I heard that Rwigema had resigned, I was not surprised. He eventually fled to the United States. The government of Rwanda told the U.S. government that he was involved in the genocide and asked that he be arrested. But an immigration judge cleared him.

Then I heard about the death of a close advisor to the president, Assiel Kabera. He was a Tutsi from my area whose wife was related to me. While I was being forced out of parliament, he was asked to make false statements against me, but refused. Now I learned that he had been gunned down in his driveway. It could have so easily been me who was killed. I thought of his wife and how hard it would be for his family. His two brothers were devastated by the assassination and eventually fled to Canada, where they still live. I thought of my own family and how Liberata and the children would have felt had I been gunned down.

I also learned that a local newspaper, *Imboni*, had published articles protesting my forced resignation. The journalists were threatened and fled to Belgium, where they still reside. Then one morning I got a call telling me about my cousin Benjamin, the one who had driven me to the Ugandan border. Kagame's spies learned that he had helped me cross. They sent a military lieutenant to arrest him, but this lieutenant took pity on him. He knew what would happen to Benjamin if he was taken into custody. So instead, he told Benjamin to run. And knowing what his own fate would be if he returned to his superior officers, he decided to flee with Benjamin. They escaped to Burundi and then to Tanzania, where they contacted the U.N. High Commission for Refugees asking for help. But the government of Rwanda (having tracked them through their spies) told the Tanzanian government that they were wanted for killing an Indian businessman and asked that they be extradited. Tanzania complied, and Benjamin and the lieutenant were brought back to Rwanda and tortured. If it had not been for a story about them that aired on the BBC and another that was published in *Imboni*, I doubt they would have survived. I was devastated to hear of the suffering these men endured because of their great sense of humanity.

I also heard about the resignation of President Pasteur Bizimungu on March 3. I knew he was going to be forced out eventually, but to hear the news that it had actually happened made me wonder where the country was heading. In the space of less than three months, Kagame had gutted the government: I was gone; the prime minister was gone; the president was gone; and the president's advisor was dead. And Kagame took over the presidency.

Epilogue

W HEN MY plane touched down in the United States on April 5, 2000, I set out to begin again. I was once again a refugee, in a country far from my homeland, where I spoke little of the language and had almost no connections. Once again I had to start my life over with little more than the clothes on my back, and the trauma of genocide and my recent escape from Rwanda hovering over me. My wife and children had just managed to leave Rwanda and go to Uganda. I comforted myself with the knowledge that they were safe, but I was devastated by this new separation.

I didn't know then that my exile from Rwanda was only the beginning. Soon after, other prominent Rwandans from every branch of government, the nonprofit sector, the military, and the media would have to flee the country: the former minister of defense, Emmanuel Habyarimana, who fled to Switzerland; the former Liberal Party wing leader, Evariste Sisi, who fled to the Netherlands; the former member of parliament, Pasteur Nsabimana, who fled to Norway; the former deputy chief justice, Gerard Gahima, who fled to the United States; the former chairman of the Rwandan Association of Journalists, Deogratias Mushayidi, who fled to Belgium; the former chairman of the League of Human Rights Organizations of the Great Lakes

region, Noel Twagiramungu, who fled to the United States; the first
secretary general and spokesman of IBUKA, a genocide survivors association, Anastase Murumba, who fled to Canada; the former chair
of AVEGA, an association of genocide widows, Chantal Kayitesi, who
fled to the United States; the former head of external intelligence,
Colonel Patrick Karegeya, who fled to South Africa—and this list
goes on. Rwandans learned the hard lesson that applied to Tutsi under
President Kayibanda: *Hunga cyangua honga!* meaning, "You flee or
you freeze!" Unlike President Kayibanda, however, President Kagame
does not discriminate—both Tutsi and Hutu are at risk.

The former president, Pasteur Bizimungu learned this lesson only
after he paid a heavy price. After being forced to resign soon after
I fled Rwanda, Bizimungu formed an opposition movement called
the Party for Democratic Renewal. Kagame's government banned the
party before it was officially launched, claiming it was unconstitutional. Bizimungu used the foreign media to call for reforms in hopes
that more inter-ethnic violence could be avoided—resulting in his arrest and imprisonment in 2002. In 2007, Bizimungu was "pardoned"
and released, but his life is still that of a prisoner. He is accompanied
everywhere by police and denied allowances entitled to him as a former head of state.

What we all have in common is that we all stood in Kagame's way
on his headlong push to realize his vision: an ultracapitalist economy
and a multiparty communist type of democracy. Free market, to-
talitarianism, and elections paradoxically coexist. This model has
translated into unparalleled order, security, and economic recovery,
and has won Kagame the respect of many in the West. Yet it has not
translated into peace and reconciliation, which are the foundations of
a *lasting* order, security, and economic development. It has not translated into the healing and transformation that would allow Rwandans
to embrace the virtues of apology and forgiveness.

In 2007, the Rwandan parliament declared that genocide ideology was widespread among children in secondary schools. In plain
words, it means that young Hutu—who were not even born or were
only toddlers during the genocide—would engage in another geno-

cide against Tutsi if they had the opportunity. A law was then passed to sentence anyone guilty of genocide ideology to a maximum of twenty-five years in prison. Whether the existence of the ideology of genocide was indeed transmitted to the younger generation as the government argues, or if this is another intimidation tactic used to silence people who cannot otherwise be accused of the 1994 genocide, it surely reminds us that reconciliation in Rwanda is as distant as the moon. Stephen Kinzer was right when he wrote in 2008 that "citizens are required to repeat platitudes about reconciliation, but hatred festers in many hearts."[1]

All this greatly concerns me, as it has since I first arrived in the United States nearly a decade ago. The uncertain prospects for peace and reconciliation occupied me as I tried to find my way in a new land, as I made the difficult transition from the life of speaker to the life of an impoverished refugee. Yet, instead of letting my mind be whipped around by the negative winds, I would refocus my thoughts on the future. I would remind myself that I could not give up on peace for future generations; I could not give up on peace for my children and all the other children of Rwanda. Being targeted by Kagame, being forced into exile, enduring beatings when I crossed the border into Uganda—all of these things could easily drag me back into the morass of anger and bitterness. But I refused to let them. What happened to me was no excuse to abandon my dream for peace. I was comforted by the recognition of the international community of the wrongs that had been done to me—and, by extension, the wrongs that were being done to Rwandans. A report by Human Rights Watch stated, "Sebarenzi fought to establish some autonomy for [parliament] and particularly to hold government ministers accountable for alleged corruption, including powerful members of the RPF. It was apparently this commitment to good government which won Sebarenzi approval among ordinary people, Hutu as well as Tutsi." In addition, the Interparliamentary Union, an association of the world's

---

[1] Kinzer, Stephen. *A Thousand Hills: Rwanda's Rebirth and the Man Who Dreamed It.* Hoboken, NJ: John Wiley & Sons, Inc., 2008, p. 4.

parliaments, wrote in a resolution that I was "an independent politician bent on denouncing abuses and enhancing the independence and role of the Transitional National Assembly, particularly with regard to oversight of government action." Although these comments and others like it helped, it did not heal my wounds.

So I turned to prayer. I asked God to show me a path that would allow me to work for reconciliation. That path led me to the School for International Training/Graduate Institute in Vermont, where I sought admission to a graduate program that was grounded in social justice and reconciliation. There I met professors such as John Ungeleider and Paula Green, who are strong believers in reconciliation. My coursework included conflict transformation, and I eventually wrote my thesis on reconciliation in Rwanda. I may have been thousands of miles from home, but my heart was still there—my heart will always be there. I eventually enrolled in SIT's Conflict Transformation Across Cultures program, which brings together peace workers from conflict-torn countries, and since 2003, have been teaching for it. I consistently remind my students of the duty and moral obligation of our generation to spare future generations the evil of violence we have endured.

Today I still live in the United States. In addition to my work as a teacher, I regularly give speeches at colleges, universities, high schools, and churches across the country about my experiences. Through my public speaking, I hope to help others find a path to forgiveness and reconciliation. I am always heartened when I hear from audience members who take my story and apply it to their own lives. I've had people tell me that my experience and the fact that I was able to emerge from tragedy with a spirit of forgiveness made them realize that they could find a way to forgive those people in their lives who had wronged them. Their reaction often is, "If you can forgive the perpetrators of such a terrible crime, then surely I can forgive my mother for not coming to my wedding," or "then I can forgive my husband for his infidelity," or, "then I can forgive my brother for how mean he was to me as a child"—the list goes on. These daily transformations, I believe, will one day transform the world. And, of course, I hope that my teaching, public speaking, and, now, this book will help Rwandans find their own pathway to peace.

During my speeches, I often share with the audience the story of an old rabbi who once asked his pupils how they could tell when night ends and day begins. "Could it be," asked one of the students, "when you can see an animal in the distance and you can tell whether it's a sheep or a dog?"

"No," answered the rabbi.

Another asked, "Is it when you can look at a tree in the distance and tell whether it's a fig tree or a peach tree?"

"No," answered the Rabbi.

"Then what is it?" the pupils demanded.

"It is when you can look in the face of any man or woman and see that it is your brother or sister. Because if you cannot see this, it is still night."

It is still night for many people. It is still night in many countries around the world. When I was born and when I was growing up, it was still night in Rwanda. And darkness still hangs over Rwanda today. Whenever I hear this story, I think of my five children: Respect (now 18 years old), Pacifique (16), Esther (12), Nicole (11), and Sandrine (9). All were born in Rwanda, except for Pacifique, who was born in exile in Burundi. Rwanda is their home. And yet it is a distant memory for each of them. My hope—my prayer—is that we will one day return to Rwanda as a family. I dream of taking my children to Lake Kivu, where I swam as a boy. I dream of taking them to see the green hills and endless blue sky; to see the country I knew before violence and bloodshed scarred it so deeply; to see the place God finds so beautiful that at night, after a day of traveling the world visiting other countries, He chooses the land of a thousand hills to lay His head down to sleep; to see the place I dream of when I close my own eyes at night. To see Rwanda.

Afterword

MOVING TOWARD FORGIVENESS
AND RECONCILIATION

———

Few will have the greatness to bend history, but each of
us can work to change a small portion of events, and in
the total of all those acts will be written the history of a
generation. It is from numberless diverse acts of courage
and belief that human history is shaped.

—ROBERT F. KENNEDY

HEN I look back on my story, I think of all that I have
been through, and, despite everything, how fortunate
I am. I survived. Time and again, I lived when others
were killed: as a baby when my mother hid with me in the bush; as a
child when I was saved by the drum in 1973; when I was imprisoned
in 1990; when I escaped Rwanda in 1991 and was lucky enough to be
outside the country when the genocide erupted, and again in 2000.
Each time, death licked at my heels and, by the grace of God, I survived. But so many people—Tutsi and Hutu alike—did not. Rwanda
is a nation of wounded souls. The last fifty years of cyclical violence

have taken at least one million lives. And those who weren't killed carry the scars: murdered family members; lives in exile; physical and emotional wounds.

Ever since the genocide, I have asked myself how the nation could heal. How could we live together again in peace? I know this question applies not only to Rwanda, but to the many societies around the world where individuals have victimized others because of ethnicity, race, religion, or other identities. I have met people from Sudan, Israel and Palestine, the Democratic Republic of Congo, Nepal, Sri Lanka, Burundi, the former Yugoslavia, and other conflict-torn societies— and they all wonder how former enemies can come together again and live in brotherhood and sisterhood. The answer is reconciliation.

Reconciliation brings enemies together to confront the painful and ugly past, and to collectively devise a bright future. It brings together communities in conflict to tell the truth about *all* past human rights violations and to create a society where they can live in peace with one another. It requires coming together and listening with compassion to one another's stories—something that is desperately needed in Rwanda, where the lives of Hutu and Tutsi are so intimately bound together.

Reconciliation is in many ways the hardest option, because it requires effort, humility, and patience—whereas revenge is quick and easy. Reconciliation is complicated. It cannot be reduced to retributive justice ("perpetrators must be punished"), as victims generally assert; nor to forgiveness ("the perpetrators must be forgiven"), as offenders and their families tend to assert. And reconciliation is far from being achieved simply through power-sharing between political parties, as politicians tend to believe. In Rwanda these perspectives have echoed loudly across the countryside: victims insisting that perpetrators be punished with the full force of the law; perpetrators insisting that their acts be forgiven and forgotten; leaders putting in place a power-sharing system (which unfortunately has been only cosmetic) and thinking that alone will take care of the problem. Reconciliation is a much more complex, delicate, and long process that includes several components: *acknowledgment, apology, restorative justice, empathy, reparation,* and *forgiveness*—and several accompanying measures, namely *democracy* coupled with *consensus, peace education,* and *international assistance.*

Acknowledgment of the wrongs committed by the perpetrator and the offering of a genuine *apology* are absolutely required. This applies to all offenses—from the most heinous to the least. No matter the gravity of the harm done, victims need their suffering to be recognized and for an apology to be offered, whether that suffering occurred at the hands of an individual or the state. In the context of Rwanda, the process of reconciliation would encompass both the genocide and other human rights violations. All offenses must be acknowledged and apologized for.

Fortunately, recent history has given us many examples of acknowledgment and genuine apology: The United States apologized to Japanese Americans for sending them to internment camps during World War II. The government of Australia early in 2007 issued a formal apology to the Aboriginal people for the decades of suffering they had endured, including the government program that took children away from their parents to be "educated" so they could better assimilate into Australian society. These apologies are acts of courage, humility, and goodness. They are reminders that we all make mistakes and are capable of horrible evils, yet as human beings we are also capable of tremendous goodness.

Sadly, very little acknowledgment or apology is taking place in Rwanda. Denial persists, which amounts to yet another victimization. Surely you've experienced a time in your life when you've confronted someone who has offended you, only to have your concerns dismissed. Maybe you were told that you're imagining things or overreacting. You know the sting of such a denial. When this happens, reconciliation is impossible. At the U.N. International Criminal Court for Rwanda in Tanzania, almost every genocide suspect has denied his horrible deeds. And the acknowledgment and apologies that *have* occurred in Rwanda have unfortunately been more expedient than sincere, because perpetrators are given reduced jail sentences for acknowledging their crimes. As a result, many genocide suspects who had spent years in prison chose acknowledgment simply to ensure that they would spend less time behind bars. Kagame's RPF is no exception: It has a hard time acknowledging the awful human rights violations it committed before, during, and after the genocide. In general, Rwandans, Hutu and Tutsi alike, tend to deny or minimize one another's suffering, as if acknowledging another's pain negates their own. So we eagerly recount our own suffering but are reluctant to talk about the tragedy our "enemies" have endured. Until we acknowledge all that happened—without minimizing, exaggerating, or equating—we will obstruct reconciliation between the two communities.

But acknowledgment is difficult. Denial persists because of the shame and guilt that accompany an admission of fault. We fear the diminishment of our social status, or having the stigma of "criminal" or "deviant" associated with our names forever. It is particularly difficult to confess when the response to that confession will be mockery or punishment.

That is why in the wake of mass violence in divided societies, a conditional amnesty is often granted in exchange for truth and apology. While this might seem odd, the insistence on truth and apology is based on the fact that you cannot build a lasting reconciliation if the truth remains hidden and if offenders—whose numbers are staggering—do not buy into the reconciliation process. If there was another way of accomplishing that, it would be done—but none exists. The conditional amnesty approach was taken in South Africa, where many blacks and whites admitted to the crimes they committed during apartheid and apologized to one another, thanks to the pledge that the truth would not be used against them. If the same environment had been created in Rwanda for low-level perpetrators (not the leaders of the genocide)—if they had been told that the goals were truth and apology to help victims recover from the losses they had suffered—then there would have been a greater chance of successfully bringing people together in a spirit of reconciliation.

This is the essence of *restorative justice*, which holds perpetrators accountable in a nonadversarial manner—in a way that condemns the offense, yet cares for the offender. It encourages offenders to take full responsibility for their actions and allows them to tell their side of the story so their victims can better understand what might have caused them to commit evil acts. It helps them repair what can be repaired to the extent that they are able. It helps them reintegrate into the community—not because telling the truth and apologizing are "the price" for reintegration, but because it is part of the self-healing process and a kind of moral reparation for the wrong inflicted on others.

The ultimate goal of restorative justice is to stitch back together the social fabric torn apart by mass violence. What other form of justice would be realistic in Rwanda, where hundreds of thousands of people were involved in perpetuating the genocide? How can you possibly bring all of them to justice through conventional courts? I strongly believe that those who masterminded the killing and those who encouraged others to kill should be punished with the full force of the law, but those "smaller fish" who were the minions of the leaders should be dealt with through restorative justice, not retributive justice. It is impossible to prosecute every single Rwandan perpetrator.

In Rwanda after the genocide, *Gacaca*—a localized court system whose judges are ordinary people with no legal education—was implemented. This system encourages confession and apology in exchange for reduced sentences. It was hoped that this system would be more restorative than punitive, but sadly, *Gacaca* emphasized punishment over reconciliation. In fact, some perpetrators who confess and apologize can still face up to thirty years of imprisonment (some of which can be reduced through community service). While perpetrators who were between fourteen and eighteen years of age who confess can be sentenced to a maximum of nine years in prison. In addition, some lose their civil rights, relinquishing the right "to be elected; to assume high responsibilities; to become leaders; to serve in the armed forces; to serve in the national police and other security organizations; to be a teacher, a medical staff member, a magistrate, a public prosecutor or a judicial counsel."[1] Further, the names of high-profile perpetrators are posted at the offices of the local administration in their town or village and published on the Internet. These punitive measures foster shame, which only encourages denial, rather than acknowledgment and apology. In the wake of mass violence, justice should be sought not for the sake of justice, but for a greater goal: healing and reconciliation.

Sadly, *Gacaca* proceedings do more harm than good to victims, perpetrators, and the community as a whole. Community members come into *Gacaca* with the goal of winning, not reconciling. During the proceedings, negative emotions run high as each side confronts the other. Participants emerge either winners or losers in the eyes of the court. They in fact emerge not made stronger, but weaker, with more anger and fear than before.

Although some truths are revealed during these proceedings—about who committed the murders, how the victims were killed, the weapons that were used, the location of mass graves—these types of truths do not lead to reconciliation. Furthermore, most perpetrators do not tell the whole truth, and victims remain unsatisfied with the whole process. Perpetrators, meanwhile, face a potential maximum sentence of life imprisonment, and yet are not allowed to have legal representation. In the end, Rwandans have received neither truth nor justice. If restorative justice—however imperfect—had been chosen I feel confident that the country would be on a path toward reconciliation, rather than a path obstructed with uncertainty and facing a risk of renewed violence.

In order for reconciliation to take place, victims and perpetrators alike must also *empathize* with one another. Empathy for perpetrators comes through active listening to their stories. It comes through the feeling that those who offended you are not evil people but people who engaged in evil behavior at one point in their lives. Such behavior is inexcusable, yet once it is put in context, we find that if we were in the same situation, we might have behaved the same way.

---

[1] Article 15 of organic law N° 10/2007 of March 1, 2007.

If we objectively think of the decades-long, poisonous situation Hutu were exposed to, we might feel empathy toward those who succumbed to evil. For example, when I was growing up in Rwanda, school children were insidiously taught that Tutsi had dominated the majority Hutu population for centuries and had mistreated them. They were taught that Hutu revolutionaries eventually ended the domination and the feudal system that oppressed Hutu, and that Tutsi still longed to retake power and resubmit Hutu. Needless to say, these teachings were toxic for Hutu and humiliating for Tutsi. Before the genocide, Hutu were consistently told, through radio and TV broadcasts, newspapers, and political meetings, that Tutsi rebels were responsible not only for launching the war, but also for the chaos that prevailed—and these accusations were not entirely false. The worst propaganda told Hutu that Tutsi wanted to seize power, kill Hutu, and dominate the survivors. So for a number of weak Hutu, killing Tutsi was "justified"—after all, the genocide was encouraged, and even mandated, by the government, local officials, and militia leaders. Given this, I imagine if a Hutu perpetrator told his victim this story of decades of brainwashing and remorsefully apologized, it would trigger empathy on the part of the victim and, most likely, forgiveness. After all, how many among us would have behaved differently if we had been exposed to such venomous rhetoric since our childhood? Until we have walked a mile in our offender's shoes, we cannot know for sure how each of us would have behaved. This is in no way an excuse, but it is worth considering.

Sadly, some Tutsi have also committed atrocities. And likewise, Hutu would most likely feel empathy for them if they compassionately listened to their stories. I think of how Tutsi inside Rwanda were discriminated against, and how refugees were banned from returning home. In refugee camps, at home, or in military training camps, young Tutsi were intentionally or unintentionally exposed to a language that fostered mistrust of Hutu at best, hatred at worst—predisposing them to violence. Then, when Tutsi finally launched a war against the Hutu government for the right to return home, they were met with aggressive rhetoric and bombs. I can understand—yet disagree with—some

Tutsi taking revenge on Hutu. Also, during the genocide, soldiers literally stumbled over the bodies of their fellow Tutsi as they progressed on the battlefield. I can imagine some Tutsi soldiers engaging in evil acts to avenge these deaths. I can also imagine a Tutsi soldier arriving at his family's home, only to find them killed, and his rage and desire for revenge. Would you have behaved differently if you had lived that life and found yourself in the same circumstances? Those of us who were fortunate enough not to be on the battleground can criticize the actions of those who were there, but until we are tested, we cannot tell. Again, nothing can justify the killing of an innocent human being, but without empathy and mutual understanding, Rwandans will always remain on the brink of more violence. I believe we can do better. For the sake of reconciliation, we need to humble ourselves, apologize, forgive, and lift each other up instead of demonizing each other.

I also believe empathy toward Paul Kagame is possible. My own empathy toward him comes when I think of his childhood and youth: He fled Rwanda when he was a child to escape the massacres. He then grew up in refugee camps where life was hard and where his father, who was well off back home, died as a result of their poor life conditions. All of this indisputably affected Kagame. Like most refugees in poor countries, he was treated as a lesser person. In his twenties, he joined the world of violence in the form of an armed rebellion in Uganda, which helped thrust Yoweri Museveni into power. He participated in military training in Cuba. As a young man he served in intelligence, where crushing enemies was a duty. When Museveni won, Kagame took a high-level position in military intelligence, another dirty and brutal job. All of that sad experience shaped his personality. He later joined the RPF guerilla movement and fought for four years in a world where respect for human rights was fiction. When I think of his own tragedy, my feelings of pain and anger at the suffering he caused me are assuaged. Again, this cannot be an excuse for the suffering he has inflicted on a number of Rwandans, but it is a reminder that we need to keep in mind the role past sufferings play in shaping an individual's behavior. I wish Kagame had emerged from this tragedy with grace, but he was not able to. Yet reconciliation is still possible. If Kagame could embrace humility, tell the truth, remorsefully apologize, and allow for reforms, I believe that Rwandans would forgive him—at least I would forgive him. This would be a chance for peaceful political change and reconciliation.

Out of feelings of empathy, perpetrators would spontaneously participate in *reparations* for victims. Reparations would therefore not be a punishment, but a compassionate response to help victims overcome the consequences of the offender's actions. That would be a significant step toward reconciliation. Together, offenders, victims, the community, and the state as a whole must work side by side to help victims. For example, Germany provides substantial financial support to Israel as penance for the Holocaust. The two countries have become allies. The United States government gave money to Japanese Americans who were placed in internment camps during World War II. But reparations need not be only financial; they can also be policy-driven. Affirmative action in the United States is a sort of reparation for slavery and segregation, giving African Americans the chance to succeed in school and the workplace.

In Rwanda, reparations have not been made to survivors. Only in some cases has property that was looted during the genocide been returned, and a handful of houses have been built by prisoners as punishment, not as voluntary reparation. But it is not too late. As a nation, we could assist victims to overcome some of the hardships inflicted on them by their countrymen. The Rwandan government and the international community have spent more than a billion dollars attempting to bring perpetrators to justice and providing food and medical assistance to them. While this is not a bad thing, I think that similar attention should be paid to victims. And these victims are more numerous than we tend to think. They include not only genocide survivors, particularly orphans, widows, and the disabled, but also Hutu whose loved ones were killed and whose property was destroyed and looted. All of these people also deserve our attention and help.

Despite the necessity of reparations, it's important to recognize that they can never fully right the wrongs that have been committed. No amount of money could ever replace my mother or father or siblings who were killed. But it is the act itself, not the money, that matters. In some situations, symbolic reparations are more appropriate. For instance, the offender can help rebuild houses that were destroyed, or help pay for the victims' children's schooling—gestures that would be greeted with genuine appreciation by the victims.

Sometimes, other interventions are necessary to put people on the path toward reconciliation, because not everyone who has suffered a trauma has the psychological or spiritual strength to move beyond their grief. It has been said that "some people have adapted to terrible life events with flexibility and creativity, while others have become fixated on the trauma and gone on to live a traumatized and traumatizing existence."[2] Those fixated on trauma are deprived of the capacity to interact constructively with their former enemies. In addition to their physical wounds, they may be haunted by images of the murder of their loved ones; the rape of their mothers, wives, or daughters; the burning of their homes. This makes some victims vehemently oppose reconciliation or commit evil acts themselves—not because they are intrinsically bad people, but because they have been wounded deeply and don't have the tools to heal those wounds and move on. When this is the case, intensive counseling and other psychological assistance are urgently needed to help these victims deal with their trauma and become receptive to the message of reconciliation. Everyone who has experienced the tragedy of war—whether directly or indirectly—would benefit from counseling, including our leaders. Unfortunately, this approach has been neglected in Rwanda.

Another necessary component of reconciliation, particularly in Rwanda, is intercommunity apology and *forgiveness*. When people have been victimized because of the community to which they belong, by people who belong to a different community, they rationalize their offenses against the other community as actions to avenge historical wrongs or preemptive attacks to prevent new victimization. Such

---

[2] Van Der Kolk, B., and A. *McFarlane.* "The Black Hole of Trauma" in Van Der Kolk, B., McFarlane, A., and Weisaeth, ed. *Traumatic Stress: The Effects of Overwhelming Experience on Mind, Body, and Society,* New York: The Guilford Press, 1996, p. 1.

community-driven victimization creates not only individual grievances among victims, but a collective grievance shared by members
of the victimized community, including those who have not been
directly hurt. That is why, even though they were never personally
attacked, you can find Hutu who hate Tutsi and vice versa—or Sunni
Muslims who hate Shiite Muslims and vice versa, or Jews who hate
Arabs and vice versa, and the list goes on. They carry with them a
collective grievance that is passed from one generation to the next.
Such grievance can survive many decades and even centuries only to
explode at a later time at the slightest trigger. That is why intercommunity apology and forgiveness is so critical. It requires telling the
truth and reaching a common history that is then taught to children
through peace education. With empathy and a desire to build a new
Rwanda, we can face our awful past with courage and determination
and pass on to future generations a reconciled nation.

All of these components of reconciliation—acknowledgment, apology, restorative justice, empathy, reparation, and forgiveness—focus
on the past, which is important because "those who do not learn from
history are doomed to repeat it."[3] Yet they must be coupled with a
forward-thinking vision. We need to look at what we can do given
our current circumstances to build a better future. No doubt one
piece of this is building a democracy.

Democracy is a crucial accompanying measure to reconciliation.
It can be said without hesitation that the major cause of violence in
Rwanda has been the lack of democracy. In essence, this is a political
problem. The solution, therefore, must also be political: building a
democracy, specifically one that takes into account the divided nature
of Rwandan society. Building democracy requires the establishment
of institutions that foster equal rights and equal opportunities, individual freedoms and liberties, human rights as stipulated by international conventions, separation of powers and effective checks and

---

[3] George Santayana

balances, and fair and free elections. In other words, rule of law must be established—a rule of law that stems from the truth that we are all born with inalienable and equal rights, and that we derive these rights from the divine. Leaders have, therefore, the obligation to materialize this truth through democratic institutions.

When I was elected to parliament and became speaker, this was the thought that propelled all of my work. I felt that being in parliament was my God-given opportunity to foster the growth of democracy, promote reconciliation, and put behind us the culture of tribal hatred. Despite the friction with Bizimungu and Kagame, parliament was able to pass key legislation related to reconciliation, establishing a national commission for unity and reconciliation and a national commission for human rights and passing bills to reinforce accountability and rule of law.

Democracy also needs to translate into day-to-day fairness. This is why I tried to ensure that my decisions as speaker were always guided by a commitment to equal treatment, which is essential to promote reconciliation in a divided society. Some Hutu lawmakers thought when I became speaker that I would treat them unfairly because I was a genocide survivor. In fact, one lawmaker told me as much and then admitted his surprise when I didn't. But I firmly believe that the suffering we endure should not be allowed to take away our kindness and our commitment to fairness. Imperfect as I am, I always did my best to treat others fairly. One of the simple ways I did this was by pushing to change the way parliament chose lawmakers to travel abroad for meetings or training. Because of the way we were reimbursed for travel, trips abroad were a good way to make extra income—something that was desperately sought after among parliamentarians who made very little money. But the criteria for selecting those who traveled abroad were arbitrary. In the end, most of the trips were made by a few powerful lawmakers, virtually all from the RPF and virtually all Tutsi. Recognizing this injustice, I proposed guidelines be established that would select who would make the trips based on competence, ethnic and political party diversity, and previous trips abroad—in other words, everyone should be given a fair chance to travel. Not surprisingly, the RPF wing leader in parliament, Tito Rutaremara, opposed the criteria under the pretext that they included ethnicity. Ironically, the lack of ethnic diversity was the thing I most wanted to correct. Ethnicity is sadly a fact of life in Rwanda. We cannot "play the ethnicity card" only when it serves us, and then deny it when it impedes our agenda. Despite this opposition, my proposal was overwhelmingly approved by lawmakers, because the vast majority, Hutu and Tutsi alike, found it to be fair and just. This is critical. Without fairness, there is no democracy; without democracy, there is no reconciliation.

That is why Rwanda concerns me so greatly. While Kagame's regime sings, "Democracy! Democracy!" there is no democracy. His victory in the 2003 elections with 95 percent of the vote is evidence of his heavy-handed control over the political process. Rwanda moved from a single-party system under President Habyarimana to a cosmetic multiparty system under President Kagame. Before war broke out in 1990, Habyarimana's regime was hailed as a model of development and stability in Africa. But that was an illusion. Tutsi's grievances were ignored and suppressed; most feigned contentment publicly only to complain privately. Hutu from the south were also unhappy with the regime. Other Hutu innocently believed the situation was fine; still others were aware of the reality and chose to remain silent—out of fear or complacency—or actively propagated injustice. Reconciliation and peace were the prime victims, and we, as a people, eventually paid the price.

Similarly, today Kagame's regime is hailed by the international community as a model of stability and economic development. Awards from around the world are lavished on Kagame. He met many times with former president George W. Bush, who in 2008 lauded Kagame as a "man of action who knows how to get things done, and who can serve as a model for other countries, like Iraq." Former president Bill Clinton has also visited him regularly and expressed his admiration for him. Former British prime minister Tony Blair serves as his advisor. What these good people have in common is that they want to help Rwandans, but they're not seeing the reality of the situation. When you look closely at what's happening in Rwanda, or when you hear from the few Hutu who honestly express their feelings, you realize that their situation is more or less equivalent to that of Tutsi before the 1990 war. In 2003, Kagame changed the terms for the president from five years to seven. In 2008, he put an end to life terms for high court judges. In addition, he changed the constitution so the president can only be brought to trial while still in office. So in essence, Kagame has given himself an unconditional and preemptive amnesty should he ever lose power. Again, some Tutsi are aware of this unacceptable situation and sadly choose to do nothing, or are afraid to speak out, or worse, intentionally whitewash the regime's repressive actions. Unless we understand that what harms Hutu harms Tutsi, and vice versa, and care for each other, we will continue to suffer.

Even the annual week of remembrance in Rwanda to commemorate the genocide deepens, rather than heals, the nation's wounds. It is a traumatizing event rather than a restorative one and, consequently, counterproductive to reconciliation. People watch gruesome films and listen to shocking testimonies from genocide survivors; the national media air sorrowful programs with melancholy songs and inflammatory speeches delivered by political leaders. Little to nothing is included to instill hope and resilience. Rather, the discourse plunges survivors into the abyss of the past, often further traumatizing them. Simultaneously, Hutu (even those who played no role whatsoever in the genocide) become fearful and ashamed. We should rethink remembrance and make sure it is guided by the goal of enhancing healing on an individual level and reconnection on the community level. We should inform Rwandans of what happened, yet emphasize our common bonds and the need to move on. We should, for instance, use remembrance to celebrate and hear stories of victims who were able to emerge with grace and forgiveness.

All of this reinforces the fact that, despite some real achievements under Kagame's rule, reconciliation is an illusion, just as it was under Habyarimana in the 1980s. I don't understand why President Kagame fosters the same type of regime that victimized him and his parents.

I suppose he fears his enemies—of whom there are many—and what his fate will be when he is no longer in power. He also may well be afraid of the outcome of a classical democracy in a majority-minority divided society, which might well translate into a demographic election in which Hutu would overwhelmingly win. He may consequently fear that Tutsi's security could once again be in jeopardy, a view shared by most Tutsi I speak with, and for good reason.

But the legitimate desire for security among Tutsi and the legitimate desire for effective political participation among Hutu are not incompatible. Some Tutsi don't want to hear about anything other than keeping power by all means necessary for security reasons. Equally, some Hutu don't want to hear anything other than "majority rule." Both groups lose sight of a host of alternatives between these two extremes. The starting point for a viable solution is to understand that we are all human beings with the same fundamental needs, notably security and self-realization. We need to understand that offending or failing to help one another is both immoral and ineffective.

And equally important, we need to understand that exclusion of the other eventually hurts us all. The Tutsi monarchy under colonial rule dominated the political arena until 1959 and ended in disarray, with the king himself fleeing into exile, where he still remains. The first Hutu president, Grégoire Kayibanda, failed to promote democracy and inclusion. His regime ended in tragedy and he died under house arrest. President Habyarimana's repressive regime ended in a catastrophe—himself dead and his innocent children forced into exile. All this seriously harmed Tutsi, but also Hutu. Incredibly, Kagame has not learned from this ugly past, and now, I worry that the current injustice will eventually hurt President Kagame and other Tutsi. This destructive pattern must end! Our heads of state deserve a better end. Our country deserves leaders who can transcend their victimization and serve all Rwandans equally. The good news is that together we can overcome what sometimes seems to be a predetermined fate. There is no obstacle we cannot overcome if we are united; if we remind ourselves of our shared humanity and common history.

One historian wrote: "Rwanda is once again at a historical crossroads where its political leadership is faced by two clear options. The first is a continuation of the civil war, as those defeated in the last round prepare for battle in the next; the second is its termination through a political reconciliation that rejects both victory and defeat and looks for a third and more viable possibility."[4] For democracy in Rwanda to prosper, the form of democracy must be carefully crafted to match the deeply divided nature of the society. Unlike most divided societies, Rwanda is polarized between two ethnic groups of uneven numerical strength (Hutu are at least 80 percent; Tutsi are less than 20 percent, and Twa are less than 1 percent).[5] What's worse is that the two main ethnic groups have a long history of mutual victimization. Given this, majority rule as it is known in most Western democracies ("winner takes all") is inappropriate in Rwanda. According to a political scientist, "There is a surprisingly strong and persistent tendency in political science to equate democracy solely with majoritarian democracy and to fail to recognize consensus democracy as an alternative and equally legitimate type."[6] The Rwandan context requires constitutional and legal arrangements that foster democracy yet translate into a win-win form of political representation. Otherwise, the likelihood of another catastrophe will remain dangerously high. Previous regimes have not understood this, nor does Kagame. It is time to be who we were created to be: people whose vision extends beyond our own egos and our own tribes.

While I was speaker of parliament, I proposed to Kagame an inclusive and reconciliatory form of democracy: *consensus democracy.*[7] Imperfect as this solution was, my suggestion stemmed from my deep desire to achieve peace and reconciliation while meeting both Tutsi's and Hutu's legitimate aspiration to political rights. Without this, I

---

[4]Mamdani, Mahmood. *When Victims Become Killers: Colonialism, Nativism, and the Genocide in Rwanda.* New Jersey: Princeton University Press, p. 270.

[5]Because of unreliable census gathering in Rwanda, the exact percentages are unknown. These are estimates.

[6]Lijphart, Arend. *Patterns of Democracy—Government Forms and Performance in Thirty-Six Countries.* New Haven and London: Yale University Press, 1999, p. 6.

[7]See Chapter 8.

worry that Rwanda will once again succumb to violence. As one lead-ing authority in conflict transformation observed, "Rwandan history has shown that exclusion of one group or another over an extended period of time is a recipe for disaster."[8] As long as one group "wins" and the other "loses," this translates into a permanent fear on the part of those in power that the other might recapture power. The winner's victory in Rwanda has always been like a cat's victory over a dog: one governed by perpetual fear, robbing the winner of whatever pleasure comes from holding power. Enormous resources, such as the mili-tary, police, and intelligence, are therefore used to protect the regime against its own people instead of being used for the common good.

But unfortunately, Kagame turned a deaf ear to my suggestion. I have not, however, let the idea go. In 2002, after I was forced into exile, I worked with some friends to create a detailed model for consensus democracy in Rwanda. We referred to the example of the United States where all states have equal representation in the Senate irrespective of the size of their populations, and proportional representation in the House of Representatives. This form can be adapted to represent Rwanda's ethnic groups. Switzerland and Belgium also have consensus models that we can learn from. There is no shortage of examples from which to devise a solution that addresses Rwanda's specific realities.

But while I think consensus democracy is necessary in Rwanda, it is not needed forever. It is possible that after some time, Rwandans will reach a higher level of consciousness in which respect for each other's rights and dignity is a given. In a civilized society, people don't care about the ethnic group or race or religion of those running for office; they care about character, beliefs, and competence. They care about who can best help them achieve their dreams and aspirations and lead the country to socioeconomic prosperity. Once we have leaders who can serve everyone fairly and citizens who demand com-petence and goodness in their elected leaders, *then* we can afford the Western style of democracy.

---

[8] Lederach, John Paul. *Building Peace: Sustainable Reconciliation in Divided Societies.* Washington, D.C.: United States Institute of Peace Press, 1997, p. 177.

In the meantime, *peace education* should be provided to our children to shape their character and make them into a peace- and democracy-loving generation. As the preamble of the UNESCO constitution states: "Since wars begin in the minds of men, it is in the minds of men that the defenses of peace must be constructed." Peace education consists of teaching people how to prevent violent conflict, how to better handle conflict, how to cope with trauma, and how to reconcile when conflict occurs—which it inevitably will. Young people should be the prime recipients of this education. While adults can change, the anger and guilt that has been ingrained in them over the years makes it difficult. Children are much more receptive.

Given this, I find it odd that in most postconflict reconstruction, countries invest billions of dollars rebuilding their infrastructures, but little to nothing teaching their children how to live peacefully. In Rwanda today, children learn math and other subjects, but nothing specific about peace and reconciliation. How can we expect them to understand how to manage conflict if we don't teach them? We would never expect them to understand grammar or geometry without education. And yet we expect them to understand nonviolent conflict management. From an early age, children should be shaped into forgiving human beings, who are not afraid to admit mistakes and make amends. But for this effort to succeed, teachers, parents, and the media must collaborate to prepare our young people to be a more peaceful generation. It *is* possible. As Harvard professor Martha Minow said, "If we can educate young people to respect others, to understand the cost of group hatreds, to avoid stereotypes, to develop tools for resolving disputes, to choose to stand up to demagogues and to be peacemakers, we might hope to prevent future violence."[9]

But individual countries should not have to do this alone. While countries can do a lot within their borders to promote recon-

---

[9] Minow, Martha and Antonia Chayes, eds. *Imagine Co-existence: Restoring Humanity After Violent Ethnic Conflict.* San Francisco: Jossey-Bass, 2003.

ciliation, the *international community* should be ready to help. In postconflict situations, countries lack the resources and expertise to begin the reconciliation process. Further, the threat of extremists in war-torn countries can also derail efforts to reconcile. Countries that emerge from war are more likely to face renewed violence. Without help from the international community, reconciliation might be impossible and mass violence might once again lurk in the shadows. Violence has erupted in Rwanda four times: in the 1960s, 1970s, 1990s, and even in the early 2000s. And the threat of violence remains, especially with rebels continuing to be active in the Democratic Republic of Congo.

Because of this, early warning signs of violence should be monitored in postconflict societies. Like all mass violence, genocide does not come without warning. People do not awake one morning and say, "I am going to kill my neighbor because he is a different color from me" (or practices a different religion from me, or belongs to a different ethnic group). The path to genocide begins long before the first shot is fired or the first machete is swung. It builds slowly, first by categorizing people. One group becomes "us"; the other becomes "them." Then the "them" group is dehumanized. The old history of victimization is revived and distorted, and then propagated through the media. The training and equipping of death squads follow. History has shown us this time and again: Jews in Germany and the rest of Europe were forced to wear yellow stars on their clothes long before they were killed. Hateful propaganda was disseminated in Rwanda years before the genocide began. The United Nations knew of arms supplies in Rwanda three months before President Habyarimana's plane was shot down, igniting the genocide. At the same time, a U.S. government intelligence analyst predicted that if conflict erupted in Rwanda, "the worst case scenario would involve one half million people dying."[10] Former U.N. secretary general Kofi Annan said in 2004: "If the international community had acted promptly and with determination, it could have stopped most of the killing, but the political will was not

---

[10] Power, Samantha, op. cit., p. 338.

there." When I read this I think of my parents, who were killed weeks after the genocide began. If the international community had acted, they would be alive today—but "the political will was not there." So the question becomes, how do you get the international community leaders to have enough political will to help? Who will hold accountable the superpowers on the U.N. Security Council vested with veto power? Ultimately, the ones who are most able to hold these leaders accountable are the citizenry that elected them. When these leaders choose to do nothing, it is the responsibility of that country's populace to be vocal in their outrage and exercise their right to protest. It is the people who have the power—a power that is exercised by organizing rallies, writing letters to legislators and newspapers, and voting out of office leaders who turn a blind eye to the suffering of other people. *That* is how the individual can make a difference.

But the true key to creating a more peaceful world is through peace education—creating a new kind of leader; leaders with the wisdom to see beyond national boundaries and beyond the color of the skin, beyond economic gains and self-interest; leaders who see that we all are brothers and sisters and deserve help when the lives of even a few fellow human beings are in danger. Our hope of preventing and stopping genocide lies in the younger generation.

But until that better educated, peace-minded generation takes hold, we need an international community strong enough to intercede when it is needed. Successful intervention requires a well-equipped and well-trained force. The current process for sending a U.N. peacekeeping force into a troubled area is long and fraught with challenges. In the time it takes to approve, fund, equip, and mobilize a force, countless people can lose their lives. That's why a strong, permanent U.N. peacekeeping force that can be sent to intervene on short notice is needed. A force like this would deter power-hungry leaders with the intent of committing mass murder. If they knew that disobeying international law would result in the quick presence of a well-equipped force, they might think twice about their actions.

However, the use of force might not be necessary for some countries. In some situations, speaking forcibly against leaders of countries or rebellions that commit atrocities might suffice. I remember in 2003 President George W. Bush warned Charles Taylor, the former president of Liberia, that he should resign to give peace in his country a chance to take hold. After this warning, the president of Nigeria, Olusegun Obasanjo, offered Taylor exile. Under this strong pressure, President Taylor resigned and left for Nigeria, where he stayed until he was eventually brought before the International Criminal Court for trial.[11] A few years later, President Bush dissuaded President Obasanjo from changing his country's constitution to allow him to run for a third presidential term. This proves that the use of force is not always necessary. Most developing countries—which are the ones most prone to mass violence—are also the most responsive to international pressure. Many would change the course of events if they felt the international community would not tolerate their evil actions. Had President Bill Clinton forcibly talked to Rwanda's political and military leaders when the genocide started, it likely would have stopped, and hundreds of thousands of people would still be alive.

If the international community could now use its influence on President Kagame instead of being blinded by Rwanda's relative stability and socioeconomic recovery, Rwandans could hope for a peaceful tomorrow. Influential people close to him, such as Tony Blair and Bill Clinton, should encourage him to work toward a truth and reconciliation commission in which truth, apology, reparation, and forgiveness can take place. They should encourage him to engage in a genuine dialogue to build a strong democracy, and to launch a peace education system. This can be done while taking into consideration Kagame's legitimate concerns and fears. On the whole, Rwandans value peace more than the past. And that may be what saves us all.

The other thing that will save us all is embracing forgiveness not only on a national and community level, but on a personal level as well. This, too, is not easy. When I returned to Rwanda after the genocide,

---

[11] As of the writing of this book, the trial is still underway.

my heart was hollow and my faith in God was shaken. I carried with me a consuming anger toward those who had killed my family. Forgiveness seemed impossible, not just for me, but for my fellow Tutsi. How could we forgive the unforgivable acts our countrymen had committed? Like most Tutsi, I maintained that every single perpetrator of the genocide needed to be arrested and punished to the harshest extent possible—execution. Only then, I thought, would justice be served. Meanwhile, I would talk about the importance of reconciliation, not understanding that reconciliation without forgiveness is like an ocean without water. It wasn't until I traveled the country with a USAID consultant visiting prisons and witnessing the awful conditions in which genocide suspects were held that I began to feel some empathy toward them. It wasn't until then that I began to see that the enemy was not Hutu or Tutsi, but a lack of reconciliation over the years of cyclical violence and, more fundamentally, a lack of the virtue of forgiveness in each of us. I began to see then that reconciliation was not only a political process that should be embraced by government leaders, but a personal journey. I realized that each of us can find our own pathway to peace, regardless of what is happening on a national level. I believe that if reconciliation, which is a two-way process, is impossible, then forgiveness is an alternative.

Forgiveness can take place even when perpetrators stubbornly refuse to admit wrongdoing and genuinely apologize; when neither justice nor reparation have been realized; when repressive regimes still reign and human rights violations still persist; when democratic reforms are slow to come, which they usually are. Despite all this, victims can begin the internal process of healing and transformation, and forgive their aggressors.

Yet forgiveness is difficult for victims. In 2008, I saw author Michael Henderson speak at the School for International Training. As he observed, "Some withhold forgiveness for fear that they might easily become a doormat for others, or that justice might not be served and cruel people will literally get away with murder, or that forgiveness and apology, particularly in terms of injustices of the past, is just the latest caving in to political correctness." But in reality, forgiveness has a much broader meaning. Forgiveness means forgoing the human tendency to get even and harbor animosity toward those who have offended us. It means choosing to repair broken relationships rather than seeking revenge. It means recognizing the humanity in others and admitting that, under similar circumstances, we might have made the same mistakes.

But forgiveness does not replace justice. Pope John Paul II once wrote: "Forgiveness neither eliminates nor lessens the need for the reparation that justice requires, but seeks to reintegrate individuals and groups into society, and countries into the community of nations."[12] It does not let the perpetrator "off the hook." Rather, it lets *you* off the hook because your life is no longer governed by the injustices you have suffered. You are no longer prisoner of the past, nor home to anger and bitterness. This does not mean that forgiveness extirpates pain or anger. I will always feel pain when I think of the death of my family. Rather, forgiveness lets you acknowledge that pain and then release it. I think back to those dark days after the genocide when I was consumed by anger. All I could think about was how gruesomely my family died; how terrified they must have been; how horrifyingly unjust it all was. I was obsessed with it, asking myself "Why?" over and over again. I felt like a caged animal, pacing back and forth but never finding a way out. Then, when I began my journey toward forgiveness, it was as if the cage door swung open and I could walk away. By forgiving, I began to see the world in an entirely different light. I realized that I had the power to set myself free. We *all* have the power to set ourselves free.

To do this, however, requires a kind of inner transformation that is not easy to achieve. It requires a high level of consciousness. It requires you to look at the world differently than you have before. And I say *you* because all of us have been wronged. While you may not have had to suffer the horror of genocide or the murder of your family, no doubt someone has wronged you—an unfaithful spouse,

---

[12] John Paul II. *Go in Peace: A Gift of Enduring Love.* Chicago: Loyola Press, 2003, pp. 29–30.

an uncaring parent, an estranged child, a resentful coworker. Pain is a spectrum, and each of us has found ourselves at some point along that spectrum, and so each of us has the opportunity to forgive. Even the small infractions we face daily—the car that cuts us off, the rude sales clerk, the ungrateful boss—present us with the chance to let go of our anger and forgive. Through my experience, I have come to embrace forgiveness as a result of three motivations: to ensure *peace for future generations,* to care for my *physical and emotional well-being,* and to care for my own *spiritual integrity.*

Peace for future generations is possible only when we can forgive one another. In the aftermath of the Rwandan genocide, it was easy to take revenge. A lawlessness and kind of implicit tolerance of revenge pervaded the country. Yet revenge perpetuates the cycle of violence. As Martin Luther King, Jr., said, "Returning hate for hate multiplies hate, adding deeper darkness to a night already devoid of stars." One need only look at Rwanda's history for evidence of this. In 1959, the masses hunted down Tutsi in retaliation for their political dominance under the monarchy. Every time Tutsi insurgents attacked Rwanda in an effort to capture power, the Hutu-dominated government took revenge on innocent Tutsi civilians. Then, in 1990, the government took revenge on Tutsi civilians after the RPF attacked Rwanda from Uganda. The RPF responded to this revenge by exacting revenge on innocent Hutu civilians. The evil of retaliation went on unchallenged and escalated. No one would have believed that the conflict would last several decades. Past generations could have spared us this cycle of violence. Had they only understood that revenge adds "deeper darkness to a night already devoid of stars," more than a million Rwandans might not have perished; hundreds of thousands of refugees might not be scattered around the world.

What's more, retaliation in intercommunity violence rarely succeeds in killing the perpetrators. Instead, the perpetrators' innocent ethnic kin are targeted. For instance, when Tutsi refugees attacked Rwanda in the 1960s, the Hutu-dominated government retaliated against innocent Tutsi civilians; the guerillas were rarely reached. When the Tutsi-dominated army attacked Congo in 1996, the victims were mainly innocent Hutu civilians, not the *Interahamwe* or former army members responsible for the genocide (who had the information and means to escape before the soldiers got to them). So more often than not, the cycle of retaliation hurts the innocent among us: children, women, and the elderly. Witnessing this madness, I realized that until each individual who is harmed can learn to forgive, Rwanda will never be a peaceful nation. If we continue to play the game of an eye for an eye and a tooth for a tooth, we will all, as Gandhi once said, be blind and toothless. Forgiveness is the most rational response a victim can make if future generations are to enjoy peace.

Of course, the desire for revenge is embedded in human nature. It's an instinct we all share, a negative instinct that results in immeasurable suffering all over the world. But in order to handle it constructively, we must recognize that it is within each of us. I felt it in the wake of the genocide, and I still feel it in the instant that someone wrongs me. But as I gained a certain level of healing and inner transformation, I found that it disappears soon after it emerges. All I have to do is remind myself how low and useless it is, and then focus on how I can prevent it from happening again. I often think of how violence in Rwanda affected my grandmother, and later my mother, and then myself. This violence should not reach my children and my grandchildren; it does not have to reach future generations. Quite simply, we have a moral obligation to ensure that it doesn't.

Again, ensuring peace for future generations starts with the individual. It would have been so easy for me to continue to hold a grudge against those who killed my family. But what would that have taught my children? There is absolutely nothing I can do to bring back my loved ones, but there is something I can do to help build the foundation for peace for those who survived. In this way I can honor the memory of those I lost. A Rwandan proverb cautions that "unwise parents pass on problems to their children." I've watched Hutu and Tutsi children play together and seen their inherent goodness. No prejudices exist. I remember my own childhood and how

I grew up blissfully unaware of my ethnicity as I played with my Hutu friends. If only our innocence had been spared adults' lingering resentments and bitterness, we would not have suffered the gruesome consequences of the cycle of violence: murder, exile, displacement, discrimination, dehumanization, arbitrary imprisonment, and political disenfranchisement.

By committing to peace for future generations, we generate a different way of looking at the past. We look at the past not to find evidence of how our enemies are evil, but to find out what went wrong and how to improve relationships. Since I learned to forgive, I no longer look back and complain that "my loved ones were killed" or "I was offended," but instead ask, "What can I do in this world to prevent what happened from happening again?"

As I said before, Rwanda is a nation of wounded souls. Yet wounds can heal. And while it may be that those who lived through Rwanda's tragedy will never forget, it is possible that their children and grandchildren will one day read about the genocide and other gross human rights violations and say to their Hutu or Tutsi friends, "Can you believe that happened? Can you believe that so much hatred ever existed?" That is my hope: that someday interethnic violence in Rwanda will be so out of the realm of possibility that future generations will read about it in disbelief.

The second reason we should choose forgiveness over anger and revenge is for our *physical and emotional well-being*. A Rwandan proverb says, *"Umugayo uvuna uwugaya uwugawa yigaramiye,"* literally meaning, "The blame hurts the one doing the blaming, while the blamed person is enjoying life." In other words, anger or resentment toward the person who hurt you ultimately only hurts yourself. Although I had heard this Rwandan proverb since I was young, I never realized how true it was until after the genocide, when I suffered from painful, recurring stomachaches. They would intensify after I visited sites of massacres or meet genocide survivors whose lives had been devastated. Yet I did not think there was a correlation between my physical pain and the bitterness I held. Instead, I became selective in my diet and took medication to ease the pain. But when I started down the path of forgiveness, my stomach pains abated. I no longer had to take medication and could eat whatever I wanted. Letting go of my bitterness literally cured me. This made me realize that my anger was hurting only myself. The people who killed my family did not have stomach pain, or if they did, it was not because of my anger toward them—I alone was the one who was suffering.

My experience is not unique. Research has proven that forgiveness has immeasurable health benefits, and that unforgivingness—which is characterized by anger, bitterness, and the desire for revenge—does untold damage to our physical and emotional well-being. According to Dr. Frederic Luskin,[13] director of the Stanford University Forgiveness Project, medical and psychological studies have shown for years that anger and hostility are harmful to cardiovascular health. These studies, he notes, show that people who have difficulty managing anger have higher rates of heart disease and suffer more heart attacks. In fact, according to the American Institute of Stress, stress-related disorders are responsible for up to 90 percent of all visits to primary care physicians in the United States.[14] This is because negative emotions release hormones, such as adrenaline and cortisol, into the body that, in turn, can trigger the development of a host of diseases.[15] As Dr. Don Colbert, who writes about the link between the body and mind, notes, "If you choose not to forgive someone, I guarantee you that your emotions of resentment and hatred will continue to poison your system . . . not only will your body suffer, but also your mind, spirit, and general well-being." Conversely, letting go of that anger and resentment enhances your well-being. Simply put, the power of positive thinking can literally improve your health.

Forgiveness improves cardiovascular and nervous system func-

---

[13] Luskin, Frederic. *Forgive for Good*. New York: Harper Collins, 2002, p. 78.
[14] American Institute of Stress, in Dr. Don Colbert, *Stress Management 101*. Tennessee: Thomas Nelson, 2006, p. v.
[15] Ibid., p.vii.

tioning. This isn't hard to imagine. Think for a moment about the tension you feel in your body when you are angry: a clenched jaw, taut or quivering cheek muscles, a furrowed brow, a strained neck, a racing heart—all of which makes it difficult for blood to circulate and, consequently, impedes your cardiovascular and nervous systems. If you continue to carry this tension with you, it manifests itself as chronic fatigue, headaches, backaches, high blood pressure, respiratory diseases, a flaring temper, sexual dysfunction, insomnia—and the list goes on. If the causes behind these symptoms are not treated, the consequences can be fatal.

In addition to my stomach pains, insomnia haunted me in the years after the genocide. Ever since I was young, I could easily fall into a deep, undisturbed sleep. My sleep was seldom disrupted, except when I had a serious problem, such as the days I spent in prison in 1990 and the night before I fled Rwanda in 2000. But after the genocide, sleep became elusive. I would spend hours in bed at night tossing and turning; playing over and over in my mind the killing of my loved ones; wondering what in the world made our Hutu neighbors kill my mother, father, sisters, stepmother, and countless others. I would think of everyone I knew in Rwanda and tick off in rapid succession the names of all who were killed. My mind would even fly back to my school days, where I would think of my former classmates and go through the same sad exercise of listing all who were dead. By the time I finally fell into a fitful sleep, I was seething with anger at all of the loss I and so many others had suffered. The next day, I would awake feeling tired, distracted, and nervous. My productivity was poor. When I think back to those nights I wonder if I would have survived had my insomnia persisted. Surely my cardiovascular and nervous systems would have eventually suffered.

Also in the wake of genocide, I found myself easily angered by my wife and two older children at any mistake they made—or any mistake I *thought* they made. I then realized that my bitterness was not really directed toward them, but instead at those who had killed my loved ones. Once I realized this, I began to understand that I had to stop feeding my mind with negative thoughts and replace them with positive ones. Instead of dwelling on death and injustice, I would remember the happy events of my life: when I graduated from high school; when my first son was born; when I saw my wife in Burundi for the first time after almost a year of separation. In every life, even the very difficult ones, there are moments of happiness that we can return to and mine for comfort during times of stress. I would also think of the extraordinary courage and kindness exhibited by so many people, such as Kamegeri.

Kamegeri was a Hutu from my area who was poor and had no power to stop the genocide—and, in fact, would have best protected himself by participating in it. But instead, he risked his life by taking Tutsi in his canoe and rowing them across Lake Kivu to safety in Congo, saving many lives. I would also think of our Hutu neighbors who hid my family and me during the violence of 1973, or of the Hutu military officer who secured my release from prison. When I thought of these people, I was reminded that goodness sometimes broke through the seemingly impenetrable cloud of evil and shed its light on those who were suffering. With this reminder, my physical pain would ease.

Of course, I am not the only Rwandan who suffered from physical problems related to my anger, and many still suffer. A great number of Rwandans continue to be angry—at their fellow citizens who harmed them, at Rwandans who stood by and did not speak out, at the international community that failed to help. Of course they're angry; they have every right to be! Tutsi and Hutu alike are angry at and devastated by the consequences of genocide, war, exile, and other human rights violations. People have lost their loves ones, their property, their livelihoods. I understand them, but by holding on to their anger, they are suffering twice: first from the pain inflicted by others, and also from the pain they have inflicted on themselves.

I remember a conversation I had with a Tutsi friend of mine twelve years after the genocide. I asked him if he was still angry at the people who had killed his loved ones. "Of course I am!" he replied.

"I understand," I said. But then I asked another question, "Do you see yourself someday forgiving them?"

"No," he simply said. "How can you forgive such people after the evil they did?"

"But that means the people who hurt your family a dozen years ago are still hurting you," I said. I explained to him that holding on to anger only ate away at himself. The people who had killed his family were still alive; they were still living their lives. They had their own demons to live with, but my friend's anger toward them did not affect them. It did, however, affect my friend, just as mine had affected me.

Ultimately, forgiveness retrains our brains to think more positively. It replaces anger with love; despair with hope; the desire for revenge with empathy. If we train our minds to focus on our blessings and our dreams for the future instead of our curses and a painful past, we become happier human beings. If we keep our friends and our family in our thoughts instead of our offenders, we become more forgiving human beings. We are not able to avoid the past, but we can choose to make only short trips to the past, to learn from it, and then return to the present. Otherwise, we become hostage to the past and suffer physically and emotionally.

The third reason to embrace forgiveness is for our own *spiritual integrity*. Every religion in the world preaches forgiveness over revenge. Christianity tells followers: "Get rid of all bitterness, rage, and anger, brawling and slander, along with every form of malice. Be kind and compassionate to one another, forgiving each other as God in Christ forgave you" (Ephesians 4:31–32). Islam says that "he who forgives, and reconciles with his enemy, shall receive his reward from God"; and "of those who answered the call of Allah and the messenger, even after being wounded, those who do right and refrain from wrong have a great reward" (Koran, Chapter 3, verse 172). Judaism states: "When asked by an offender for forgiveness, one should forgive with a sincere mind and a willing spirit . . . forgiveness is natural to the seed of Israel" (Mishneh Torah 2:10). And Buddha said, "Holding on to anger is like grasping a hot coal with the intent of throwing it at someone else; you are the one who gets burned." Also, the Dalai Lama strongly calls for forgiveness, not revenge. He notes that dwelling on the past feeds anger and resentment that then give rise to further disturbances in our minds and cause our continued unhappiness.[16] And Hinduism professes, "Splendor, forgiveness, fortitude, cleanliness, absence of malice, and absence of pride; these are the qualities of those endowed with divine virtues" (Bhagavad Gita).

Those who engage in revenge, condone retaliation, or sermonize hatred against their offenders are not true believers. Suicide bombers who claim to kill and die in the name of Allah do not represent Islam. Those who kill in the name of God work against their religion's teachings; they betray their faiths. I find it a great wonder that all faiths, regardless of their differences, share a belief in the golden rule: do unto others as you would have them do unto you. For instance, Judaism says: "What is hateful to you, do not to your fellow man. This is the law: all the rest is commentary."[17] And Islam teaches: "None of you [truly] believes until he wishes for his brother what he wishes for himself."[18] The golden rule is, in essence, the incarnation of goodness, and it compels us to ask ourselves before we act, "Is what I am about to do—whether justified or not—what I would want done to me?"

All faiths also believe in the capacity of human beings to be transformed and free of prolonged anger, hatred, and violence. Buddhism calls this enlightenment—when a person chooses to relinquish anger and hatred in order to free himself from suffering. Eckhart Tolle says, "Enlightenment consciously chosen means to relinquish your attachment to past and future and to make Now the main focus of your life."[19] In other words, you can forgive and transform yourself only when you are capable of freeing yourself from the past. Enlightenment, therefore, makes people grow in consciousness and reach a level of goodness characterized by love, forgiveness, and compassion.

---

[16] Dunchunstand, Eileen Borris. *Finding Forgiveness: A 7 Step Program for Letting Go of Anger and Bitterness,* New York: McGraw Hill, 2006, p. XII.

[17] Talmud, Shabbat 31a.

[18] Number 13 of Imam "A-Nawawi's Forty Hadiths."

[19] Tolle, Eckhart. *The Power of Now: A Guide to Spiritual Enlightenment.* Novato, CA: New World Library. 1999, pp. 137–138.

A similar transformation is possible in Christianity. One of the core beliefs of this faith is that individuals can dramatically change from a state of sin to one of grace. Christianity tells us that we can relinquish our habits of hatred, revenge, verbal and physical violence, and malice to grow and embrace the goodness embodied in love, forgiveness, and compassion. With this transformation, we become new creations.

My spiritual beliefs have been crucial on my journey toward forgiveness. Without faith, I don't think my other motivations (peace for future generations and physical and emotional well-being) would have been strong. In my case, forgiveness, as a way of life, has been sustained by my faith. In fact, strong faith represents a powerful foundation from which forgiveness instantly flows; it provides a new way of seeing the world; a new way of looking at the sufferings we go through; a new way of looking at our offenders.

I grew up in a Christian family, attending the Seventh Day Adventist Church. Almost every Saturday, we would go to church and I would worship as I had been taught. But when I was a child, going to church was more for fun than worship. Still, I internalized some verses that no doubt shaped at least part of my adult behavior, including the verse from the New Testament that reads: "Do not repay anyone evil for evil" (Romans 12:17). This clearly is a command not to take revenge. God said: "It is mine to avenge; I will repay." In other words, the offender will pay, but we, the victims, should not take justice into our own hands. Doing so would only lead to anarchy and to the cycle of violence among God's children.

As part of my faith, I believe that God does indeed repay offenders, even if we don't always see it. I think of all the genocide leaders who are either in prison or in hiding. Theirs is not a happy life. Many members of the *Interahamwe* were killed. Even murderers who go free, who never acknowledge their crimes or express remorse, in some way suffer—if not in this life, in the next. Regardless, it is not my place to take revenge, not only because my faith condemns it, but because it is ultimately useless. When you seek revenge, you are simply following the steps of your offender's dance. I remember when I became speaker of parliament a friend told me that I should use my position to take revenge on those who killed my loved ones. "If revenge was the right thing to do—if it somehow drove away my bad dreams—if it was solution to the endemic conflict between Hutu and Tutsi, I would do it," I told him. "But it's not."

Opting for kindness in the face of evil is often mistaken for weakness, but in truth, it exhibits profound strength. It is easy to lash out at someone; it takes great fortitude to restrain yourself and act with kindness. The Bible tells us: "If your enemy is hungry, feed him; if he is thirsty, give him something to drink" (Romans 12:20). I often think of this when I remember my encounters with the mayor of my family's village in prison. By giving him money and showing kindness, rather than bitterness, I acted in accordance with my faith. As Martin Luther King, Jr., said, "Darkness cannot drive out darkness; only light can do that. Hate cannot drive out hate; only love can do that." When we respond to hatred and aggression with love, we help bring in the light.

Imagine that while participating in a peaceful demonstration, you are beaten by a police officer. The same officer arrests you and escorts you to jail. As he walks you to your cell, he sneezes. What do you say? As angry as you might be at him for his unjust behavior, you should turn to him as you would a friend and tell him, "Bless you," or whatever other kind words you choose. No matter how he responds, even if he ignores you or rudely tells you to "shut up," you have demonstrated grace, and that act increases the amount of good available in the world.

It can also unwittingly change the behavior of the perpetrator. At the very least, showing kindness toward an offender will puzzle him and most likely decrease his or her animosity. Offenders live in fear of revenge—it is what they expect. So when the victim demonstrates love instead of hatred, it often compels the offender to re-evaluate himself and his life. It brings some light into the offender's heart. It can lead to an apology that otherwise would never have come, and consequently lead to healing and reconciliation. In fact, perpetrators are often so ashamed and so fearful of revenge that they cannot take the first steps toward reconciliation. It is therefore up to the victim to help the offender begin that journey. To borrow from Martin Luther

King, Jr., this is in essence the paradoxical power of the victim to restore the offender's blighted humanity.

I was once asked by a student, "Can you forgive the people who killed your parents?" I responded that it is the genocide that is unforgivable, not those who perpetrated it. Of course, I wish I could receive acknowledgment and genuine apology from the killers of my parents. I would then forgive them from the bottom of my heart, as my faith has predisposed me to do. Yet even though I have not received an apology, I don't carry any hatred or bitterness against my parents' killers. When I was speaker of parliament and visiting my parents' village in Kibuye, I saw the mother of the men who are believed to have killed some members of my family. When she saw me, I could see the shame in her eyes. I could have turned away and said nothing, or spewed words of anger and hatred toward her and her sons. But this was also the woman who helped hide my father during the violence of 1973. And I knew that she also had been hurt by the genocide. Her husband was in prison and most of her children had fled the country. She was virtually alone. She, too, had suffered. When I saw her, I saw her not only as the mother of my family's killers, but also as the protector of my father. So I embraced her.

We should all embrace forgiveness. And in doing so, we must understand what that means. Forgiveness is not just a sacrifice one makes to rebuild a healthy relationship between a parent and child, a husband and wife, or even two communities—it is beyond that. Forgiveness is not just a practical means of preventing the physical and emotional harm unforgiveness wreaks—it is beyond that. Forgiveness is not just a way of embodying one's spiritual beliefs—it is beyond that. Forgiveness opens our hearts and allows us to be better human beings.

Each of us can reach a place of forgiveness in our own lives. As I said before, because we all have been hurt, we all have the opportunity to forgive. As difficult as it is, it is possible, and once forgiveness is embraced, it becomes second nature. Where negativity and anger once took up residence in our minds, we instead find acceptance and peace. Over the years, I've learned how to nurture forgiveness within myself. I equate forgiveness to a flower: It grows only if I water it. I nurture it by, for example, practicing positive thinking, kind speech, good manners, empathy, and reflection. When we do that, forgiveness is no longer a sacrifice or challenge, but a way of life; a lifelong journey. I am still on that journey, and always will be.

Children already live this way. When children get mad at one another, their anger can be quite fierce, but they quickly put it behind them and come together again as friends. There are no grudges, no lingering animosities. They live in the moment. Their life is not governed by what happened ten months ago, or even ten minutes ago. So any wrongs done to them by their playmates simply dissipate. Sadly, as we grow up our lives become less and less about *now* and more and more about *then*. We dwell on all the negative events in our lives and lose the ability to forgive. Our bodies might grow up, but we lose that childlike goodness. We become un-grown-up adults. But we can find that childlike place in our hearts again. We can return to it and banish the cycle of blame and revenge. We can transform ourselves—and in so doing, we can transform the world.

Robert Kennedy once said, "Few will have the greatness to bend history, but each of us can work to change a small portion of events, and in the total of all those acts will be written the history of a generation. It is from numberless diverse acts of courage and belief that human history is shaped." It reminds us that our individual acts—the small kindnesses we show to one another as human beings—can in fact change the world. We all have the power, and the responsibility, to do it. Start now.

Acknowledgments

———~w~———

I owe much to the memories of my parents, my brothers and sisters, and members of my extended family. Without my parents' discipline and love, my journey of transformation would not have begun.

I think of those who protected my family in 1973, who secured my release from prison in1990, and who supported me through prayers and other support during the dark days prior to my exile in 2000. I remain indebted to those who did their best to help me get out of Rwanda in 2000—especially my brother Emmanuel Niyomugabo, my brother-in-law Emmanuel Naho, Emmanuel Uwumukiza, Benjamin Rutabana, and Janvier Rugema.

My gratitude goes to the government of Uganda, and particularly to President Yoweri Museveni, for welcoming me and my family and providing us sanctuary. Amnesty International and Human Rights Watch contributed to my protection and the government of the United States arranged our safe departure from Uganda.

Allan A. Hodgson has helped me in many ways and has been a blessing to my family. Augustin Kamongi and his family welcomed me into their home and have been good friends to me. Mimi Townsend has provided me with spiritual support and encouragement. Jeff Unsicker, Jim Cramer, Abdoul Diallo, and Robert J. Schweich made it possible for me to continue my graduate education at the School for International Training in Brattleboro, Vermont. Paula Green introduced me to the field of conflict transformation and has been a true friend and now colleague. To all of you, I express my deepest gratitude.

I would like to thank Laura Ann Mullane who helped me write this book at every step. Her involvement, skill, and kindness were invaluable to me. I thank my agent, Faith Hamlin, for her encouragement and unwavering support. For her enthusiasm and commitment to get this book in print, I extend my appreciation to Malaika Adero, editor at Atria Books. I also thank Ginni Stern for her help in the early stages of preparing this book. My friend, Constance Clarke, read the manuscript and provided helpful insights in many ways.

Finally, I express my love and gratitude to my wife, Liberata, and to my children, Respect, Pacifique, Esther, Nicole, and Sandrine. Their love and trust have comforted me throughout the writing of this book. They are my constant companions in my journey of transformation.

Throughout my life I have been the recipient of love, support, and kindness from many people. I thank you all from the bottom of my heart.

Index